Say It Is Pentecost

Say It Is Pentecost

A Guide Through Balthasar's Logic

Aidan Nichols OP

T&T CLARK
EDINBURGH

T&T CLARK LTD
59 GEORGE STREET
EDINBURGH EH2 2LQ
SCOTLAND
www.tandtclark.co.uk

The lines from *The Mystery of the Charity of Charles Péguy*
by Geoffrey Hill are reprinted by permission from
Collected Poems (Penguin 1985) and *New and Collected Poems 1952–1992*
(Houghton Mifflin Co, Boston and New York 1994).

First published 2001

ISBN 0 567 08752 2

British Library Cataloguing-in-Publication Data
A catalogue record for this book is available from the British Library

Typeset by Waverley Typesetters, Galashiels
Printed and bound in Great Britain by Biddles Ltd, Guildford

Or say it is Pentecost: the hawthorn-tree,
met with coagulate magnified flowers of may
blooms in a haze of light

Geoffrey Hill
The Mystery of the Charity of Charles Péguy

Contents

Preface   ix

  1   Introducing Balthasar's Logic   1

PART 1: TRUTH OF THE WORLD

  2   Being and Truth   9
  3   Subject, Object – and God   15
  4   Inwardness and Freedom   23
  5   Image and Reality   35
  6   Being Situated   45
  7   Mystery   51
  8   Truth Worldly and Truth Divine   55

PART 2: TRUTH OF THE WORD

  9   The Johannine 'Entry'   63
 10   Logic and Love   67
 11   Ana-logic: Tracing the Trinity   69
 12   The Self-expression of the Logos   73
 13   The Place of the Logos in God   81
 14   The Emergence of the World through the Word   91
 15   Cata-logic: Fulfilment from God   95
 16   The Word Is Made Flesh   101
 17   And Made Sin: The Logic of Contradiction   119

PART 3: TRUTH OF THE SPIRIT

 18   The Spirit's 'Entry' into Logic   127
 19   Christ and the Spirit   131

20   The Holy Spirit, the Interpreter   135
21   The Spirit as Personal Being   139
22   Dyad in the Triad: The Father's 'Two Hands'   147
23   The Spirit and the Church: Logical Preliminaries   161
24   The Spirit and the Church: Subjective and Objective   171
25   The Spirit and the World   187
26   Return to the Father   191

PART 4: A RETROSPECTIVE GLANCE

27   Epilogue to the Trilogy   197
28   Postword   211

Select Bibliography   213

Index of Subjects   215

Index of Names   225

Preface

With the present work, I come to the end of my task of providing Balthasar's prolix trilogy – *Herrlichkeit, Theodramatik, Theologik* – with an interpretative summary. The last member of the trio, the theological logic, is also the shortest. But since it contains, in its opening volume, Balthasar's metaphysics and epistemology – a synthesis of Christian Scholasticism and the classical German philosophical tradition, theologically re-worked – it is hardly the least demanding. The effort of understanding is rewarded, however, with a fuller grasp of Balthasar's contentions in the aesthetics and dramatics, as well as in the remaining volumes of *Theologik* itself.

Readers of my two earlier commentaries, *The Word Has Been Abroad* and *No Bloodless Myth*, will have found *some* material on *aisthēsis* and the drama, respectively: enough to explain the terms 'aesthetics' and 'dramatics' which control the sub-titles of these 'Guides'. But of logic as ordinarily understood – whether the traditional syllogistic variety, or the modal logic favoured in the later Middle Ages as again today, or the symbolic logic of the mathematically inclined, they will find little if any trace in *Say It Is Pentecost*. As with Hegel, Balthasar's logic is his ontology, his study of being – though to be sure there are discussions here of language, in which being comes to expression. Not that the second and third volumes of *Theologik* – on the difference made to ontology by Christology and Pneumatology – are an afterthought in this respect. For Balthasar, as his (separate) *Epilog* to the trilogy, also discussed here, points out, understanding of the missions of Son and Spirit not only confirms the judgments about the world's being as divine epiphany made in the opening ontology but also shows the being of the world flowering under the sun of transfiguring grace.

This makes appropriate the choice of title and epigraph, for which I am again indebted to the distinguished poet, my fellow-countryman, Geoffrey Hill. The completion of the present study seems a good time to thank too all those in T&T Clark's publishing house who have made the production of these books so singularly free of heartache. Writing them has sometimes been a labour, but it has been a labour of love on behalf of the faith of the Church which Cardinal Balthasar so signally served.

AIDAN NICHOLS, OP
Blackfriars, Cambridge
Memorial of the Holy Name of Jesus, 2000

1

꧁꧂

Introducing Balthasar's Logic

Balthasar did not his complete his theological logic until he had written his theological aesthetics and dramatics. But before he started on his aesthetics and dramatics he had already written the first volume of that logic. Containing as it does his general ontology, it is important for its expression of certain general principles of Christian thought later pre-supposed by the theological aesthetics and dramatics, and for introducing us for the first time to some of the root philosophical concepts set to theological use in those works.[1]

General principles

In the foreword to the original, 1947, edition, Balthasar insists that he does not want to be so original as in any way to displace those fundamental principles relevant to the theme of truth which the masters of the Western tradition, from Aristotle to Aquinas, have put forward, and which sub-sequent Christian philosophy from the high mediaeval period to the time of writing has the more solidly established. And yet, alternatively, human thought will surely never exhaust the truth which is its own proper object. So Balthasar's aim will be to introduce into the traditional theses some 'new developments', developments which cohere with what he calls the 'ever renewed perspective' that the passage of time brings in its train. The ethos of his study will be faithfulness to the spirit rather than the letter of the *philosophia perennis*.[2] When re-published in 1985 as the opening volume of a trilogy under the overall title of *Theologik*, the foreword to *Wahrheit der Welt*, 'The Truth of the World', turned out to have expanded so as to take in Balthasar's now widened conception, the second and third instalments of which would be called respectively 'The Truth of God' and 'The Spirit of Truth'. The overall aim of Balthasar's theological logic – in effect his *ontology*, for, like Hegel, he can think of no logic which is not 'onto-logic', the truth of *being* – is now re-defined in *Trinitarian* terms. A 'theo-logic' addresses the question of what is meant by 'truth' in the context

---

1 See the two previous studies in this series: A. Nichols, *The Word Has Been Abroad: A Guide through Balthasar's Aesthetics* (Edinburgh 1998); *idem*, *No Bloodless Myth: A Guide through Balthasar's Dramatics* (Edinburgh 2000).
2 'Vorwort', *Wahrheit*: I *Wahrheit der Welt* (Einsiedeln 1947).

of the 'event' of God's revelation through the Incarnation of the Logos
and the Outpouring of the Holy Spirit. This Christological, Pneumatological and therefore ultimately Trinitarian setting for theological logic
requires us to investigate what 'laws' of thought and language can be
said to underlie the expression of the content perceived and experienced
in theological aesthetics which, in another perspective, is also the
'confrontation' between divine and human freedom set forth in the
theological dramatics. But Balthasar regards this as a question which can
hardly be raised until we have clarified what we mean by the 'truth of
being' in the first place, for this is the most fundamental question of all,
unavoidable if we are to grasp something of the Logos, the foundation of
'logic'.

So despite the concern of volumes II and III of the *Theologik* with Father,
Son and Spirit, and the re-definition of theological truth which their self-
manifestation brings in its train, Balthasar remained convinced of the
appositeness of Volume I, which links his work to Scholastic metaphysics,
and indeed to the entire tradition of ontological thinking, both pagan and
Christian, in the Western world. As he writes, situating the task of Volume
I in the context of the three great serial trilogies as a whole:

> From the outset, the whole trilogy has been articulated in terms of
> the transcendental determinations of being, and indeed with
> reference to the analogical relationship which they bear, by their
> validity and their form, in the being of the world, and in divine
> Being: there is a correspondence in the 'aesthetics' between worldly
> 'beauty' and divine 'glory', and in the 'dramatics' between a worldly-
> finite and a divinely-infinite freedom. Here, accordingly, in the theo-
> logical logic we shall be pondering the relation between the structure
> of created truth and that of divine truth. Following this, we must
> look into the question as to whether divine truth can represent
> itself within the structures of created truth and (in diverse forms)
> come to expression there. Theological findings about God's glory,
> goodness and truth naturally presuppose not only a formalistic or
> gnoseological but also an ontological structure in the being of the
> world. Without philosophy, no theology.[3]

The settled conviction of Catholic divinity that it cannot do without a
philosophical mediation if it is both to grasp as fully as it can the content
of its own divine resources and 'give a reason for the hope that is in'
believers faced with a sceptical world (cf. 1 Peter 3.15) is Balthasar's
wholly adequate justification in writing *Wahrheit der Welt*.[4]

Incarnation and ontology

In the 1985 Foreword to the ontological trilogy Balthasar makes it clear
that the question of the analogy of being, so far from constituting a

---

3 'Zum Gesamtwerk', *Theologik* I *Wahrheit der Welt* (Einsiedeln 1985), cited below as
  TL I, p. vii.
4 A conviction re-expressed at the highest level in the 1998 encyclical of Pope John
  Paul II, *Fides et ratio*.

separated natural theology, paralleling, in uneasy independence, the deliverances of revealed doctrine, is intimately connected with the latter. For ontological thinking is crucially relevant to the Incarnation. The Incarnation is literally unthinkable unless a positive answer can be indicated to the question, Is 'worldly logos' – the intelligibility implicit in the world's being – capable of bearing the weight of the divine Logos were he to make himself known in his own world? And anticipating somewhat his own response, Balthasar speaks of the way in which being has a 'polarity structure' – a term he drew from his one-time mentor, the Polono-German Jesuit Erich Przywara[5] to whose contrasting poles of essence and existence, general and individual, he adds others which come to light both in aesthetics (such as form and radiance) and ethics (like obedience and freedom). This polarity structure of all existence, while manifesting the ontological difference between the being of the creature and that of the Creator (because, owing to the divine simplicity, the latter 'is' all that he 'has'), also suggests a 'positive moment' where the creature displays a certain likeness and so comparability with its God. For between these poles there plays a fullness of inner life – a continuous epiphany of the divine liveliness. Still, for Balthasar, to show how finite being might be considered the image and likeness of absolute being is only possible once we have begun to think in a thoroughgoing Trinitarian fashion.

The first volume, *Wahrheit der Welt*, will therefore play a rôle at once modest yet crucial. Exploration of the inner-worldly structure of truth – that is, of the ever-deeper strata of being as no less ever-deepening ways in which truth explicates itself to the knower: this is Balthasar's subject. He will remind readers of many points familiar to the ancients and the Fathers yet subsequently lost to view – without, however, departing from the main lines of the Thomist tradition, the 'great' tradition, as he terms it.[6] The book's closing chapter will show how these inner-worldly structures of finite being point on towards a transcendent divine Logos – even though for philosophical thinking God and his truth come into view simply as the world's beginning and end, as the First Vatican Council's Constitution on faith and reason, *Dei Filius*, makes clear. Balthasar realises that, to the reader unforewarned, it may seem strange that he can pass, in the second volume of *Theologik*, to an unashamedly theological account of the same topic: treating the truth God has made known through his free revelation as the final norm of worldly truth. The first volume simply presumes that divine revelation does not cancel out worldly truth but rather fulfils it in raising it up.

Revelation and philosophy

He uses the expanded preface of the ontological trilogy to justify this *démarche*. First, and taking up a major emphasis of his principal Francophone teacher, Henri de Lubac:[7] in its concrete existence the world is

5 For Przywara's role in Balthasar's development, see Nichols, *The Word Has Been Abroad*, pp. xiii–xiv.
6 *TL* I, p. x.
7 For Balthasar's relation to de Lubac, see Nichols, *The Word Has Been Abroad*, pp. xiv–xv.

already placed in a supernatural dimension by the grace of God. There is
no such thing as a theologically neutral world for philosophy to investigate.
It follows that, while philosophy may certainly abstract from the supernatural in order to lay out some basic structures of the world and our
knowledge thereof, the closer it comes in this task to its object in the latter's
concrete character, and the deeper it penetrates our equally concrete modes
of knowledge, the more it will have to do with theological data – whether
the philosopher concerned is aware of this or not. For the supernatural is
at work as a leaven in the natural, or is present (in another metaphor) as
its atmosphere. It would be foolish, in Balthasar's opinion, to attempt to
banish supernatural truth from the philosophical enterprise. It is one
thing for a Plato or an Aristotle to incorporate *de iure* theological elements
within a *de facto* philosophy without being able to know that is what they
were doing. It is quite another for one to undertake, after the Gospel's
definitive illumination of rationality, a 'purification' of philosophy in a
secularising spirit – though of course such a reductive return to a purely
immanentist philosophical truth is the common denominator linking
modern rationalisms of various kinds. A Catholic thinker by contrast will,
in Balthasar's words:

> describe the truth of the world in its prevailing worldly quality
> [*Welthaftigkeit*] without thereby excluding the possibility that the
> world thus described contains elements of directly divine, super-
> natural provenance.[8]

Moreover, and in particular, there may be truths pertaining to the 'first
gift' of created nature which are available now *only* through the enlightening power of revelation. Balthasar proposes this as a way of
understanding the First *Vaticanum*'s claim that the divine existence is
accessible to human reason.[9] His hopes, at this juncture, of the possible
conversion to Catholicism of the great 'Neo-Orthodox' Protestant dogmatician Karl Barth[10] may have influenced him here, for such an interpretation
would have enabled that doughty exponent of *revelatione sola*, 'by revelation alone', to accept the Council's dogmatic decree on faith and reason.
In the world of antiquity, so Balthasar notes, people havered indecisively
between a polytheism of personally conceived deities, as with Homer,
and an impersonal mysticism of unity, as in Plotinus. The only way to

8 Ibid., p. xii; cf. pp. 21–2. See also on this H. U. von Balthasar, 'Der Begriff der Natur
   in der Theologie', *Zeitschrift für katholische Theologie* 75 (1953), pp. 452–64.
9 Though at the First Vatican Council no explicit mention was made of the condition
   of sin as reducing the human capacity to know God, there was – via the text of
   Thomas' *Summa Theologiae* – an implicit reference, for Thomas is reflecting on the
   concrete, post-lapsarian human being who carries in his flesh the rationally
   debilitating consequences of original sin. The development of this point by Pope
   Pius XII in his encyclical letter *Humani Generis* might suggest that while human
   reason, weakened though it is by sin, can none the less reach God as the beginning
   and end of created things through the means placed at its disposal by created reality,
   there is still a *moral* necessity for supernatural revelation. At the Second Vatican
   Council, *Dei Verbum* will reverse the sequence of *Dei Filius*, speaking of a natural
   revelation in the creation only *after* it has dealt with the supernatural revelation in
   biblical history.
10 See Nichols, *The Word Has Been Abroad*, pp. xvi–xvii.

overcome the unsatisfactory finitude of the many gods appeared to be through the positing of a non-personal principle of unity behind the divine world. By contrast, after the coming of Christianity, a thinker like Aquinas is able to speak of a 'natural' desire for the vision of the only and personal God. But did such a desire come to light naturally or supernaturally? Leaving that question open, Balthasar for his part will set out to describe the 'truth of the world' without distinguishing what in his understanding comes from natural, and what from supernatural, sources. In practice, in the construction of a Christian ontology, this demarcation line cannot be precisely drawn.

This does not mean, however, as Balthasar is at pains to point out, that he proposes to sink philosophy and theology as mere ingredients in some vast soup, for in the remaining volumes of the ontological trilogy his task of describing truth as conditioned by the Incarnation and Pentecost will be completely determined by the historic revelation. Indeed, Balthasar uses this opportunity to enter a caveat against any 'Rahnerian' misunderstanding of his project. There will be no question here, as in Karl Rahner's Theological Idealism, of dismembering the divine self-manifestation into on the one hand 'categorial' and on the other 'transcendental' aspects, such that the line of particular historical development which links Christ, the Spirit and the Church is to be distinguished (as merely 'categorial') from some more comprehensive, historically all-embracing, 'transcendental' sphere, with the concomitant danger that Christian truth becomes at best a key to, and at worst simply an illustration of, what is in any case already given in the universal God–world relationship. Here, looking back from the vantage point of 1985, he could appeal to his own *Theology of History*, published in 1950,[11] to suggest an alternative scheme. The mystery of the active influence of Christ's Holy Spirit must itself be understood in so universal a way and Christ, in his historical and resurrectional reality, be grasped as so much the 'concrete universal' that it strikes us as perfectly natural for the radiant light of the Spirit of Pentecost and the Christ of the Paschal Mystery to penetrate to the furthest boundaries of space and time.

But there is a second reason too which legitimates the apparently effortless transition, within the *Theologik*, from the philosophical programme of Volume I to the Christological and Pneumatological interpretation of the truth of the world within the mystery of God in volumes II and III. The inner fulness of philosophical truth – quite apart from any theological light which may fall upon it – is much richer (so Balthasar claims) than many post-Renaissance philosophical systems will concede. If, following the example given by St Thomas in his integration of the contrasting Platonic and Aristotelian world-views, a variety of philosophies, each with their own favoured insights, are permitted to 'infiltrate' each other, then natural reality has a chance to appear in its own largeness, fullness and manysidedness. And this in turn makes possible a proper evaluation of the work of grace, for grace can only display itself in its true colours where just such a 'fulness' offers itself as its raw material – as the 'matter' which grace will penetrate, form, raise up and perfect in its activity.

11 *Theologie der Geschichte* (Einsiedeln 1950; 1959³; Et *A Theology of History*, London and New York 1964).

If this preparatory philosophical homework is neglected, then theology will be the sufferer. Balthasar's ideal, then, is that philosophy and theology should 'draw life from each other'.

A philosophy that renounces the transcendent ends up, he believes, of necessity, with what amounts to forms and varieties of Positivism, sterile systems that go by various names: functionalism, logicism, linguistic analysis. Then truth itself as a transcendental determination of being becomes perfectly superfluous. Theology finds itself left hanging in the air, and can take refuge only in the most unsatisfactory of solutions, whether some kind of existentialism, or an exegetical rationalism, or a political theology that turns belief into praxis. Here what are at best *partial aspects* of theological truth, now left un-integrated, lead into the sand. But, Balthasar thinks, a programme of re-integrating philosophy with theology is only plausible if the analogy between divine prototype and worldly reflection is restored to its former centrality in Western thought. Kant and Nietzsche were not far wrong in centering their attack on traditional metaphysics on *the transcendentals* – for the latter give us access to the heart of the God–world relation. And in any case clear-eyed modern man, contemplating his world, can only treat the transcendentals as illusory: where is this all-governing truth, goodness and beauty? Alas, the perversions of being and its basic determinations which human freedom has (whether maliciously or negligently) perpetrated in the history of culture have had the effect of suppressing our awareness of the mysterious depth of reality, and so leading us to misdescribe it. 'X is nothing other than' is the typical formula of this betrayal. In reality, in the last analysis, everything knowable must have a 'mysteric' character, on the simple grounds that all objects of knowledge have a *creaturely* character, which must mean that the final truth of all things is 'hidden in the mind of the Creator who alone may utter [their] eternal names . . .'[12]

12 *TL* I, p. xvii.

PART 1

TRUTH OF THE WORLD

2

❦

Being and Truth

The facets of being

Readers who are chiefly anxious to get to the meat of Balthasar's theological doctrine will understandably want to hurry through the philosophical discussions in *Theologik*, largely confined as these are to its opening volume. This would be a mistake. 'Truth of the World' does not only provide us with the wider philosophical–theological presuppositions of Balthasar's theological aesthetics, itself the propadeutic to his theological dramatics. The work under consideration also gives us philosophical entrée to some key concepts later actually to be deployed in the theological exploration of the 'Glory of the Lord' and the 'Theo-Drama' of God's saving work.

Now Balthasar's ostensible subject is *truth*. Any logic is concerned with some at least of the conditions which must hold good if true propositions are to be affirmed. Balthasar's sub-title, however, in this opening volume of the 'theo-logic', is 'the Truth of the *World*' – just as the succeeding volumes will go on to have as their explanatory rubric 'the Truth of God' and 'the Spirit of Truth' respectively. Placed as he is in the great tradition of ontological metaphysics, Balthasar does not for a moment suppose that the topic of truth can be properly introduced without at the earliest possible moment pointing out the interrelation of truth with being. As he writes:

> Truth is not just a property of knowledge; it is above all a transcendental determination of being as such.[1]

Crucial to *Theologik*, then, will be the character of being itself.

Here a word of warning, for the Anglo-Saxon reader in particular, seems in place. In a philosophical tradition such as that of England and America where most philosophy takes the form of either commonsense discussion or logical analysis, Balthasar's notion of the metaphysics required by Catholic theology may come as something of a shock. In the tradition to which Balthasar belongs – a Christian Scholasticism still very much in touch with its ancient Hellenic sources but reinvigorated by the questions posed by post-Cartesian philosophy in nineteenth- and twentieth-century

---

1 *TL* I, p. 11.

9

Germany, metaphysics must go deeper than common sense, yet do so by words ('essence', say, and 'existence') that are not coinings by intellectual technicians but play a part, in however unconsidered a fashion, in ordinary discourse. The chosen idiom of Balthasar's philosophical writing will mean for us a fairly demanding journey – but I should not be inviting readers to accompany me on his way unless I thought it a highly rewarding one as well.

To anticipate: what Balthasar will show us is that the truth of being, as we unfold it in philosophical reflection, turns to us four facets. Being deploys its truth as *nature* (here the relation of object with subject, and its further implications, will draw Balthasar's especial attention), as *freedom*, as *mystery* and as *participation*. That is to say: the truth of being is given with the nature of things, yet it yields itself only in the interplay of the subject with the object; it exceeds our images for it, our language about it, yet does so only because in the last analysis it is a participation in the infinite. It is of course that final conclusion which will open out Balthasar's philosophical contemplation of the 'truth of the world' to a theological exploration of the truth of the Word and of the Spirit, the twofold 'economy' which transports us to the Source of all truth, the divine Father.

Balthasar's own preparatory comments on the ontological character of any enquiry into truth worth the name prepares us for its positive possibilities. The first thing to which he would have us turn our attention is what we can call the *plenary* character of the intuition of the truth of being. To realise that truth governs the reciprocal relations of being and thought is, in epistemology, journey's end. Yet it is only our beginning in the kind of ontological investigation Balthasar wants to pursue. Moreover, we should be deluded if we imagined that in this matter – as with any foundational philosophical enquiry – a line will ever be drawn to bring our reflections to their close. In Balthasar's metaphor, the screw that bores down into the mysterious abyss of the real never comes to a final halt on brute resisting bedrock. Not that a comparison taken from mechanics is especially congruent here. In lyrical, even exalted, mood, Balthasar makes appeal to the Aristotelian theme of the endless wonderment of the philosopher in the face of reality. Without the 'primordial fact', the *Urtatsache*, that is the existence of truth, one would look, in this domain, somewhat foolish. But the task is to go deeper into *what the fact means*. So Balthasar moves on to happier similes of lovers and water babies. The 'fact' of a romantic proposal may initiate a lifetime of personal relationship. The 'fact' of jumping into the water is the *sine qua non* of learning to swim. Similarly, Balthasar is saying, there are some primordial intuitions which we never leave behind because the intelligence lives ever after through their medium. The marvellous discovery of the truth of being – perceiving the entry into intellectual day both of existence (what it is to be) and of essence (what it is to be something) – is surely one such. Thanks to the inexhaustibleness of such an insight, this *Ausgangspunkt der Metaphysik* – 'beginning for metaphysics' – is no mere temporal 'kicking off' point, but an abiding source of illumination. Here, to invert T. S. Eliot's words, In my beginning is my end. From this fount of vision, unending vistas open. No metaphysician, not even St Thomas, can do more than gather a few blooms from the country thus laid open to view, giving us thereby *some* conceptual grasp of its flora. To capture 'the richness, fulness, atmosphere, fruitfulness and splendour of the whole landscape . . . of the immeasurable fields of truth' lies beyond any man's achieving.[2]

The transcendentals again

These abundant metaphors (and metaphors of abundance) also signal Balthasar's refusal to limit the Christian philosopher's concern with truth to a mere apologia against scepticism, and bring before us a second basic feature in Balthasar's approach to the truth of being: the inseparability of truth from goodness and beauty. Beauty, truth and goodness are co-equal transcendental properties of being – properties found everywhere in different ways. None of them can be encountered except in some condition of mutual compenetration with the others. All three are necessary if there is to be a manifestation of being's intimate richness – that is, an unveiling of its truth.

> Only a living and durable unity of the threefold attitude – theoretic, ethical, aesthetic – can lead us to the true knowledge of being.[3]

The more these three attitudinal elements differ formally, and so have necessarily to remain distinct, the more important it is not to lose sight of their 'common root and continual circumincession', a metaphor taken, evidently, from the theology of the inner-Trinitarian relationships. No one of these three attributes can be concretely described without drawing in the other two. Just as John Henry Newman had seen the intellectual and the volitional, mind and heart, as interwoven in the act of faith, so for Balthasar, looking ahead to his aesthetics and dramatics, a doctrine of revelation and salvation – which are the correlate and the content, respectively, of the act of faith – cannot prescind from the way being is disclosed in expressive gesture, truth in beauty and goodness. Modern rationalism, by reducing truth-theory to verification and abandoning the good and the beautiful to subjective arbitrariness, has torn apart the image of being. The flight to irrationalism – a periodic recourse of offended sensibility from the Romantic movement onwards – makes confusion worse confounded. It is for Balthasar the vocation of Christian philosophy today by recovering the unity of the transcendentals to salvage thought itself.

Being and appearing

Exploring the truth of being, like married life or standing on water, is, we have seen, in one sense pre-given in an intuition that 'truth exists'. Balthasar investigates that *Vorbegriff*, or first stab at the concept of truth, by way of leading us from his most general opening remarks, into a consideration of truth as nature, and in so doing usefully complements his comments so far. He insists that, contrary to what the unalerted reader may fear, the topic of being is not arcane. For being shows itself in appearance. (Here Balthasar makes us aware of his sympathy for the phenomenological

2 *TL* I, p. 16.
3 *TL* I, p. 18.

thinking favoured by many late nineteenth- and early mid-twentieth-century German philosophers from Brentano to Husserl and Heidegger. His phenomenology, we should note, is, however, always in the service of a Christian ontology in the mode of a repristinated Scholasticism and even, ultimately, Thomism – unlike theirs.) Truth is being's property of unveiledness, uncoveredness, revealedness, non-hiddenness (literally, in Greek, *alētheia*). Over against a positivistic phenomenalism, Balthasar asserts that *being* (nothing less) is what appears. Over against a Kantian noumenalism, he affirms that being does indeed *appear*. And the unity of these two statements yields up to us the nature of truth. Truth is being's ability really to appear as it is.

Encounter with truth – being appearing – is both a closure and an opening, an end and a beginning. G. K. Chesterton once remarked that the only point of opening your mind is to close it again as quickly as possible on something solid. Balthasar would agree with this gastronomic metaphor but add with the Italians, 'L'appetito viene mangiando': 'with eating there comes appetite'. Balthasar's explanation is, however, as one might expect, less homespun, and in its course he complements the Hellenic concept of truth as disclosure with the Hebraic one of truth as faithfulness or that which can be relied upon. To say that in truth being is unveiled (Greek) requires analytically that being be unveiled to someone, to a knowing subject. The authoritativeness of being (Israelite) guarantees the solidity of knowledge – an attribute of truth which Balthasar refers to in biblical Hebrew as *emeth*. In its faithful reliability, truth does two things for us. First, it draws to a close search's uncertainty and what would otherwise be its 'false infinity', its fruitless unendingness, as well as its hesitancies and conjectures, replacing this unstable condition of things with its own solid evidence. But secondly, in and through this overcoming of a false infinity, it generates a true infinity instead. From truth now made present there spring up a thousand seedlings of cognition. By uncovering being, and hence the internal relations between being's various regions, truth opens up perspectives on realms still unknown.

> Truth never closes the subject within narrow, constraining limits, but on the contrary opens and liberates, not only in relation to itself and in itself, but also in relation to other truths.[4]

There *is* such a thing as real progress in knowledge and certitude, but every genuine advance in knowledge reveals the realm of the true and knowable as ever greater, ever more unlimited.

The rational and the whole

And this enables Balthasar to identify the senses in which rationalism both is and is not correct. In the sense that truth is apt to be grasped, it is rational: a fragment of the universe is penetrated in its meaning and nature. Yet inasmuch as the fragment is just that, a parcel of the total truth which remains veiled, transcendent, the knowledge of the fragment arouses in the knowing subject the desire for something more. It stimulates in fact

4 *TL* I, p. 30.

that movement of *eros*, of desire for the infinite, which Balthasar had first studied in Gregory of Nyssa.[5] He insists, however, that these two moments are not to be contrasted as rational over against irrational, for in their unity they constitute in fact the indivisible structure of human understanding. The understanding that truth prompts is, as he puts it, both adjudicatory and intuitive. It *both* masters or judges *and* is carried beyond itself.

> The rational aspect in the narrow sense of the first moment is in immediate continuity with the widening perspective which opens it out onto the domain of the still unknown knowable. Or better: it is only truly rational in the measure that the particular knowledge detaches itself from this hitherto unknown, yet in principle knowable background.[6]

Despite Balthasar's antipathy to system, *holism* is very much his watchword. It is the dimensions of that whole which the rest of *Theologik* will attempt truly to convey.

---

5 H. U. von Balthasar, *Présence et pensée: Essai sur la Philosophie religieuse de Grégoire de Nysse* (Paris 1942).
6 *TL* I, p. 31.

3

☙❦❧

Subject, Object – and God

From the subject to God

Balthasar's remarks so far have implications, clearly, for that highly controverted topic of philosophical discussion, the subject–object relationship. In one sense, inasmuch as the revelation of being is a property inhering in being itself – for being of its nature unveils itself, it is 'transcendentally' characterised as truth, then the knowing subject must at all costs adapt himself to this vital disclosure. His knowledge must let itself be measured and determined by the object, what traditional philosophy calls the *adaequatio intellectus ad rem*. And yet it is not the hallmark of subjects to become simply Geiger counters for the registering of objective data. Subjectivity, indeed, includes the ideas of self-determination and creativity. In a distant echo of the divine intelligence which in an unconditional sense creates the object it knows (namely, the world), human subjects also creatively 'pose' their objects. Since the revelation of an object has its meaning only when it is offered to a knowing subject, we can even say that the object finds its own full sense only in that subject. Created knowledge for Balthasar is, therefore, at once receptive and spontaneous, or, in his preferred vocabulary, 'measured' and 'measuring'.

Here, in a phenomenological idiom, he renews the commonplace distinction of Aristotelian Scholasticism that the mind – which for Balthasar is always that of a *spirited animal* (he stresses, in other words, the share that sensibility has in such intelligence) – operates as *both* the 'possible' or 'patient' intellect, receptively, *and* as the 'active' or 'agent' intellect, spontaneously. At the same time, however, Balthasar stresses that an appropriate division of labour between these two will vary greatly from one area to another. For truth may be almost entirely *theōria*, contemplation, a looking, or nearly exclusively *poiēsis*, 'poetry', a making.

Because the subject is self-aware, disclosed to itself, 'unveiled' for itself, he or she can 'measure' themselves by the norm of truth and thus in turn be 'measured'. Keeping his distance equally from empiricism and Descartes, Balthasar maintains that the two discoveries – of the 'I' and of the world – coincide. By an absolute simultaneity, the subject becomes both self-aware *and* conscious of invasion by the truth of other realities beyond it. And, indeed, as Balthasar writes,

The more perfectly a being possesses itself, the more free it is, the more open it is, the more receptive to everything that surrounds it.[1]

And so, by an inversion of Leibniz's monadology, the Balthasarian subject is *as such* a being with windows, a being hospitable to other realities. It would be no privilege for an existent – a subject in whom being is unveiled – to be so equipped with innate truths that it needed no enlightenment from outside. So as to be able to taste the richness of being, a certain poverty is required, a capacity, as Balthasar remarks, to be 'listening out for a foreign revelation'. It is for him an essential law of finite spirit that the higher the spontaneity the more perfect the receptivity, an axiom which he illustrates in characteristic style, by reference to the experience of love. Love would 'willingly renounce all its knowledge, if it could only receive it anew from the one it loves', whereas, by contrast, innate ideas would be 'opposed to all true dialogue, wound courtesy, make love impossible'.[2] Relating that back to truth, we can say that the more spirit masters truth the more it is mastered by it – a statement which echoes Balthasar's early attempt to present a just doctrine of transcendence over against the Promethean and Dionysian proclivities of modern German literature in 'Apocalypse of the German Soul'.[3]

In that work, Balthasar concluded that only reference to God as the ever-greater reality towards which the human spirit strikes out in its own movement of self-transcendence in the midst of the world can resolve the riddle of existence posed from Lessing to Rilke. Here too, Balthasar introduces, this time in more straitly philosophical mood, his concept of God. In the act of knowledge, the embodied mind encounters a twofold limitation. On the one hand, this particular object which engages its interest at some given time is to be distinguished from the unlimited background of beings from which it emerges. On the other hand, the being that, precisely in this meeting with the object, is unveiled to the subject itself in its self-awareness can hardly be called being in the absolute sense of that word either. The experience of illumination by which the subject grasps itself and learns what being is does not throw light for the subject on being in its totality. But just this very fact teaches the subject that the truth, whose light allows it to measure the object – a light, moreover, that is itself the illumination of being – is not limited to the point-like finitude of the subject's own self-awareness. And so the subject, in Balthasar's words:

> knows that in making use of its own norm for the knowledge of the object, it is not dealing solely with a subjective norm, but participating in an objective norm, and in the last analysis, in a norm that is infinite, absolute.

The light of the finite subject is a limited sharing in a light unending. Its thinking is inserted into an infinite thinking of being and can only serve

---

1 *TL* I, p. 37.
2 *TL* I, p. 42.
3 See my *The Word Has Been Abroad*, pp. xi–xii.

as a measure because it itself is 'measured by an infinite measure which is no longer measurable, but measures all the rest'.[4]

And this is the divine thinking and being, the presence of which is the *conditio sine qua non* of all finite subjectivity and knowledge. Though what is known immediately is not God (here Balthasar wishes to bypass that heretical cul-de-sac in nineteenth-century thought that is Ontologism) but the contingent world of the human spirit, still God is known tacitly in that very contingency. Balthasar is able to appeal to St Thomas' *De Veritate* in support of his claim that the knower, in every act of self-awareness, as in the entertainment of every object, knows God in implicit fashion: *omnia cognoscentia cognoscunt implicite Deum in quolibet cognito*.[5] He adds, however, a more Augustinian reflection of his own, to the effect that the knower can only know himself and other things *through* God, in a witty transformation of the famous Cartesian formula (the *Cogito*), *Cogitor, ergo sum*: not 'I think' but '*I am thought* – and therefore I am'.

And so the reason why philosophical Idealists will never persuade the generality of human beings of the well-foundedness of their position turns out to be: religion. The primordial act by which persons perceive them-selves as subjects is the same act in which they know themselves to be 'posited and grasped by an Other, placed before him and at a distance from him'.[6] It is within this respectful distance between God and the creature that other free beings can put in an appearance likewise. How do we know about 'other minds'? Only the acceptance of an analogy – *not* identity! – between the divine 'I' and the creaturely 'I' can persuade to that other analogy, this time *within* the world, which both unites and distinguishes different 'centres' of self-awareness and truth-possession.

> Now the truth appears in the world as shared among countless subjects, open the one to the other in an attitude of spontaneous *disponibilité*, and awaiting each from each the communication of that share in truth accorded by God to each one as participation in his [God's] eternal truthfulness.[7]

For Balthasar the clearest sign of God's transcendence, over against the finite self, is found in the fact that to be *like* God, in possessing a luminous self-knowledge, the finite subject must be utterly *un*like him in requiring the mediation of some foreign object. In his own words:

> [the subject] takes cognizance of its likeness to God in the exact measure that it has to recognise its essential ordering to another – to recognise, that is to say, its creaturely condition.[8]

The subject can only draw close to the divine Truth by distinguishing itself more and more from that truth – that is, by receiving the truth of other things in ever readier *disponibilité* towards them. And yet this very

4 *TL* I, p. 45.
5 Thomas Aquinas, *Quaestiones de Veritate*, q. 22, a 2, ad i.
6 *TL* I, p. 48.
7 *TL* I, p. 49.
8 *TL* I, p. 46.

openness to truth is itself the gift of God to the constitution of the subject. So it comes about that, to continue the citation:

> the finite subject, thanks to its commerce with truth, is so to speak projected increasingly towards the divine truth, because it recognises in every finite encounter with the objects of the world, the ever greater amplitude of the truth of God.[9]

As always in Balthasarian thought, comparability and incomparability with God increase in direct proportion – that claim constitutes what can be called his 'mystical' reading of the *analogia entis* doctrine, indebted as that was, through Przywara, to the Fourth Lateran Council.

From the object to God

The same conclusion – that the subject–object relationship cannot be thought through without reference to the concept of God – also emerges if we come at the problem from the side of the object, rather than the subject.

At first sight, it might seem that the sheer fact of the being of the object should suffice to render it knowable – after all, the subject knows whatever it knows under the aspect of being in general, which is its sole form of a priori knowledge. Balthasar warns, however, that such a decision would be hasty. Too often in the history of epistemology the ultimate conditions which render an object knowable have simply been deduced from the conditions of human knowledge, with the result that ontology became a mere projection into being of the structure of our knowing – an inadmissible procedure. Being has its own laws which are not simply those of knowing.

Balthasar has already established that the two inseparable properties of truth are *measure* and *light*: measure is a being's aptitude for being known, light is the effective knowledge brought by a subject. As he writes:

> It cannot just be assumed that a being possesses measure and therefore knowability unless it stands in the light of an efficacious measuring.[10]

For an object to be knowable it does not suffice for it to be measurable. It must also (so Balthasar now goes on) *be measured already*. Since it cannot be self-measured when considered as an object (and even a subject may, and must, be considered as an object when objectified by another subject), and since, furthermore, the finite subject pre-supposes that any object it knows is already measured in and of itself, it follows that the measure of the object must be located in the infinite Subject – in God. A being which was not known by God would possess no measure and thus no truth. The truth of beings abides in God and he or she who wants to know them *fully* must get to know them in the divine light.

The *divine knowledge*, then, founds the truth of the existent, and gives it all the relations it enjoys. The divine idea is immanent in a being as its

9 *TL* I, p. 47.
10 *TL* I, p. 50.

'internal plan, its nature, its meaning'. If the existence of things cannot be identified with their being without also taking account of their *essence*, the kinds of things they are, then that essence is never 'something complete in itself'. It cannot be detached from God's idea of it, and therefore from his power to modify it in the course of the story of a life. And this is never more true than when the 'essence' we are speaking of is that of the human being.

In the case of man, individuality and species remain, but the decisive orientation – salvation or loss, the gift of grace abounding or imprisonment in spiritual dryness and loneliness – these are realities that can and do change, for their measure is found in eternity. A being 'never so fully possesses its own norm that it need not constantly, and increasingly, receive that norm from God'.[11] For Balthasar *both* the permanence of things, and so the universal validity of knowledge, *and* their dynamic quality, and so the transformative openness of beings to the God of history and the future, are equally important.

The subject and the object

What then, on this account, does the overall pattern of the subject–object relation look like? Given his reliance on the Aristotelian and Thomist notions of the mind as simultaneously receptive and spontaneous, and facilitated in both respects by the sensibility it draws from its material embodiment, it will scarcely come as a surprise to learn that Balthasar's portrayal of the commerce between subject and object takes concrete form in an account of *images*. *Conversio ad phantasmata*, 'turning to the images', is, after all, the rubric that governed Thomas Aquinas' account of how embodied beings know. But the atmosphere of Balthasar's account is hardly that of ancient or mediaeval philosophy. He has set his Aristotelian and Thomist inheritance in a new context drawn from post-Cartesian discussion of how the object can enter the realm of the subject and vice versa – and, most importantly, from the way such 'realist–idealists' as Schelling, with their emphasis on inwardness and freedom, treated that issue.

He explains that the object can only attain to its own proper perfection outside itself, in the world of subjects. It is by penetrating that world more and more that it comes to its full dimensions.

> Who would dare to affirm that this tree, stripped of its sensuous qualities and reduced to an unknown 'vital principle' would still be the being filled with beauty, meaning and precious advantages such as evidently it was thought by its Creator.[12]

This does not mean that the truth of things is transformed into a purely subjective truth, for the field of the subject's sensibility is also, in its spontaneity, part of nature, as is the yet higher spontaneity of the mind's formation of concepts by which, in a rule-bound way, the two spheres of object and subject are made one. Balthasar attacks in so many words the

11 *TL* I, p. 55.
12 *TL* I, p. 60.

'naïve realism' which would see sensible qualities as simply adhering to the object outside the realm of subjective perception. For such a defective realism, the object emits images which are only the 'duplication' – not an essential development – of its nature. Here the realm of sense is betrayed by the mistaken assertion that things need no 'space' in which to express themselves and acquire a language, for they possess expression and a proper name already in themselves. Lamentably absent on such a view is:

> the marvellous mystery of that twofold growth where object and subject penetrate each other, the mystery of the reciprocal service which they render each other in the birth and discovery of truth.[13]

This is not to say, however, that the diametrically opposite critical position is any better. (Kantian) criticism separates the subjective and the objective contributions to the object of knowledge, producing – wherever subjective participation is eliminated from truth and rejected as essential to the object – an immense impoverishment of the content of the truth of the world.

So for Balthasar there is no opposition between the subjectivity of the realm of sensation and the latter's participation in the truth of the object. The object always retains its own centre, from which it strikes out onto the fields of knowledge, there to win the spurs of its own completion.

Balthasar admits, however, that such an idea is less liable to easy acceptance than its complement: the notion that the subject needs the object for *its* deployment, waking as it does, like Sleeping Beauty, only when stirred from slumber by a stranger, becoming aware at once of self and world. Without the world, indeed, the subject remains only a 'formless myself', deprived of 'figure', 'plan', 'imprint', 'character'. When the subject comes to himself, he always finds himself to be:

> a being already absorbed by the permanent task of offering house-room to a world of objects, and of giving a form to himself.[14]

The rôle of the image

The relevance of images to all this lies in the fact that a subject's grasp of some object always takes as its starting point the images produced by the object in the sensuous sphere which the subject inhabits. This is simply (to repeat) the traditional Thomistic doctrine of the *conversio ad phantasmata*, a 'turning to the images', as the beginning of the movement of knowledge.

> The object has notified its presence in the subject by a sign which is first and foremost pure sensuous expression, and, in this capacity, manifests neither the essence of the object nor that of the subject as they are. And yet this expression of the object in the language of sensuous images is all that the subject gets in terms of the immediate grasp of the object. Even if it later manages to reach the being and

---

13 *TL* I, p. 62.
14 *TL* I, p. 65.

invisible essence of the object by way of the images, it will never encounter that being and essence save in the expressive sensuous image.[15]

Balthasar's idea of the image or sensuous sign will be vital to his later theological aesthetics with its centre in Jesus Christ as the Word Incarnate, the visible image of the Father, the sensuous sign *par excellence* of the invisible economy of the divine Logos. Here we can note how Balthasar first presents his semiotics – his theory of signs – at the philo-sophical marriage feast of subject and object. There, sensuous image and intuition of sensuous image form a perfect couple. The receptive and the spontaneous sides of the imagination are in balance, the working of the object in the realm of the subject counterpoised by the working of the subject as a creative reproduction of the impression issuing from the object. Little by little, the subject learns to read the significance of the signs that surround him. He discovers the difference between expression and what is expressed, and so can take the measure of the object, and thus identify its truth. Balthasar is careful to include here both the individually personal and the culturally social: experience and tradition. As he writes:

> On the one hand, truth, in its matter and in its form, is offered from without: it is thanks to experience and tradition that the subject's treasury of truth is bit by bit accumulated. On the other hand, the subject, as soon as it awakes to self-consciousness, is enabled by its own norm to test the ever richer treasury of truths, and pattern it in harmony with the norm of the person.[16]

As the subject grows in experiential maturity, he takes on more and more the form of the world, and yet, by the same token, the image of the world becomes ever more personal to him.

What is happening is that the subject decodes in the image a significance and a spiritual system of relations which *do not exist in the sensuous order as such.*

> To confer a meaning on images, it is necessary to recognise on their behalf an essence and existence they themselves do not possess. One bestows an essence on them when one sees them as the appearance of an *ensemble* endowed with meaning which does not itself appear; one lends them an existence when one sees in them the signs of things that exist in themselves.[17]

To be objects fitted for mind, images need this twofold interpretation, for they cannot interpret themselves. They cannot reveal their own meaning any more than the letters of a book can state what the words mean of which they are the parts. But just this incomprehensibility invites the spirit to seek a meaning in them, to decipher them. The 'all too obvious manifestness' of the images – their stunning impact – itself suggests some hidden mystery. And fortunately the subject has the capacity to:

15 *TL* I, p. 70.
16 *TL* I, p. 67.
17 *TL* I, p. 146.

bring to life the confused diversity offering itself to intuition by accentuating the essential traits of the given, and pushing the inessential to the background; to interpret a certain figure as the inevitable effect of a certain invisible power; and, lastly, to illuminate the object of vision by inserting it into larger *ensembles*, or more universal and already familiar concepts.[18]

This is a passage of considerable importance in the light of Balthasar's later theological aesthetics. Confining himself for the moment to the language of Thomism, Balthasar simply asserts that in this complex action two things happen simultaneously: an illumination of the image which transforms it into a concept (*abstractio speciei a phantasmate*) and the insertion of spiritual meaning into the image (*conversio intellectus ad phantasma*). If we may borrow a phrase from the aesthetics of Balthasar's Neo-Thomist contemporary, Jacques Maritain, this amounts to a 'creative intuition'.[19] Thanks to its spontaneity, knowledge divines the spiritual by drawing it from the sensuous (and this is a process of divination, not an immediate vision of essence, as the possibility of false interpretation shows). But at the same time, this creatively intuitive act is none the less sustained, and indeed demanded, by the image itself.

And here Balthasar adds a point that looks directly ahead to the theological aesthetics: it is by taking as a hypothesis the notion that the images of some constellation of impressions all issue from a midpoint which itself does not appear that one makes sense of them. The fluctuating images now appear as so many presentations from different angles of the same reality – a statue I circumambulate, a landscape through which I amble, or so many cinematic frames of different phases of its movement – as with, for example, a planetary circuit that I study. Be this as it may our spirit is so constituted that it can never stop asking after the meaning of things, and so has never ceased to interpret the world of images as an *ensemble* of meanings.

We shall return to the topic of the image under the rubric of 'truth as mystery'.

18 *TL* I, p. 72.
19 J. Maritain, *Creative Intuition in Art and Poetry* (New York 1953).

4

🙟🙠

Inwardness and Freedom

This pair of terms already put in an appearance in the last chapter, as indicators of Balthasar's debt, in his repertoire of themes, to the German philosophers of the nineteenth century. It was only predictable that, in the wake of Romanticism and the dissolution of the old establishments in a Europe prey to revolutions, such motifs would gain a higher profile in speculative thought. Perhaps with just that background in mind, Balthasar opens his account of truth as freedom by reassuring his readers this will be no launching of a ship named *Anarchy*. Even the divine freedom, a sovereign freedom if ever there was one, is exercised in accordance with the divine nature.

The freedom of the object

Balthasar begins his treatment in a very unusual place – with the liberty of the *object*. Here his concern is with the freedom of some being to let itself become an object of knowledge to others. Underneath even the most austerely theoretical of Balthasar's enquiries into the metaphysics of knowledge we frequently find spiritual themes, whether from the New Testament or from the Ignatian *Exercises*. To share one's substance with knowing agents is to give, to serve. What is elected by such liberty is a sharing of some object-of-knowledge's unique and irreplaceable *Selbstsein* – that which makes it more than simply one 'case' or example among a hundred. After all, were the knowledge of particulars never more than a discretionary application of general knowledge,

> existence would have lost every meaning, for being would have been deprived of that property which alone makes its possession desirable: namely, its constantly renewed uniqueness and therewith its character as something intimate.[1]

With the being he bestows on every creature, God grants, relative to the kind of being it is, a power of action, and, more especially, some sort of spontaneity in matters relating to its self-manifestation – a sort of distant echo of the perfect divine freedom. Even sub-spiritual creatures, Balthasar

---

1 *TL* I, p. 82.

23

maintains, have some analogue to the interior–exterior distinction, some 'within' protected by shell or carapace. Here Balthasar was greatly influenced by Goethe's philosophy of nature. As he would write in *Herrlichkeit*:

> Goethe cannot be seen as a naive objectivist; 'Nature' is implicitly understood as the mutual reciprocity and indwelling of subject and object . . .

and, citing the *Anschauender Urteilskraft*,

> all that is in the subject is in the object and something more besides; all that is in the object is in the subject and something more besides.[2]

Balthasar's philosophy of nature, like Goethe's, is preoccupied with 'grades of intimacy', the varying degrees to which beings possess this crucial property of interiority, necessary condition as it is for the 'freedom of the object'. Balthasar is unwilling to admit that any being lacks some rudimentary 'intimacy', for the abstract, approximative and revisable character of the scientific explication of natural phenomena suggests that even here reality

> will always remain essentially and necessarily richer than every knowing enquiry, and even on the lowest rungs has so inexhaustible a truth content that the researchers of all periods can busy themselves with it, without ever reducing it to a heap of facts, non-mysterious, fully surveyable.[3]

When the interiority of being condenses in the forms of vegetative life, the contrast between inner and outer becomes more acute. Even in the lowest life forms we find a mystery of unity: an organism can at one and the same time reaffirm its identity in regard to a large variety of exterior pressures, influences and factors, and also be so little unified that it can reproduce itself – that is, let duality come forth from unity. Philosophically, the reproductive power of organisms might be thought of as a testimony to the potency of their inner unity: they can engender unities of the same nature as themselves without suffering any loss. Alternatively, it can be considered as a deficiency of unity whereby some compensation is sought for inner defect by way of extending their own life in the form of (henceforth) two independent unities. These are the kinds of *aporia* which natural science will never resolve, as is pointed out – wisely, Balthasar thinks – by Goethe himself.

With animal life, being's intimacy enters a new phase. Now inner space begins to grow light, and to become accessible to itself. That is, the object is becoming subject, thereby raising a set of knotty philosophical problems. How can a subject be made an object, granted that the subjective is precisely *not* the objective? Is it possible to know a subject in the selfsame subjectivity, 'enlightened by the same light'? The possibility that it is the very subjectivity of knowledge which is incommunicable is often overlooked

2 *The Glory of the Lord: A Theological Aesthetics*, Volume 5: *The Realm of Metaphysics in the Modern Age* (Et Edinburgh and San Francisco 1991), p. 369.
3 *TL* I, p. 86.

when it comes to thinking about an interchange between minds, but it is inescapable when what we are concerned with is the interiority of animals. We can know *that* animals perceive, but *how* they perceive is something we can never co-experience with them. The world appears in the animal kingdom via a tremendous variety of images, corresponding to the environment of each species and harmonised with its feeling. We cannot know how the world appears to the many-faceted eyes of an insect, or to a bird or fish whose eyes point in different directions. Nor is this simply a question of difference of organ, for *Sinnlichkeit ohne Geist* – a sensuous grasp of the world without intellectual spirit – is something quite alien to us. And, none the less, all of these beings are grounded in the common medium which is life.

And here Balthasar does not hesitate to speak of the animal creation as occupying a mid-way position between the absence of freedom and its presence. Although their expressive gestures are made according to necessity not choice, animals none the less take part in their own exteriorisation, their 'truth'. For they share by 'knowing feeling' in the process of their own formation. And the fact that they speak the words of nature (rather than being, as are plants, the spoken words of nature) means that the truth of animals (as compared with that of plants) is both more mysterious and more accessible.

In the human being, consciousness becomes *self*-consciousness which entails, of course, a process of *Verinnerlichung*, 'interiorisation'. The inner world now becomes light for itself: man, by his self-possession, is a *free* being. *Geist*, spirit, is self-disposing. Truth as self-revelation is a free action, and so one heavy with responsibility, with moral significance. If the spirit is to be truly free it must be so not just before such communication but in it and after it. Balthasar stresses that what is proper to spirit is a truthful self-revelation which does not, however, renounce the interiority or 'being for oneself' which alone makes spirit's self-communication precisely a revelation. In a lapidary formulation:

> It [spirit] must have the possibility of giving itself to the other, without the other having the possibility of capturing it.[4]

Spirit's possession of a truth all its own, which others can only enjoy with its consent, is at once something qualitatively new when compared with the rest of life, and yet also the fulfilment of an ever-clearer tendency within nature itself.

When human beings reveal themselves in freedom, the result is a *testimony*, not just an expression.

> The speaker institutes a non-verifiable equation between the content of what he says and its form, and stakes his honour on the rightness of the equation concerned.[5]

Here the notions of *veracity*, on the communicator's part, and *faith*, on that of the communicatee, enter into the story. To try and remove from the picture the features of witness and trusting faith would have the effect of

4 *TL* I, p. 98.
5 *TL* I, p. 99.

sundering *Selbstsein*, self-being, or being a self, from truth altogether. Whilst we are not obliged to believe everything others say of themselves, a certain disposition to credit the self-testimony of others (a human analogue of faith) necessarily precedes and accompanies whatever effort we make to check up on their veracity. The communicatee witnesses to his own freedom in the reception of the word of another by associating himself with the recognition of the freedom which that word expresses. These notions, brought together under the heading of 'truth as freedom' will play a modest but crucial part in Balthasar's later theological dramatics.

An unexpected adjunct, in a work of modern metaphysics, is the discussion which follows on the holy Angels, those immaterial spirits whom revelation discloses as a category of beings higher than humankind.[6] Like St Thomas Aquinas, Balthasar regards angelology as raising questions of the highest philosophical importance. Sheer *Selbstsein*, such as angelic mind must possess as pure spirit, will be marked both by a far greater self-transparency than our own and a more marked capacity to communicate itself without. Balthasar represents the angelic world as the 'highest realisation of created freedom in the truth'. Aquinas' idea that each occupies its own species underlines the point that these beings are irreplaceably original in their individuality. For Balthasar this means that their communication, their 'word', is to the highest degree (for a creature) a creative act. An angelic word is free not only in the decision to speak but also in the form it takes: he compares it with the artwork of a human creator. Just as a symphony can only be by Haydn or Mahler, say, so the word of an angel can only be *this* angel's word and no other.

And the ultimate explanation of the freedom which characterises creatures in such diverse modes is the divine creative act from which they spring.

> The creative word of the 'Let it be!' which is the original cause of all extra-divine existence can only be a word spoken in absolute freedom. So the revelation of God contained in the creation, however much it achieves accomplishment in created nature, remains a work of freedom. Every flower, mountain, human being speaks of this freedom. To be sure, as creature every being in this world *necessarily* discloses the Creator, but in that moment it also reveals the non-necessity of creaturely existence and thus the Creator's *freedom*.[7]

A new initiative of grace is needed, however, if man is to proceed further along these lines – to receive, through the illumination of faith, the revelation of what God in all mystery is in his inner essence.

That discussion of the kinds of creature there are opens a more compendious ontological discussion. 'Everything that is and that happens is a carrier of meaning, is expression and reference.' The signifier is neither to be fully unified with the signified, nor is to be wholly separated from it. That is what the lesson of interiority teaches. And from it a further truth emerges: being and value (in the corresponding English discussion one

6 *TL* I, pp. 103–6.
7 *TL* I, p. 106.

finds 'fact' and 'value') do not belong to two sharply distinct realms. True, since a created being is non-necessary its existence remains extrinsic to its essence, and yet existence as the existence *of* the essence must bear along the features of the latter, and notably of the values it contains. Not all values, admittedly, are realised; certain ideal exigencies of things fail to become actual. But this in no way implies that reality itself is deprived of value. The dichotomy of fact and value expresses the tragic sundering of the practical and the intuitive intellect and, beyond even this, a collapse of nerve before the central problem of being itself. It is the interiority of things that gives them value, and makes them distinct from mere positive facts to be quantitatively assessed – not their capacity to arouse in the observer a *Wertfüllen*, a 'feeling of value'. Essence is always more than is already realised, for to it there corresponds a proper way of being (*Seinsart*) which does not just coincide automatically with the way of being of its present existence as an observer concerned with verifiable facticity could describe that.

And here Balthasar begins to reintroduce the important notion, drawn from Przywara, of *polarity*. A human being, he points out, remains self-identical in his essence from cradle to grave, even though 'in fact' he changes constantly *als existierender*, 'as an existing being'. At the same time, however, we can also speak legitimately of his essence participating in such a *perpetuum mobile* of change.

> The sphere of essence extends without discernible rupture from reality to ideality, from the figure (*Gestalt*) formed in concrete existence (*Dasein*), changing as this does through space and time, right through to the stable, normative idea which persists through all fluctuations in the real.[8]

We must speak of a polarity in finite being which amounts not to a metaphysical juxtaposition of elements but to the quasi-immanence of two terms one within another. Over against the 'father of phenomenology' Edmund Husserl's 'bracketing of existence', so as to concentrate, in his phenomenological logic, purely and simply on the world of essences, the Existentialists are right to see existence as absolutely inseparable from the sphere of essence. But Existentialism in its turn has only been able to offer a description of the essence of existence! Thus the history of recent philosophy shows that each of the two terms, essence and existence, orients thought towards the other via their common mystery, being. Where essence is the privileged object, it teaches that it cannot be understood without the consideration of existence, the simple fact that being has won the victory over non-being. Where existence is what interests, it refers the student to the interiority of being. Thus the mystery of being reaffirms itself time and again in and through the reciprocal implication of essence and existence, and shows itself in its unity as both. Each created thing has received from its Creator the gift of sharing in the infinity of its origin. Though it is not itself infinite, its being is too rich to be comprehended in exhaustive fashion.

8 *TL* I, p. 110.

The freedom of the subject

All this has been said under the rubric of the freedom of the object. There remains to be considered, albeit rather more briefly, the freedom which the subject may be said to dispose of. 'More briefly' because, for Balthasar, in surprising contrast to everyday supposition, it is the less significant of the two liberties. He emphasises the primordial receptivity of the subject, and only treats of the spontaneity of spiritual intelligence in strict dependence thereon. Subjectivity for Balthasar is an open vista onto a field already requisitioned by objects, objects which can either manifest themselves to such a subject or remain hidden in their silence. Either way, the subject remains constrained by the law of the object in his own thinking. To be enriched by other beings (the primary purpose of opening one's mind, in the remark by G. K. Chesterton already cited) asks first and foremost of the knowing subject 'the service of things'. Here we have what might be termed an 'evangelical ontology' where the subject comes not to be served but to serve, an analogy in the order of knowing and being of the advent of the Son of Man in the order of redemptive action.

Still, were there no freedom at all involved in the spirit's knowing activity, it would not be spiritual (*geistig*) activity at all. The spontaneity of knowing expresses, in point of fact, the interiority of the subject – a new topic in Balthasar's account of *Intimität*. As *person* the subject has freedom to direct himself towards those objects he wishes to receive within himself, to become familiar with. Among the vast gallery of objects that press upon us, we can only choose to know a selection – a sign both of the narrowness of our awareness and of the 'ordering and constructive freedom of spirit, which from out of the mass of stuff offered chooses that alone which suits its spiritual building'.[9] (It is, then, liberty not to see as well as to see.) There is voluntary closedness towards untimely truth as well as voluntary openness towards the truth that is sought and desired. The choice of what we will know, and of what will contribute to our world-image is already a free, ethical *prise de position* in regard to the great issues of life. The will is already engaged in the process whereby knowledge is acquired. The very openness of the knowing subject to the world already implies at any rate *voluntas ut natura*, will as part and parcel of our nature – the anticipatory sketch of *voluntas elicita*, my personal liberty. The interiority of the subject consists in the fact that, subjacent to its state of openness, there lies hidden in its being the movement of self-opening. In other words:

> Behind its spiritual light as intelligence there dwells within it the abiding will to self-opening and to openness.[10]

Here Balthasar insists that he is not espousing an irrationalist position for which the order of will is infinite and conditioning, that of thought finite and conditioned. The volitional opening of which he speaks is, rather, the supreme meaning of *ratio* itself. No being has meaning unless it possess a

9 *TL* I, p. 115.
10 *TL* I, p. 117.

Für-sich-sein, or 'being-for-itself'. But such *Für-sich-sein* has no sense unless it is capable of a movement of self-communication (*Mitteilung*). And indeed these two terms – being-for-itself and communication – form together the 'unique and indivisible illumination of being'. In a difficult statement, Balthasar speaks of this voluntary openness as

> the supreme justification of all being in its essence as in its existence, the 'forth-setting' (*Voraus-setzung*) to which every positing (*Setzung*) at last lets itself return and without which all being and history would remain unintelligible and meaningless.[11]

And in a Eucharistic metaphor he remarks that the will to self-revelation from the side of the object and the will to self-opening for the understanding of the object from the side of the subject are but the dual form of a single *Hingabe* – gift of self – manifested under two species. This concept of self-donation will be vital for his mature dogmatics.

And this in turn leads to the insight that *love* bears some relation to *truth*. The concept of love is as integral to that of truth as the concept of will is to that of knowledge – and for exactly the same reason.

> Love is by no means on the far side of truth. It is that which within truth ensures an ever new mystery over and above all unveiling; it is the eternal more-than-what-we-already-know without which there would be neither knowing nor knowable; it is that which, within the real, never permits a being to become a mere fact and that which never permits knowledge to rest on its laurels but makes it serve something higher still.[12]

Truth, then, springs from love, and love is more original and comprehensive than truth. And this has obvious implications for the 'liberty of the subject'. First, a free, conscious turning to the object of knowledge involves a serious and lasting *disponibilité* towards the latter. Subjectivity becomes sheer *Aufnahmefähigkeit*, the 'capacity for welcome'. It becomes all ear. Its will to do justice to the object's communication is also love, a preference for the good and truth of the other. But then, secondly, this attitude on the subject's part can and should intensify. So as to let the object achieve its virtualities in the subject, the natural willing of openness to the other must be raised up into the realm of the subject's freedom: now, through the creative looking of the loving knower the loved being can put forth aptitudes perhaps unknown even to itself. Balthasar's chosen metaphor for this is a climbing plant mounting up thanks to a trustworthy trellis which supports it.

This mystery of freedom in knowledge is, Balthasar remarks, 'like all true mysteries', a mystery of love. For the ideal image of the loved object which the knower in love hides within him is as much subjective as objective – subjective, not in the sense of fantastic but in the sense that its truth only becomes real truth by means of a subject, just as a fruit only matures in a specific climate. The possibility the loving knower sees is

---

11 *TL* I, pp. 117–18.
12 *TL* I, p. 118.

objective, then: it is incarnate in the being of the loved. It is not a question of positing some ideal reality in a transcendent sphere, for the true dwelling of these ideal images is the personal love of another being. Lover and loved collaborate in the realisation of the image, such that the border between subjective and objective can never be drawn with exactness. And if the two contrive to let the ideal become fully identical with the real then the object takes possession of its own truth, since

> that which was hidden in it has been unveiled, the possible has been realised, and that conformably with its original idea. And yet the idea has been perceived by the lover and as it were re-created by him. It is his ideal which has been really formed in the loved one, such that the latter must henceforth give thanks for what he is to the lover who has given him the true image of himself.[13]

The lover lets the material imperfect image of the loved one collapse into the abyss of non-being. By not attending to it, to certain real defects, it permits it to disappear. By acting as if the ideal were already real this attitude enables it to become so – from which Balthasar draws the conclusion that there is not only a truth which unveils. There is also a truth that veils, that hides. Only by the knowledge that the apparently unreachable ideal is perceived in one by anticipation can it become reachable reality. And referring to the way in which the dissection of an organism necessarily means its death, the destruction of its truth as a living thing, Balthasar writes (and here he has psychoanalysis particularly in mind):

> It belongs to the truth of the living thing that a part of itself must remain hidden. And it belongs to the truth of the free and spiritual being that a part of itself must be consigned to forgetfulness. Not every truth . . . has a claim to eternalisation. An ordered cosmos of truth comes to birth only through selection and preference: much that is hidden must be brought forth, and much that is disclosed be returned again to hiddenness.[14]

But if through his knowledge man contributes to the actualisation of the real, does this not mean he can also risk leading the objects of knowledge into temptation by imposing on them the products of his own fantasy? Indeed it does, which is why, for the creative aspect of his 'doing the truth', he needs a *Leitbild*, a directive image whereby the image of his knowing of another can be formed. Now the knowledge which is not measured by things but measures them, measures them because it contains the truth they must realise as best they can, belongs only to God. The divine knowledge is in no way a 'registrative' knowledge; rather does it engender the truth it knows. By his creative action, moreover, God can bestow on his intellectual creatures something of this power of his – so long as we understand that statement according to the 'law of the analogy of being and of secondary causality'.[15] In the case of artistic knowledge, where what is made cannot be known till man has conceived and fashioned

13 *TL* I, p. 123.
14 *TL* I, p. 126.
15 *TL* I, p. 127.

it, this is obvious. But Balthasar extends the range of this thought (for otherwise there would be no analogy between the divine knowledge and human knowledge *per se*). Only by placing himself in the divine perspective can someone propose to another the ideal image he should realise, just as only by inviting the other to look towards God can he assist him to conform himself to this image. Without God this 'supreme operation of human knowledge' would be Promethean, and therefore wholly inadvisable.

> Only when one can refer a human being to God, when one can make it credible to him that his image perceived in love is also the image conserved for him in God, does one have the right to cooperate in the formation of the truth of the world.[16]

And, for that, it is an indispensable condition that one has received from God the grace of loving and contemplating human beings in God. There alone, in God, do the image of knowledge and the image of God coincide.

Prudence and totality: the 'administration' of truth

Balthasar's final thoughts under the heading of 'truth and freedom' concern the use, conduct or 'administration' of truth. Both the object and the subject, Balthasar has so far shown, possess the truth in the form of *an sich*, as *nature*, and in the form of *für sich*, as *freedom*. Insofar as they belong to nature they are set in movement towards truth even before they are aware of the fact. This is so for the object in its opening up *vis-à-vis* itself, and of the subject in its opening out onto others. But insofar as object and subject possess freedom they can actually intervene in the *déroulement* of these processive movements. They can share in the elaboration of the truth, for God has willed to associate men with him in the administration (*Verwaltung*) of truth.

The exigence of witnessing to truth is, in Balthasar's view, inscribed within the being of man. Unless he responds to it he goes, spiritually speaking, towards ruin. Still he must *freely* consecrate himself as a witness to truth. But when should he testify to the truth, to whom, to what degree, and in what manner? Similarly, one can ask, When is it a duty to give a hearing to the possible truth offered by another – for one cannot concede equal attention to every truth or putative truth on life's way. Balthasar appeals to the virtue of prudence to answer these questions: situations are simply too many and various for exact norms to be supplied. There are few domains where so much scope, and responsibility, is accorded to this virtue. So much so is this the case that prudence alone, without the assistance of a higher norm, cannot justify her determinations. That 'higher norm' is one of two, Balthasar thinks: either egoism or love. This follows from what has been already said about the epistemological rôle of love.

> Insofar as love is the truth-engendering movement itself, it alone holds the key to the use of truth (*Wahrheitsanwendung*). It is the true measure of all communication and all reception.[17]

16 *TL* I, p. 128.
17 *TL* I, p. 132.

All expression of truth which is not at the service of love is compared by Balthasar to an erotic exhibitionism. It fails to respect the inner law of its subject. If truth, however, considered as the unveiling of being, has its measure and limits in the laws of love, love itself has neither measure nor limit outside itself. Love does not only limit the self-revelation of the subject, it also respects the mystery of the other person, and forbids all invasiveness of approach. Furthermore, it also dictates what John Henry Newman would have called a 'principle of reserve'. It may constrain us only to reveal truth in a reserved, reticent fashion. An unmeasured love may still need to measure out truth, portion by portion, as it can be borne.

> Truth as we know it in the world always consists of individual dis-
> closures, propositions, judgments, which unveil a determinate per-
> spective. Each of these perspectives has its finitude, and has to be
> completed by others. No worldly truth is absolute – not even if it is
> genuine, real truth. It is only truth if it is in continuity with the whole
> truth, if it is really an expression (even if only a limited and measured
> one) of an unconditioned and unmeasured revelation and gift of
> self. So in the human use of truth every finite communication of
> truth must express an unmeasured will to self-donation (*Hingabe*).[18]

And so this is quite different from a 'being economical with the truth' which disguises a merely political will to manipulate others or at any rate to achieve a compromise by telling one one thing and another another, where both hear something to their liking. Each partial expression of truth must be animated by a hidden spirit of integral truth, a complete 'truth-attitude' (*Wahrheithaltung*) which should underlie it. 'Every misuse of truth consists in the granting of independence to the fragmentary to the disfavour of the whole.'[19] Ignorance of more than a fragment of the infinite truth is no crime. What *is* criminal is a self-satisfied closure to vaster and more complete perspectives. Only love guarantees that this will not happen, because in love one opens oneself without reserves – and hence opens oneself to every truth which transcends some personal viewpoint.

> Love is that receptivity which gives every foreign truth credit so
> that it may disclose itself as such. It is the most universal of all a
> prioris, for it presupposes nothing other than itself.[20]

And now Balthasar can state a most important principle of his entire philosophical theology – highly relevant, as we will note in connexion with his *Epilog*, to his presentation of a proper Christian apologetics. No rule in the use of truth can be higher than that of *totality*. The more some partial perspective is able to integrate within itself a large measure of truth the better has it staked out its claim to truth. By contrast it is typical of heresy and sectarianism that they hive off a fragment of the truth in opposition to the whole. The antidote to this is, once again, love. Love is happy to admit every truth, whatever its provenance, but it is also clear-

18 *TL* I, p. 137.
19 *TL* I, p. 138.
20 *TL* I, p. 139.

sighted and far-seeing enough to be able to establish a hierarchy among truths themselves. In particular, it can distinguish enveloping truths from enveloped truths, the comprehensive from the included. This faculty is its greatest resource in the 'conversation of *Weltanschauungen*'. And if, then, it wins a triumph over an adversary it does so less by the precision of its replies than by the plenary quality of the truth it offers.[21] And Balthasar makes clear that he is thinking ultimately of the divine love of the truth of Judaeo-Christianity when he writes that love does not so much judge as leave the judgment to the more radiant light of revelation which flows from the evidence itself.

21 *TL* I, p. 140.

5

Image and Reality

Balthasar has several times had occasion to refer to the mystery of being, or the mysterious character of truth. Now he turns to deal expressly with *truth as mystery*. From the perspective of the object, first of all, reality – so we have seen – forms an ordered series where the higher the being the more interiorised it is. As our eye moves upward on this scale, we find things increasingly evading the clutches of that facile knowing – knowing as registering mere being-there – typical of Positivism, and becoming instead more and more the locus of a free revelation. At the same time, something becomes plainer and plainer – the fact that being is essentially a 'marvel full of mystery', its sheer presence stupendous richness. Indeed, it is being's nature to be richer than what, of being, one can see and grasp. Mystery does not lie on the further side of truth: it is truth's own immanent, enduring property. In the real order, to know an object is to be enriched by a lasting mystery.

But the question is, Does such mystery attach only to being or also to truth itself? We have already discovered, in relation to the freedom of the subject, that truth is not a 'mere fact to be taken for granted' but something co-produced in the 'loving self-gift of a subject'.[1] What is understood is conditioned by the loving gaze of the one who understands. Disclosure, precisely in its freedom, remains something mysterious. To draw out this mystery-character of truth, Balthasar goes on, we must leave off consideration of the subject–object relation, for this is a very abstract enquiry, and embark on an exploration of how in lived existence all this strikes us. (Here Balthasar's vocabulary – taken from the *Lebensphilosophie* of early twentieth-century Germany, and from the increasingly influential Heideggerian Existentialism of the 1930s and 1940s – shows his desire to answer better the challenges of these philosophies than contemporary Neo-Scholasticism was doing.)

The translucence of the image

We shall not by now be surprised to hear that the primary way in which, in all concreteness, object and subject are mutually open one to the other in interaction is that of *images*. This will be Balthasar's starting point for a

1 *TL* I, p. 144.

journey to realms revealed by the interplay between these 'poles of
knowledge'. In a key statement for his account of truth as mystery:

> The human spirit, gazing on images, contributes a dimension of
> depth, which they do not themselves possess. It draws from them a
> wholeness of form (*eine Ganzheit der Gestalt*) which is more than the
> simple contours of the appearance alone.[2]

Phenomenalism, the notion of a world of images as sheer surface – a
world with no depth of existence or essence – is purely an abstract thought
which would never occur to instinctive awareness. The human spirit passes
via images to the depth of the object which the images re-present. The
images 'just have to' lean on the non-revealed depth of a truly existing
essence if what they communicate is to become intelligible to the eyes of
the subject.

Here, however, Balthasar enters a caution for, when reflection about
the status of the images gets underway, people can easily follow false
trails. For instance, they can readily become sceptics, perceiving only in
abstract fashion the relation between the world of images, which is visible
but without essence, and the essential world which is invisible and situated
'behind' the images. What Balthasar seems to have in mind is one strand
in Platonism, where only commerce with intelligible ideas and essences
yields truth, the world of images granting but deceitful opinion. The result
may be that one closes the doors of the senses so as, rather, to listen
interiorly to the voice of reason or receive spiritual illumination – the way
of classical rationalism and idealist mysticism respectively. Images are
reduced, either absorbed into the concept or into the immediate reality of
spirit. In the end, the rationale of the existence of sensuous appearances
becomes impossible to grasp.

The opposite tack is to look for the essence in the inessential, renouncing
any truth beyond phenomena, and locating truth in the flux of images.
Here appearance and truth become identical, pure change the persisting
essence and sheer irreality the form of existence. These are the paths
trodden by empiricism and by the mysticism of immediate experience.

If the first approach wants the truth in an idea without an image, then
the second seeks it in an image without an idea – and so both alike arrive
at an empty mystery. This is Balthasar's version of Kant's dictum in the
Critique of Pure Reason that 'thoughts without content are empty; intuitions
without concepts are blind'. As he explains, by way of dismissal of the
cul-de-sacs up which these roads lead:

> The pure concept of rationalism is as empty as the 'ground of the
> world' of idealist mysticism, and the unknowable thing-in-itself of
> empiricism is as empty as the pure becoming of experiential
> mysticism.[3]

From this void the subject can but return to itself in disillusioned self-
preoccupation. Since, seemingly, what the world offers is reality deprived
of all graspable figure, consciousness seeks salvation within its own

2 *TL* I, p. 147.
3 *TL* I, pp. 150–1.

resources and tries to create an order as the result of personal effort. In this 'Copernican epistemological revolution' all 'objective interiority', as Balthasar terms the native withinness of things, disappears into that of the subject, and the images become no more than incomprehensible externalisations of inner space.

But if, as Balthasar has steadfastly proclaimed from the outset of his treatise, truth is really the unveiling of being – being's ability to appear as it really is – then this *aporia* can be resolved after all. Naturally, truth does not have its seat in images – appearances – *as such*, for these can only have meaning if the centre to which they relate is situated beyond them. However, no more is it to be expected that truth lies *beyond* the appearances, for that is the non-disclosed, which by definition does not appear. The truth of the matter is that the world of images constitutes the means whereby the non-apparent being of objects interprets itself, that is (if the pun may be allowed) *comes – to be interpreted*. Thus, whereas aestheticism falsely thinks the images are the be-all and end-all, anti-aestheticism equally falsely disregards them as of no avail.

The place of meaning

Meaning or significance (*Bedeutung*) would be impossible unless surface were already charged with all the ideal content of depth. From the hidden centre there takes place an 'ex-pression'. The image is not an artificial doublet of reality, and yet being does not have its dwelling there. Balthasar's comparison is a painting which represents a third dimension it does not itself possess. What the image is not is precisely what gives it its image–essence – the capacity of being to let an image of itself appear. This 'plastic power' is what enables the image to signify, and gives it a content and density which surpass what we would consider to be the imagistic alone.

> Thus it is that the significance is wholly to be seized in the image, without however being limited to the [material] reality of the image. In this unbreakable duality the mystery of truth begins to show itself as a plenary mystery.[4]

Balthasar calls this environing world of images in which we live a 'single field of significances'. The reality expressed there can never be adequately described, for nature's *Ausdruckssprache*, her 'expressive speech', is addressed not to conceptual antennae but to antennae Balthasar terms, paying homage here to Goethe, *gestaltlesende*: literally 'form-reading'. Balthasar's early love of Goethe – and notably his philosophical fascination with the latter's emphasis on the 'vital form' of concrete, living things – had been confirmed by his study of Guardini at Berlin. For that Catholic philosopher, things cannot be grasped in their originality without *both* intuition which gathers in their 'existential' richness *and* a conceptual apparatus that registers the depth of their 'essence'.[5] Our most important

---

4 *TL* I, p. 154.
5 R. Guardini, *Der Gegensatz: Versuche zu einer Philosophie des Lebendig-Konkreten* (Mainz 1925).

epistemological equipment is, accordingly, a capacity for a *comprehending seeing* which can read off, and so assimilate, the significant forms of things. And when image and idea – expression and what is worth expressing – match perfectly, the result is a symbol greater than the sum of its parts, so great, indeed, that it is, Balthasar remarks, a quasi-infinitude. Much the same thing has been said in English by Samuel Taylor Coleridge, with his notion of the 'translucence' of the image, and of symbols 'consubstantial with the truths of which they are conductors',[6] though Coleridge quite lacks Balthasar's capacity for steadily advancing an account of the real at large through sustained philosophical exposition. Here for the first time, Balthasar comments, we have the premonition that mystery may be a lasting property of truth itself. It is inseparable from the most perspicuous disclosure – and not just from the *de facto* opaque.

To this aspect of truth is joined beauty, for the beautiful is that property which enables truth to radiate out, to subjugate those who perceive it by its splendour, its clarity and the perfection of its expressive power. And in a definition crucial to the theological aesthetics Balthasar calls beauty:

> the inexplicable active irradiation from the mid point of being to the expressive surface of the image, irradiation reflected in the image itself and granting it a unity, depth and richness far beyond its own power to contain.[7]

Beauty gives truth a grace-character. Knowledge calls out for clarity and conquest: the response of 'Got it!' But a mountaineer in conquering an alp has not got it henceforth in his pocket. Beauty – this counterweight for recognising the abiding 'excess' in reality which can never be reduced fully to concepts – is necessary if a truly integral attitude to knowledge is to be ours. So it is that, with a work of art, one could know it by heart and still find it fresh every morning.

It is not surprising, then, Balthasar thinks, that the knowing subject is often tempted to confine its satisfaction to the world of images and its immanent significance. Regarding the world as a 'song without words' which it would be impudent to explicitate is the characteristic approach of aestheticism. Yet profound as the sense of the images already is, if that depth is itself cut off from ontological rooting – if we abandon the attempt to conjoin the world of images to a wider whole – all its spiritual significance withers and fades. Beauty when human beings aim to experience it in its abstract purity soon engenders a deep melancholy. The inquietude and appeal which we find sparked off in us by the images calls from us a movement Balthasar terms (using a Hegelian pun) *erinnern* – a movement both of going further into the interior of being and of transforming the sensuous content of thought into the spiritual. The images do not deceive: they proclaim both the real mystery they house and their own fragility and insuffiency. Appealing both to Augustine and to Hegel: thanks to their comparative lack of being, the images return to the source from which they come and by this very movement draw attention to the depth whence

---

6 S. T. Coleridge, *Lay Sermons*, ed. R. J. White (London 1972), p. 98.
7 *TL* I, p. 156.

they came. Incapable of showing more than they have shown already they return to the ground of being, and let the essence (*das Wesen*) address through them as they fade an almost intermediary-less word, before falling back into silence.

Balthasar is at pains to stress that the movement from sensuous immediacy to spiritual reflexion should not be regarded as a victory of concept over image. The image remains as indispensable as before – but this time by making known, so to say, its own withdrawal, in rendering itself superfluous, and thereby drawing attention to the essence. Balthasar finds – fancifully, some will think – a kenotic quality to the presentation of being through phenomena. He invites us to glimpse here, in other words, a faint reflection of the central event of cosmic reality: the self-emptying of the Logos, in the Manger, on the Cross.

> The truth which is identical with the unveiling of being (*Sein*), with the offering of self (*Preisgabe*) it makes to the knowing subject, indeed, in a kind of abasement of its sovereignty, so as to become a 'matter' for an alien knowing, this truth has the precise form of a mutual renunciation of essence and image, ground and appearance, whereby essence consents to step forth in appearance, to offer itself as an 'open thing' in the world of images, while the appearance on its part wants only to be a function of the revelation of essence. And so in the interior of being a mysterious movement arises, which neither monism nor dualism can represent, but which presents in its deepest reality the structure of truth.[8]

Neither pole, that is, neither being nor appearing, can be separated from the other, any more than they can be confused therewith.

Up to now we have been looking at the movement whereby truth presents itself to us in being considered as an object of knowledge. To this movement there corresponds a correlative happening in the *subject*. By renouncing sensuous perception inasmuch as (but *only* inasmuch as!) the latter constitutes an immediate datum, and abrogating through thought the 'closedness' or hermetic character of signs that are meaning-laden, certainly, yet without ever laying their own meaning bare, a spiritual subject that cannot come to the whole truth except by *reflexion* enters into the depths. Such reflexion – which takes place in *concepts* – may seem rather impoverished when we contrast it with the richness of images. (So for that matter does essence when compared with appearance.) But what is happening, Balthasar opines, is that the thought of the subject is modelling itself on the structure of the object. This it can do, however, in no way other than by reference to the images, the phenomena (*conversio ad phantasmata* again!), for without them the concept can receive neither life nor truth. Actually, the most satisfactory way to receive a reality, for Balthasar, is by a combination (what he terms a 'reciprocal reflection', *Ineinanderspiegelung*) of intuition and concept. Abstracted from the sensuous, the concept must then lead away from its own abstractness, so as to move towards the concrete plenitude of intuition. In knowledge, the

8 *TL* I, p. 165.

act of abstraction from the sensible coincides ever more precisely with the orientation of the spirit towards the sensible. The act in which *intellectus agens* – the spontaneity of mind – turns towards the sensible to touch it with its light and raise it into its sphere is at the same time the act in which the spirit leans for support on the sensible so as to fill out the empty unity of spirit with the manifoldness, *Vielfalt*, of the sensuous. In this movement the reality of the essence apparently strips itself of mystery to show itself as pure enlightened concept. In fact, however, the mystery deepens. It *is* a mystery that the immediate disappearance of the surface in the depth can let the depth be glimpsed as such and yet never appear immediately.

And this leads Balthasar to his attempted solution of that age-old problem in the theory of meaning (and reference): the relative priority of the concrete individual or the universal category. For while what is given in sensuous knowledge is something particular, that to which the concept is ordered is first and foremost the essence as universal. Thus:

> As humanity only comes to be as man, so the [individual] man only comes to be as humanity. They presuppose each other. If there were no humanity – no reality of inter-connexion of the stock to express and guarantee continuity of essence and being, no individual would be possible. But inversely if the individual person did not find himself in immediate relationship with this abstraction that is humanity, no universal nature would be possible either.[9]

Balthasar's mediation between universal-realism and individual-nominalism is subtle – or rather he aims to avoid both. This is just as well because in the paradigm case of most interest to him (humanity 'versus' individual men) he will need to affirm *both* the solidarity of the human community *and* the uniqueness of individual actors if his project of a 'theological dramatics' is ever to be realised. Stoutly insisting on the reality of a common essence in which individuals communicate, he adds that, whereas the *individual members of a species* can be counted and agglomerated, one can never add together *persons*. A person, in the measure that he or she is unique, reflects in their irreducible individuality the absolute unicity of the divine being. Later, when engaged on writing *Theodramatik*, his account of the uniqueness of persons will be both more Trinitarian and more charismatic – in the sense of that word which denotes the Holy Spirit's allotting of vocations in the body of Christ.

Not that Balthasar's purview is restricted to the special case – in the theory of universals and singulars – of mankind and men. An analogous ambiguity would attend the case of a bird or a book. 'One' of these things, commonplace as they are, raises the whole question of the 'aporetic' quality of that foundational property of being which is unity. As with essence and existence, and essence and appearance, so too with universality and singularity. Thought cannot close the gap; it can only circle round a mystery. It is not logical grammar which is at fault in failing to provide a generally accepted theory of reference, for reality itself requires of thinking a ceaseless oscillation

9 *TL* I, p. 170.

from the universal, which is empty, to the particular, and again from the particular, with its plenitude, to the universal. And vice versa: from the particular, which is limited, to the universal and again from the universal, with its vastness, to the particular.[10]

Here too, then, mystery cannot be eliminated from truth.

The word

When the exterior expression of some being is not simply sensuous sign but language, then the possibilities both of deceptive presentation and of faithful presentation of the hidden essence become more intense. The freedom of spiritual nature, in the case of human beings, sees to that. Natural expression still takes place – for instance by intonation and facial gesture – but is subordinated to spiritual, *geistig*, meaning. Analogously to what he has said of the image, Balthasar speaks of the word as so supercharged with spiritual content that it can accomplish the work of disclosure much more by *eine dienende Selbstaufhebung* than by *herrschende Selbstvorhebung*, more by a 'serving self-effacement' than a 'dominating self-affirmation'. By contrast with the sensuous sign, its language is much poorer: it makes known a maximum of spiritual content by a minimum of sensuous material. None the less it is in human language that the image reaches its most perfect transparency *vis-à-vis* the essence. *Verbal language* is the paradigmatic form of spiritual speech – though there are also the languages of art and of human gesture to consider too.

Obviously, in a 'theo-logic', *words* are going to be, for Balthasar, a pretty important topic. To speech belong those 'general concepts' – doubtless modified to some degree with the passage of time – which countless millions of speakers in human history have drawn on, as from a common patrimony. In one sense, accordingly, speech is a 'function of being in the world and in the community'.[11] That may sound anodyne enough – but what will then happen to language considered as free spiritual self-expression? It is, presumably, Balthasar's literary passion which leads him to feel so strongly the force of this objection. The common concepts which, in Neo-Scholasticism, are an altogether comforting sign of the self-identity of the human species and the permanence of some basic features in its experience of the world can also be a menace to the free spirit in its search for exact expression, and an invitation to spiritual laziness in speaking. Balthasar's ontology of the human being is far too robust, however, to yield to this individualist account of 'perfect' language use. An infant at arms is destined for spiritual consciousness, but it hardly enters the world as pure spirit. Its growth implies learning to play on many registers.

Nothing is smoother and more uninterrupted than this emerging of the human spirit from the realm of unconscious nature; as imperceptible as the growth of the bodily organism is the unfolding of the bud of the living form of human truth.[12]

10 *TL* I, p. 174.
11 *TL* I, p. 181.
12 *TL* I, p. 180.

An essential part of introduction to the world is initiation into universally valid traditions and forms of human communication – and it is in this context that personal spirit develops further, both in the 'subjective' direction of exploration of its own profound freedom and in the 'objective' direction of taking the measure of cosmic space. Getting to know the 'I' and getting to know the world are (as usual in Balthasar) simultaneous happenings, not alternative options.

Sign of his belonging in the tradition of Augustinian Thomism, Balthasar gives much weight to the *verbum mentis*: the inner 'word' of the human spirit whereby understanding takes shape, at once distinguishing the 'I' from the world (and so giving it spiritual freedom) and declaring its intimate connexion with the world (its freedom is, not least, the liberty to give the inner word outer expression). The spiritual word, through its openness to the world and so to every existent, not only mediates knowledge of self, it also enables my potential knowledge of other beings to become actual – through the power that is speaking and listening. The unheard word of the mind becomes sensuous expression at work both to teach and to learn in the world, and that in unlimited fashion. Here the temporal priority of sensibility and of the image – of which Balthasar has made so much – gives way to the real priority of spirit – for what is there in the richly ramifying realm of the sensuous, the phenomenal, the imagistic, that I cannot in principle draw on as a communicative agent, a user of the word? The 'world of images', so dear to Balthasar's poetic Scholasticism, takes on a new vocation – to be a repertoire for inter-subjective communication and understanding for use in a greater spiritual space. 'Intersubjective', because, just as the universal and the singular proved to be unthinkable one without the other at the level of being, so now Balthasar considers himself to have shown that at the level of knowing there is no possibility of à la carte selection between the personal 'I' and the social world of subjects together. I cannot see my own face – though others see it – unless I use a mirror. Just so where my grasp of my own spiritual being is concerned. I shall come to know it in some fashion as it becomes visible in the 'mirror of the circumambient world and its objective responses' to my addressing it.[13]

Thus the word – even, or indeed especially when we conceive it as the expression of a free spirit – is a *dialogical* word. Truth itself, consequently, enjoys a 'dialogical, social, character'.

> The *logos* of being – which seemed at first no more than a mysterious reduplication of being in the form of image, expression, concept, havering between unity and duality within being's enclosure, now opens out into an inter-subjective *logos* which, oscillating between oneness of essence and multiplicity of persons, has as its result the unity of the word in the form of speech and response.[14]

Such natural truth – the 'truth of the world' – is hardly being *simpliciter*, for then it would be one with eternal truth and have no need to be

13 *TL* I, p. 190.
14 *TL* I, p. 192.

constantly recuperated in this manner. But neither is it sheer becoming, a flux with no more achieved stability than the procession of phenomena.

According to Balthasar, the ontological preconditions of a sound epistemology already suggest the pertinence to knowing of analogues, at least, of such quintessentially religious attitudes as faith and love. The communicative movement Balthasar has described under the heading of truth's dialogue nature would entail a burdensome proximity to others if it were not inspirited by love. Likewise, a moment of faith and trust – fiducial faith would be the phrase in a strictly theological context – is indicated by the terms of the exchange between free spirits in which the communication of truth (or putative truth) occurs. There must be *some* willingness to credit the authority of a witness (or the witness of an authority) if society's intellectual life is not to collapse in universal scepticism. More strongly, no one takes responsibility for the truth of an affirmation he or she makes unless in the last analysis they are willing to let the totality of their life and actions (and, if need be, sufferings) support it.

> Trusting self-gift (*vertrauende Hingabe*) remains the a priori of all true knowledge between free spirits and in this attitude there is fulfilled the objectification of the subject in the object as well as the objectivity of the object being received *vis-à-vis* the subject. Thus faith is so little in opposition to knowing (*Wissen*), or even in tension with it, that the unity of faith and knowing signifies perfect knowledge (*Erkenntnis*), perfect openness for the truth.[15]

Moreover, not only do these spiritual preconditions of natural knowledge already suggest some formal features of revelation thinking where faith and love are all-important. More than this, they sketch out, however inchoately, the contours of the content of divine truth which – so succeeding volumes of *Theologik* will show – is also a 'unity of self-determination and dialogue' and an 'eternal livingness of word and self-gift'.[16]

15 *TL* I, pp. 198–9.
16 *TL* I, p. 200.

6

꧁꧂

Being Situated

One might have thought that Balthasar had so far been rather successful in integrating the intimately personal with the publicly common in his account of truth. But before crossing the threshold of mystery – which will bring us to the climax of *Wahrheit der Welt*, the contrast and comparison between truth worldly and truth divine – he wants to clarify further the relation between truth's universal validity and its personal validity, essential truth and the truth of personal existence.

Universal and personal

What he wants to scotch is the notion that concentration on the latter – in some sense religiously inevitable inasmuch as real assent to Christian revelation can only ever be given by *persons* – threatens the universal truth-claims of an objective metaphysic. How does he achieve this laudable goal? He argues that the beings whose essential characteristics it is the task of metaphysical enquiry to elucidate are situated in time and history – with the result that their 'idea', though in one way given and determinate, is in another way a project and open to the future. And he adds that this is the case precisely by dint of certain virtualities in their essential idea – so the truth of personal existence is in no way to be regarded as counterposed to the truth of essences, of kinds of nature. Freedom, after all, is a property of certain sorts of nature, precisely. And the adage 'the individual is ineffable' does not mean that individuals are unknowable but simply that they cannot be translated into terms of universals *without remainder*. So 'nature' and 'situation' need to be comprehended *together*.

Still, it follows that if being can be 'individualised' so also can truth – which is never other than the truth *of being*. First and foremost, this is a matter of the features which belong with some essence, or at any rate may do, the *Soseinsmerkmale* of some subject, its traits of its 'being-so'. Here essence and situation constitute together the subject-in-its-context, or what Balthasar terms – in a coining he will develop theologically for the Word incarnate in his relations with others – a 'constellation' (*Konstellation*). Everyone judges reality – and so grasps truth – from within his or her 'constellation': there is always personal angle, a point of view. Nor is this to be regretted inasmuch as it guarantees truth its 'intimacy', its inwardness in the subject's life. However, this is no charter of epistemological individualism, much less of solipsism. Every subject is responsible for filling out and enriching their own 'perspective' by reference to those of others, in that way 'discovering ever richer relations within the infinite field of truth and making their own an ever more comprehensive standpoint'.[1] Though he speaks of perspectives, Balthasar does not, we should note, embrace perspectiv*ism*, for he insists that, just because this multiplicity of viewpoints gives access to a single truth, the aim is always to co-ordinate them in the interests of gaining a total vision of the unity of reality – even if this is an asymptotic ideal, which the human creature can never actually achieve (not, at any rate, this side of heaven). This may look like Hegel: the thinker should become, if at all possible, one with the *Weltgeist*, the 'spirit of the world'. But the Existentialism and Personalism of Balthasar's philosophical contemporaries had taught him a lesson (one need only advert to the warnings entered by Kierkegaard, fountainhead of those philosophic streams). The intimacy and 'personality' of truth could not survive, in point of fact, so cosmic an uprooting from one's own situation – unless, that is, some way of integrating the personal with such totality thinking were to come to light (there is a reference here, of course, to the transformation in the conditions of our knowing wrought by *revelation*).

Essential and existential

But there is another manner in which the truth is ineluctably 'individual'. Truth is also 'singularised' (*vereinzelt*) when we think not of essence, *Sosein*, but of existence, *Dasein*, in which 'the personality of being comes to fulfilment for the first time'.[2] The phrase 'personality of being' is certainly a strange one, but that is not so odd if at this point we begin to cross the threshold into mystery – as Balthasar maintains. It is in personal existence that the full power and wealth of being comes to expression. To be *für sich*, a personal subject, is not just to have one more quality among a host of others that essence can show. It is to enjoy incomparability, a 'preciousness for which nothing can substitute', since I cannot barter my 'for myself' for any other. The truth I have made my own through my own freedom, in spiritual blood, tears and sweat, I *can* give to another, but in so doing I give them myself.

> In such exchange of personal truths spirits feed one another with their own substance.[3]

And here is where mystery opens up. Analysis and reflection never 'get to the bottom of' personal existence, because time and again it is that incommunicable and fathomless reality that defeats the analyst, the thinker. Nor is this, as the secular Existentialists think, simply a matter of the 'tragic sense of life' , the insoluble puzzle of being a self. It is the *giftedness* of existence which is the source of its groundlessness in the finite order. Hence the necessity of *gratitude* to what lies beyond that order. Ontology calls forth from us, accordingly, some kind of *faith*. All this has

1 *TL* I, pp. 208–9.
2 *TL* I, p. 211.
3 *TL* I, p. 213.

been more pointedly said by G. K. Chesterton than I could ever make plain by paraphrase of Balthasar's prose.

> We thank people for birthday presents of cigars and slippers. Can I thank no one for the birthday present of birth?[4]

More difficult to penetrate – for non-Thomists, at least – are Balthasar's ruminations on the 'real distinction' between essence and existence (a cardinal point for the later Thomistic school), and notably (and this is, rather, a contribution of his own to the Scholastic tradition) the claim that this distinction entails an ontological importance for the temporal dimension that can scarcely be overestimated. No account, however full, of essence can, as such, speak to us of existence; yet some being's existence never shows us the full panoply of possibilities of its essence. And that polarity points us to the theme of *time*.

> Existence in the world (*weltliche Dasein*) can be regarded as, so to speak, the form of being come forth from the fullness of being (*existentia* in the literal sense of that word). Its emergence (*Aussensein*) makes itself known in the way the contours of essence (*Wesen*) narrow down that fullness of being (*quidditas* stands to *esse* as *limitatio*). And yet in every case, at every moment, that essence takes the measure of its being from the everlasting totality of being. This it does through its striving to have part in being's fullness and in that way to preserve itself in being.[5]

That reference to 'striving' (*Bestreben*) opens the door to the topic of temporality, of movement in time. It will be of especial importance for the final volume of Balthasar's theo-dramatics, when nearly forty years later he has to describe how in the final act of the saving drama time-bound creatures like ourselves may plausibly be said to enter the life of the eternal Trinity. For while time has its origin in the real distinction between essence and existence (real in the creature, but not so in the Creator, for whom to be divine *is* to be, and that in unrestricted fullness) and so would appear to have, in the creation, purely negative connotations (our being temporal is another way of saying we are not God), the same 'striving' for the fullness of life (the heart of temporality on Balthasar's analysis) is also a faint echo of God's own supreme vitality. So *temporal* being also has positive connotations. It is a reflection of the riches of the divine life. We are not so ontologically alien to a goal in God as might at first appear.

When in this perspective we consider truth as the unveiling of being we see, or should see, that it bears the character of presence. It is something that makes its advent, and in this way always possesses some sort of future dimension.

> It is like the opening of a door, the entrance of a person, the happening to us of an event, the arrival of some news, the beginning of a history, the welling up of a spring, the shining of a light.[6]

4 G. K. Chesterton, *Orthodoxy* (London 1908; 1996), p. 73.
5 *TL* I, p. 219.
6 *TL* I, p. 221.

Existence is essentially source-like; it is always linked with hope; and, ordered as it is, in one way or another, to fuller being it is, in Balthasar's curious term, 'comparative' of its very nature. When in every present moment the real is made over to its beneficiaries there is something *excessive* about that happening which is generative of the future, just as there is also (and this is a theme more frequently sounded in metaphysical description of the finite order) something both transient and non-repeatable which refers it to the past. Balthasar does not want us to live, in other words, in a neophiliac haze of excitement about the future possibilities of things, so that we lose all sense of the preciousness of what is given us only to pass away. None the less, his emphasis lies on the future, to the point that he can say of the life of eternity:

> it is a life whose present contains within it an eternal future but no past, whereas eternal damnation would be a life the whole of whose present is turned toward the past and is thus the sheer negation of hope.[7]

Once again, we find Balthasar preparing the way for a theological ontology that will allow sense to be made of the creature–Creator union in bliss promised by the Gospel. As he comments

> Eternal life would be the perfect fulfilment of the eternal enhancement (*Steigerung*) contained in being itself; it would be the comparative of life become permanent condition.[8]

Nor is this merely theoretical; there is an obvious practical application. Living for the eternal future (as the religious do) is not (as Nietzscheanism alleges) a de-naturing of the human being. On the contrary, it is to act with, not against, the grain of one's being.

Truth in history

But in this crucial segment of *Wahrheit der Welt* there is not only in view – one surmises – a philosophical opponent outside the Church: there is also a theological opponent within it. When Balthasar tells us that truth's disclosure of being is the more faithful to eternal being and truth the more future-oriented it is, we can hardly help hearing in his words a message of support for the 'new theology' of Pius XII's pontificate – for one of the principal issues at stake between the Thomists and the New Theology men was precisely the question of the permanence of truth and the sense in which philosophical and theological progress are possible.[9] At the same time, however, Balthasar denies that progress in the assimilation of a truth that always keeps its 'comparative' character can ever be rightly regarded as anything other than a fuller appropriation of the 'ever greater wideness and fullness of existent things'.[10] He issues a call, then, to retain (with the

---

7 *TL* I, pp. 223–4.
8 *TL* I, p. 224.
9 See my essay, 'Thomism and the *Nouvelle Théologie*', *The Thomist* 64 (2000), pp. 1–19.
10 *TL* I, p. 228.

Scholastics) the ontological foundations of thought. The urgency with which truth calls out to us in new situations is, he says, by no means chiefly a matter of the social location of thinking, its sociological conditioning. Rather does it derive from the continual novelty characteristic of being itself. Balthasar suffers from no allergy to Scholasticism. His wish is to retain, indeed, the *philosophia perennis* but in rejuvenated form.[11]

Despite all the personalism of Balthasar's epistemology, he insists as much as any Idealist on the organic interrelatedness of truth. In an anticipation of his encomium on the philosopher-poet Charles Péguy, which will form the climax of Volume III of the theological aesthetics, he contrasts the kingdom of truth, a noetic counterpart to the communion of saints, with the kingdom of lies, where there can be no communion, not even in error, since the lie isolates precisely by attacking the unity of truth. Equally, despite his concern with history – for history in his eyes is nothing other than the 'totality of all the concrete situations of truth',[12] he will have it that the interlacing narratives of individuals and communities, the modes of interpretation proper to epoch and culture, convey not a chaos but a single, self-identical truth, '*the* truth in its historical concretion'.[13]

And Balthasar looks ahead to his work on the theology of history (the book of that title had appeared in 1950, just three years after the first edition of *Wahrheit*) when he writes that while the philosopher of history can suggest certain 'frameworks', even 'laws', of general applicability to the realm of historical becoming, nothing can substitute for the unique image (*Bild*) produced by one historical constellation or another. Nor should the metaphysically minded philosopher of history reduce the variety of historical situations to mere instances of metachronic norms. Leave each its particularity – but with the goal of getting an overall view (*Gesamtschau*) of the concreteness of truth. In those words, Balthasar distinguishes from Positivism his critique of the over-ambitious historical theories of his older contemporaries – in Germany, a Spengler; in England, a Toynbee.

11 For Balthasar's relation to the *nouvelle théologie*, see F. Bertoldi, 'Appunti sul rapporto tra H. U. von Balthasar a la Nouvelle Théologie', *Communio*, Italian edition, 105 (1987), pp. 108–22.
12 *TL* I, p. 230.
13 *TL* I, p. 232. Italics added.

7

꧁⚜꧂

Mystery

Actually, this section of Balthasar's study, whose provocative title – in a rational ontology (but this is an ontology of reason under grace!) – is here reproduced, turns out to be tantalisingly brief. Balthasar does little more than gather up threads already laid along the labyrinthine ways of 'Truth of the World', prior to weaving these into the account of the world *in its relation to God* which will constitute the transition to the second and third – the more explicitly theological – volumes of *Theologik*. After all, did he not declare in his introduction to the theological logic as a whole that (in my summary):

> In reality, in the last analysis, everything knowable must have a 'mysteric' character, on the simple grounds that all objects of knowledge have a *creaturely* character, which must mean that the final truth of all things is 'hidden in the mind of the Creator who alone may utter [their] eternal names'.[1]

The question before him now is whether – on the basis of what we have discerned of the dimensions of the real so far – telltale signs of that mystery-character of being can be identified. He thinks they can.

The 'signs' in question are twofold. In the first place, they concern truth's nature as the 'non-hiddenness' of being, a major motif in Chapter 2 of this study. Things declare themselves, in their existence and their essence – as *that* they are and *what* they are – but their confession is not, in Balthasar's words, 'indiscreet'. Thanks to the 'intimacy' of being – the inwardness of *their* being – things are 'unveiled in a veiled fashion (*als verhüllte enthüllt*) and in this form do they become the object of knowledge'.[2] That sounds paradoxical, but it is not a sheer antinomy. It has a sufficient explanation in what Balthasar has already said about the interrelation of existence and essence, essence and expression, situatedness and time. What these themes had in common was that they enabled Balthasar to point up the overflowingness or excessiveness (*Überschuss*) of the real's riches – and the attitudes (not just feelings, for there is cognition here) which that

---

1 See above, p. 6, with an eternal citation of *TL* I, p. xvii.
2 *TL* I, p. 234.

51

'excess' draws forth from us (wonder, enthralment, joy, gratitude, and so forth) constitute our registering of being's mystery.

There follows an excursus on the relation of all of this to love as a primal human act. Only if being is *thus* – only if the more disclosed it is the more inexhaustible it appears – is it in the long run tolerable for knowledge, because only something endowed with mystery is tolerable for love. If a lover considered they had (epistemologically speaking) exhausted their beloved, this would be the infallible sign that love was at an end. Where mystery ceases, love has to re-create it – and Balthasar is ingenious in the examples he gives (the devising of a legend, the withdrawal of a sacred object from the public gaze). Love lives when its object remains *das immere Grössere*, the 'ever-greater'.[3] This impulse for veiling (to call it a mystificatory impulse would be precisely to miss its significance!) is perfectly compatible with – and always exists alongside – an impulse to know, to *un*veil, to seek the other in their pure transparency.

> In a being that loves, there can be much mystery, but this mystery is light. In love is endless depth, but no darkness at all.[4]

Trust, for instance, is often needed when we cannot penetrate the mystery of an other, but trust illuminates the loving relation, it does not darken it.

One might feel that this was at best a suggestive analogy for a general ontology, but Balthasar insists it is because 'love' dwells at the heart of being (two years previously he had published a work entitled 'The Heart of the World')[5] that these ruminations are of universal significance. Love is the 'worshipful kernel of all things',[6] and so human love's dialectic of both unveiling and veiling finds its ultimate meaning in a cosmic mystery of giving or communicating which, by its very lavishness, exceeds all our grasps. What *Scham – la pudeur*, the French call it – is in human loving – the modesty by which we offer ourselves, lost in wonder, in grateful welcoming of the unveiling of another human being, has its cosmic counterpart (so Balthasar seems to be saying) in a renouncing of the will to master reality and its replacing by the simple act of letting truth, in all its overwhelmingness, stream in. It is fitting that love should seek the cover of night, precisely in order to support its own excess of light.

An even less likely source for a universal metaphysic is another phenomenon in human relations which Balthasar discusses at this juncture: the 'creative' overlooking of a loved one's deficiencies, as the latter are judged, and found wanting, by virtue of the lover's idea of his friend. The magic of love can sometimes bring about, by such means, the integration of elements in the other woefully lacking before. Of course what Balthasar has in mind in these comparisons is the best-case scenario: the divine love which is unlimited in its capacity to energise and transform the real.

The second manner in which Balthasar would approach, via its signs and evidences, the 'mystery-character' of being, is the transcendentals:

---

3 *TL* I, p. 238.
4 *TL* I, p. 239.
5 *Das Herz der Welt* (Zürich 1953; Ostfildern 1988⁴; Et *The Heart of the World*, San Francisco 1980).
6 *TL* I, p. 242.

and notably *verum, bonum, pulchrum*, the true, good and beautiful. His Preface alerted us to the claim that no forgetfulness of being has more damaged the West than the falling into oblivion of the interrelation of these three which, in all being, are one. Here, in short compass, he would raise our consciousness on the point.

It would be strange if, at this juncture in the first volume of the theological logic, we had no inkling of what he might mean by the transcendental determination of being that is *truth*. In truth, being experiences its openness for others, its accessibility, as the true enters the possession of another. Balthasar recalls his earlier discussion of 'light' and 'measure', for this is, to his ears, the primordial language of truth. A being's ground epiphanises, and so is light – to itself and for others. And this happens in measured fashion, with appearance and reality in full correspondence. So Balthasar links *goodness* to the communicativity of being. Appealing to the ancient adage *bonum diffusivum sui* – goodness spreads itself – he speaks of being rejecting the avariciousness of a being-only-for-itself and, in opening out in communication, receiving in return its own proper weight as a value, as valued by others. Its not holding on to its own preciousness shows being's prizeworthiness, its transcendental determination as good. Nothing is more primary than this, the foundation of being *is* communication; being and the good are convertible, then, or, in a less Scholastic and more Balthasarian tag, being is groundlessly outpoured love.

Still, the formal concept of the good adds something to that of the true, for the correspondence of ground and appearance which is the focus of our concern with the truth of being, might only be a matter of correctness, appearing in a light that was cold, that rendered no one blessed, since the aspect of value had not yet made its presence felt. The good is not merely that which fills my need (though it does fill it); if so, it would evaporate with need's satisfaction. Goodness is principally in things, as love gives being its value.

That the ground of things is loving communication – 'beyond' which lies no further ground on which to stand – is for Balthasar the proper starting point of a metaphysics of *beauty*. The disinterestedness of the beautiful – something noted by philosophers of very different stamps – is crucial. 'It shines on all who behold it as the sun upon a landscape',[7] and this utter absence of envy in the way it is shared and given signalises its origin. The 'aimlessness' of loving communicativity – being's only 'foundation' – is its hallmark. Beauty is the sheer streaming forth of the true and the good for its own sake, which is why it arouses an indescribable joy. (It is also why beauty, as a transcendental determination of being, one that inhabits, without being constricted by, a plurality of categories, can enter into seemingly opposing elements – the high formality of classicism, the formless longing of Romanticism – or what Balthasar calls, with a retrospective glance to *Apokalypse der deutschen Seele*, the Apollonian and the Dionysiac.)

Truth, goodness, beauty, so we hear one last time, are ontological properties so constituted that one cannot be grasped without the others. That is why Balthasar's masterwork must be a trilogy: not logic only, but

7 *TL* I, p. 254.

dramatics and aesthetics as well. Collaboratively they 'prove' the
inexhaustibility of being's riches, that its mystery is not twilight but the
sun's excess. For, as Balthasar puts it, and here the theological underpinnings of his ontology find acknowledgement for what they are:

> What is more inconceivable than that the kernel of being consists in
> love and that its emergence as essence and existence has no other
> ground than groundless grace?[8]

8 *TL* I, p. 255.

8

Truth Worldly and Truth Divine

What then are the relations between worldly truth and divine truth as Balthasar sees these in *Wahrheit der Welt*? In describing worldly truth, Balthasar has presented it, tacitly at least, as having a definitely contingent character. No purely immanent phenomenology of truth in this world is possible, for him, that leaves aside the relation between finite truth and infinite truth. And now, in conclusion, he turns to this in its own right.

The infinite hinterland

He has already established that if being is in principle knowable this must be because it is in itself 'measured'. A self-enclosed being measured by no knowing would not possess a measure and could not, then, itself be measured. It follows for Balthasar that the knowable is what has ever been known. Only if absolute truth – where eternal being and everlasting knowing coincide – has measured an object can it be presented as knowable to finite intelligence. Thus:

> the analysis of finite self-awareness does not fructify in merely the discovery of an empty, limitless horizon – that of being in general as a transcendental *a priori* enabling all finite knowledge; it also allows one to conclude, in an express and rigorous fashion, to the existence of an infinite awareness, as the condition of possibility for finite subjects.[1]

From what has been said already of the freedom and intimacy of truth, it should be clear that no pantheist or idealist attempt at realising an assimilation (immediate or progressive) of finite subject and infinite subject can be legitimate. For the more perfect the knowing subject is (the more independent of sub-spiritual nature) the more intimately free and personal is its sphere of action. The *infinite* freedom given with *infinite* self-awareness guarantees the infinite Subject an *absolute* transcendence *vis-à-vis* all the world's subjects and objects.[2]

1 *TL* I, p. 258.
2 For a good statement of what, historically, Balthasar feared here we can turn to the metaphysics volume of the theological aesthetics: 'It is true that Schleiermacher, who in the spring of 1802 heard Fichte lecture on his philosophy of the absolute

The structure of finite truth is inseparable from its contingency, which reflects its created character. It is this character which, from the first awakening of consciousness, distinguishes it from divine truth. As Balthasar writes:

> If in the first act where the finite subject takes the measure of itself and of being in general, God, as the infinite Subject, reveals himself – in a way, to be sure, that is veiled and indirect – as the necessary source of all worldly truth, he distinguishes himself at the same time from every finite consciousness precisely in this knowledge of his truth as the mystery, hidden in itself, of infinite personal Being.[3]

It is important to Balthasar that whereas the existence of God is necessarily implied in all knowledge of the truth, this disclosure of his being is directly bound up with a grasp of his primordial liberty. The absolute Subject, possessing in himself the measure of every being, requires no relation with which to express himself simply by nature, just as he has need of no passive reception of anything. (Here, in an extraordinary way, Balthasar re-expresses the God–world relationship doctrine of Scholasticism in the language of German Idealism whilst also rendering it palatable, through his emphasis on the sovereignty of divine freedom, to the biblical Neo-orthodoxy of Barth!)

So finite truth always has the quality of a free gift of God, drawn up from the wells of his infinite truth-resources. By means of it God shows his hand as the Creator, that is, his communicative goodness. What he manifests of himself is entirely deposited, Balthasar writes, in the natures of the objects known and the subjects' knowing. Only from their being – and notably from their contingency, combined with their value, their positive properties – can we infer what God has desired to make known of himself in the created world. In revealing himself as the Creator, God shows that he is at once the deep source of the world and the absolutely hidden being. He unveils himself in the exact measure required for teaching the creature that he remains the Creator who is both free and hidden in his own mystery.

---

sense of dependence, will similarly attempt to interpret this teaching in Christian terms, as Augustine aimed to deepen the teaching of Plotinus by Christianising it; but the point of departure for both remains quite distinct, for in Plotinus the decision has not been made (or not clearly so) for the 'living God' of the Bible, while Fichte passionately rejects precisely this form of aliveness. No Christian school of thought, be it Protestant or Catholic (Maréchal, for instance, and his followers), will in the long run be able to resist the strength and the pull of the fundamental acts of decision in the three Idealist systems when they 'engage' with the latter in order to effect a dialogue with them. Neither can we be deceived by the fact that, compared with the philosophy of the Spirit of the Enlightenment, we find in all the Idealists a feeling for the dimensions of negative theology: God cannot be reduced to an object and yet is precisely as such (*pace* Kant) the One who manifests himself in the world: does not this draw very close to Plotinus, Erigena and Nicholas of Cusa? But philosophical necessity binds God and his revelation, man, one to the other. Man is himself the manifest God.' *The Glory of the Lord* V *The Realm of Metaphysics in the Modern Age* (Edinburgh and San Francisco 1990), p. 548.

3 *TL* I, p. 260.

Here then is the final – fully theological – explanation for why truth is mysterious. Beyond every finite truth lies this infinite hinterland. That side of the character of truth which he explored in the last chapter under the heading of 'mystery' can only really be understood when we look at it in the light of the analogy between infinite and finite truth, divine truth and worldly.

> It is *because* the divine truth, as the truth of an *absolute* interiority, necessarily remains a mystery in each and every disclosure, that each truth in this world bears something of the same mystery-character around with it.

And he adds that:

> the mystery which attaches to worldly truth is a mystery given to the being of the world as its *own*, to dispose of in personal intimacy proper to itself in a free and spontaneous manner; and yet at the same time this mystery remains always a gift, held only as a participation in the absolute interiority of that divine truth from which it draws its mystery-character.[4]

The sign of this is that being is never so much given away to us that we can cease to be for ourselves a perpetual mystery.

The world as divine epiphany

By stressing the 'gift' character of finite truth – for all that God has made known of himself in such general revelation is 'deposited', *given*, in the 'respective natures of the objects known and the subjects knowing', Balthasar can make the transition from a way of talking about the God–world relationship characteristic of philosophical and theological idealism to one more typical of philosophical and theological realism – from, if you like, the vagaries of a Catholicised Hegel or Schelling to the terra firma of the *philosophia perennis*. And yet even when speaking of God as the Creator of beings, rather than as the ultimate Condition of subjectivity, Balthasar still retains the accents of Romanticism and its offspring Symbolism: this is St Thomas rigged out in the Parnassian clothing of Mallarmé. Balthasar writes of the created world as

> having the aspect of a vast image of the divine being, as the latter expresses and manifests itself in a symbolic language. To know how to decipher the world as such a field of symbols, is to understand at one and the same time the world itself and the God who expresses himself therein, in the measure he wills. The proportion that is defined by the formula 'Matter is to spirit as the world is to God' constitutes indeed the best means of approaching the problem of the knowledge of God. Whoever has made the attempt, both theoretical and practical, to regard everything corporeal as a symbol and an expressive field for spiritual truth will find themselves

4 *TL* I, p. 262.

perfectly prepared to interpret all creation as the Creator's symbol and expressive field likewise.[5]

The creative act of God in bringing forth the world in freedom establishes an all-pervading analogy between finite truth and infinite truth. *Like* divine truth, the truth of worldly beings is mysterious, yielding itself only in part to appropriation by others. *Unlike* divine truth, the truth of worldly beings receives its mystery character by participation – a sharing in the absolute inwardness of the truth of God, whereas divine truth is *essentially* hidden – something Balthasar links to God's primordial freedom, for no factors 'beyond' him determine his decision to communicate his being to what is other than himself by creating. *Unlike* the truth of God, worldly truth's lack of final foundation derives from its reception of its ground from something that is not itself – namely, God – whereas, while the divine truth is equally without foundation, this is only in the sense that God's truth rests on nothing other than itself, nothing other than its own infinity. So between finite truth and infinite truth there is likeness and unlikeness simultaneously. This relation is to be spoken of, therefore, not equivocally, as though worldly truth and divine truth were without any connexion, nor univocally as though they were just two examples of the same thing, but *analogically*. Indeed, their analogy makes possible all other analogies found within the world. It is the God–world relationship which gives to anything within this world its finally determinative meaning.

Balthasar points out that in theological logic what is from the creature's side *participation* is from the Creator's side *revelation*. Viewed from the created pole, the relation between finite and infinite truth appears as a relation of internal participation, a relation so rigorous indeed that should worldly truth (*per impossibile*) detach itself from divine truth the former would cease to be. Viewed from the uncreated pole, the same relation appears as a free disclosure with no kind of necessity about it at all. Yet, thanks to God's sovereign goodness, the creature comes to be as a 'relative centre of truth', able to recognise truth and express it for itself. And vital to the appropriation of truth by the spiritual creature is hearing the attracting call of God through the creation, where the overflowing richness of the world is meant to direct us to the infinite Value which is its source. Created being, intended to be transparent to infinite truth, can also be misinterpreted by us, so that its qualities as participation and revelation are turned into immanent and essential properties of the finitude we share – and this self-divinisation on the part of the creation is its ruin.

We could learn our lesson here, Balthasar suggests, if we attended sufficiently to the signals given us by finite truth when we think about what acquiring knowledge of such truth entails. For the finite character of worldly truth is well expressed in the main forms of human knowledge of that truth: (1) 'analysis' – the delimitation of what is to be known by distinction from other areas of possible knowledge, what we call, tellingly, *definition*; and (2) 'synthesis' – which is a matter of placing individual truths, thus defined, delimited, into larger and larger contexts. Each of

5 *TL* I, p. 264.

these procedures, if taken in isolation, lands up in false infinites – the first in knowing more and more about less and less, the second in ever-increasing generality that is not only increasingly empty but actually less and less *known* where any concrete application is concerned. Only by proceeding simultaneously in both directions, contrary as they are, can human knowledge escape the domination of false infinites. This, to Balthasar's mind, is the telltale sign that worldly truth, like the being of the world, is suspended over nothingness into which it would collapse unless sustained by the creative divine hand.

What, by contrast, gives human knowledge right direction is precisely awareness of the primordial analogy between God and creature, a continually renewed perception of ourselves as beings placed in a condition of dependence and service before the mystery of the absolute majesty of God. The most important cognitive attitude we can ever adopt is one which awaits from God alone the measure of the truth we would know. That 'logical worship', the obedience of reason, is owed to God simply by virtue of a correct understanding of the character of the human mind and of its divine Source.

And this in turn constitutes the fundamental openness of man to divine revelation in the historical sense of that phrase. Should it please God to see an increase of his glory in linking the creature's knowledge to his own, should he find it good that the creature share in his own knowledge of his truth, then I ought to seize this truth with both hands. For there must I find the true extent, the proper dimensions, of my being – true and proper because according to the measure that God generously (we might also say *lovingly*) wills.

PART 2

TRUTH OF THE WORD

9

The Johannine 'Entry'

Nothing said in Volume I, as Balthasar remarks at the outset of *Theologik* II,[1] can prepare us for the Saviour's philosophically shocking affirmation of his identity with Truth itself. 'I am the Truth' (John 14.6), a statement which, not unreasonably, he describes as representing a quantum leap compared with the investigations of the same subject (truth) in *Wahrheit der Welt*. Only the self-disclosure of the divine Glory in Jesus Christ, as studied by theological aesthetics, and the presentation of the divine philanthropy with Jesus Christ as the central protagonist of the action, transforming fallen finite freedom in conjoining it to all-holy infinite freedom in his saving sacrifice, in the way that is displayed to us by theological dramatics, can make us ready to hear these words. But, as Balthasar points out in introducing the second and third volumes of the theological logic, devoted respectively as these are to the Son and the Spirit, any division of labour here between a Christological and a Pneumatological divine logic must necessarily be artificial. If the hidden mystery of God, which has shown itself aesthetically and dramatically as the absolute beauty and goodness of triune Love, has truly revealed its real colours in the incarnation of the divine Logos, who is the Word, Son and Interpreter of the Father, then how could we ever hope to understand this Christological display without the Holy Spirit who introduces us into the truth of the Son and therefore into the Son's relation with the Father? After all, the Word promised his disciples the Spirit for the time of his return to the Father, and in any case all that he had done and suffered to reveal the Father, from his Incarnation, through his Passion to his resurrection, had happened in the Holy Spirit whom the Father had sent upon him in immeasurable fullness (cf. John 3.34, a text of the utmost importance to Balthasar's Triadology).

None the less, in the context of a theological logic – that is, within an evocation of the saving revelation by reference to that transcendental determination of being which is truth, we can and must isolate one question that requires for its answer special, sustained reference to the divine Son, and that is, However could the eternal Logos of God manage

---

1 'Vorbemerkung', *Theologik* II *Wahrheit Gottes* (Einsiedeln 1985), cited below as *TL* II, p. 11.

to express himself within the finitude of a creature – the humanity of the man Jesus? It is to this question that the whole of the second volume of Balthasar's theological logic will be addressed. Which is not to say that he will try to exclude reference to the Holy Spirit: it is a matter of the *focus* of his interest, not its limit.

Actually, the Jesus of St John's Gospel describes himself not only as truth but also as one come to bear witness to the truth (John 18.31), and this Balthasar sums up by saying that he presents himself as the truth inasmuch as he is sent by the Father for the salvation of the world, in such a way that he reveals the Father's will and work. He alone can both be the truth and testify to it since he is the only One who is sent by the Father to make him known. Here the words and the deeds done in the flesh must not be parted. When, in the Johannine Prologue, that Word which was in the beginning with God and was itself God is declared to have become flesh, and as flesh – that is, as an embodied mortal human being, to constitute the exegesis, the explanation, of the Father, this is said not only of that man's spoken words but also of his entire corporeal activity. As the truth, Jesus explains the thought and action of the Father who so loved the world as to send his only Son; hence he can *be* the truth only if he is not just the one given by the Father but also actuates this giving in himself, that is, in his voluntary sacrifice. Before Pilate he will witness both to his truth, and, in this sense, to his absoluteness, and to the fact that he has received this truth from above, from the Father, and so to his relativeness, or better, his relationality.

And here, in the meditation on St John which introduces *Theologik* II, Balthasar finds himself already obliged to draw in the Spirit. The interpreter, Jesus Christ, himself needs interpreting in turn if he is to be at once entirely 'referred' to a truth other than himself and yet defined as this very truth. At the culminating point of the interpreter's career, when his interpretation of the Father is – as he himself cried out on the Cross – 'finished' (John 19.30), water and blood flow from his riven side (John 19.34), signalling the appearance of a co-witness who will be, as Balthasar puts it, the Son's 'monstrance', pointing the way to the truth of the interpreter, Christ, rather than his, the Spirit's, own. 'The Spirit of truth will lead you into all truth because he will not speak of himself but will take what is mine and proclaim it to you' (John 16.12–13a, 14b): he will make it credible, as an advocate can render a position irrefutably credible, and convict of error the opposing position, though the Spirit will do this not, in the main, forensically, exteriorly, but interiorly, generating faith in the truth thus attested and explained and making those who have such faith co-witnesses with him. 'The Spirit of truth . . . will bear witness to me; and you also are witnesses . . .' (John 15.26–7). By introducing the disciples into the entire truth, and thus also to that which Jesus had not yet said at the moment of the Supper, for then his Cross and Resurrection were still future, the Spirit will lead them into the authentically eschatological truth, at once rounding off the interpretation of the Father given by Jesus and yet opening out that interpretation to endless sub-mediated explanations – Balthasar's version of the 'development of doctrine' – until the End comes. This will involve, however, no new truth but the ever-renewed bringing to mind of the inexhaustible depths of

Jesus' explanation of the Father. And so the single truth – that explaining of the Father through the Son which is itself explained by the Spirit – is in the last analysis a Trinitarian truth, though because this is a truth unveiled in the world, and for the world, it is not that of the immanent Trinity in itself, even if it does represent that absolute Godhead to the world, being as it is the world's only means of access to that ultimate Source.

In the separate *Epilog* which he wrote as a brief postlude to his finished trilogy, Balthasar calls the object of the aesthetics a *Sich-zeigen*, a 'self-showing'; that of the dramatics a *Sich-geben*, a 'self-giving' which assumes the *Sich-zeigen*; and that of the theological logic a *Sich-sagen*, a 'self-saying', which incorporates them both.[2] For this truth is glory and goodness: splendid deed. The truth which Jesus is, both as interpreter and interpreted, is not an abstract theoretical truth but a concretely contemplated truth since it is the truth of the Word become flesh. The humanity of Jesus, since its subject is the Father's consubstantial Image, is the more than simply analogous representation of God in the world – more than simply true, that is, with the truth of the analogy of being, for here the concrete analogy of being *appears in his own person*, as both God and man. The expression of the Father in the incarnate Word not only makes the divine truth, glory and goodness visible, for considered as the self-expression of the first-born Son it *is* that truth, glory, goodness itself.

The theological aesthetics had already discovered, in the total unfolding of the Word through the scenes of Jesus' life, death and Resurrection, how God clarifies his own truth as gracious or self-giving love. And the theological dramatics has spelled that out in terms of the action of Christ in tears and blood. Here, in a theological logic dedicated to the Son, one can take a step further, and say that the splendid goodness of truth is disclosed not only in the fateful career, up to Easter, of the Word made flesh but also in the gift at Pentecost of the entire relation between Father and Son, a gift communicated through the Holy Spirit. As the interpreter, the Spirit transmits to the world the gracious truth of the Father and the Son not simply exteriorly, as the Advocate who defends the truth of doctrine, but interiorly, as the 'Anointing' spoken of in the Johannine Letters, for he is the One who gives believers a share in this relation between Father and Son in such a fashion that they may know that relation for themselves.

For Balthasar, it is only when truth is apprehended in a way at once Christological and Trinitarian that it can be presented as really a truth that has fullness. 'Fullness' here means the inclusion not only of the other transcendentals – beauty and goodness – but also the intimate and indissoluble relation of Son to Father and Spirit which is those transcendentals' source. Such Christologico–Trinitarian truth must be accorded absolute primacy over whatever *within* this world can be designated as 'true' – a point entirely compatible with Balthasar's phenomenological description of the intrinsic openness of worldly truth to divine truth in the first volume of the theological logic as well as a powerful way of underlining the specificity of the truth-claims of Christian revelation in polemic self-differentiation from liberalism.

2 *Epilog* (Einsiedeln–Trier 1987), pp. 45–66.

10

Logic and Love

And here, in order to bring out the difference between what is basically a philosophy masquerading as a theology, on the one hand, and authentic theology, on the other, Balthasar contrasts examples of each – Hegel's *Logic* and the properly theological logic implicit in the Prologue of the Fourth Gospel. For Hegel, while the concept in its maximum development as the absolute 'Idea' gives the truth of all being, all essence, yet none the less philosophy never *begins* with that concept – that is, with the truth. For the philosopher to presuppose the truth would be for him to found his project on mere assumption, what Hegel calls simple 'assurance', whereas where truth is genuinely thought through it must prove itself in thinking. So the philosopher starts with – as Hegel puts it – the most miserable of all contents: with such notions as being, nothing, becoming, something and so forth. Then, little by little, philosophy raises itself dialectically to absolute fullness. By contrast, the theologian – as Balthasar points out on the basis of the Johannine Prologue – *begins* with absolute fullness. He or she starts with God's own self-interpretation to the world, a self-interpretation which is utterly plenary, unsurpassably full, even though it is a fullness which the Holy Spirit is to expound in and graft on human minds by a process always progressive, never concluded. None the less, there is, Balthasar goes on, *something* in Christian theology that corresponds to the 'wretched beginnings' of the basic notions with which Hegel commences his *Logic*. And this is the poverty of the fleshly existence of the Word of God: not, of course, a poverty of abstraction, like Hegel's inventory of rudimentary notions, but a poverty of love, because a poverty that the Word freely embraced so that we might become rich (cf. Philippians 2.7).

Nor is this merely a rhetorical comparison, for *Theologik* II as it unfolds turns out to offer a logic of divine love. This is in any case unavoidable if the question about the truth of theology is also a question about theology's Object: the God who in his covenant, and finally in his incarnate Word, has become a God for us and with us. Moreover, if, as in Jesus' summary of the Torah in Matthew, Mark and Luke, God is to be loved with one's whole 'understanding', *dianoia*, then thought too is to be placed at the service of the love of God – something which, again, the concluding pages of Balthasar's phenomenology of worldly truth had, even at the natural level, foreseen. As what Thomas, in his lectures on St John's Gospel, called *totius Patris expressio*,[1] the expression of the Father in his entirety, the Son became incarnate precisely as an act of love. Thus Balthasar can go so far as to say that a cognitive relation not at the service of love could not maintain, within theology, a legitimate claim to constitute part of theological logic. The Writer to the Ephesians sets forth the aim of such *dianoia* as 'to know the love of Christ which goes beyond all knowledge' (3.19) – beyond, that is, all human cognitive possibilities which, if they are to converge at all, must do so in the service of love.

Yet can a logic which eliminates itself in love still be called a *logic*? The early twentieth-century philosopher of human action, Maurice Blondel, provides Balthasar with materials for a positive answer to this question in his early essay on the 'Elementary Principle of a Logic of the Moral Life' where Blondel speaks of moral action as simultaneously appropriation and renunciation – as it were, affirmation and negation – and in both respects something that has an eye to the global meaning (what he terms 'the real *logos*') of human existence.[2] There is a logic of existential choice, for good or evil, which according to Blondel has meaning only in relation to the absolute Logos, divine and eventually divine-human, as response to the One who is the totality of the good for man. What a *theological* logic can add to Blondel's contribution is the awareness that the logic of God must always be *Trinitarian* through and through. And so if the Logos in person, Jesus Christ, is to express the divine totality – not only himself, the Son, but, in relation to himself the Father and the Spirit too – then the human logic in which he does so must itself be in the image and likeness of the *triune* God. There must be, in the truth and being of the world, some capacity to reflect the Trinity to which the Logos, in the 'explanation' he gives of himself in his self-expression, can refer.

---

1 Thomas Aquinas, *Lectura super Ioannem*, *lectio* I, n. 29.
2 M. Blondel, 'Principe élémentaire d'une logique de la vie morale' (originally 1903), in *Les premiers écrits de Maurice Blondel* (Paris 1956), pp. 123–47.

11

꧁꘎꧂

Ana-logic: Tracing the Trinity

Hence Balthasar studies first of all what he calls 'ana-logic', that is: a way *leading up to* the self-expression of the divine Logos in his incarnation, from the side of the world. Since what the Logos discloses is the Trinity, such an ana-logic will consider possible traces of the Trinitarian mystery in the creation and our reflection upon it – a well-known feature of patristic and mediaeval theology here revived by Balthasar on a renewed basis which turns out to be essentially twofold.

First, he offers an explanation, indebted to Paul Claudel, of the triadic structure of all worldly logic, for there can be no 'A' without, on the one hand, the indefinite series of non-'A's which co-determine 'A', and, on the other, some relation on the part of the indefinite series of delimiting determinants to an *un*-delimited determinant – without which we would be involved in an infinite regress. B. C. D., etc. may, taken abstractly, be negations of A, but taken concretely they are A's co-constituents – something which could hardly be thinkable without the crucial pre-supposition that they share a common finitude, itself distinguished from yet related to a Source of all that is. Here Balthasar puts into Germanic philosophical form the genial insight of the French poet in *Art poétique* that to know – *connaître* – is always in some sense to be in together at a birth – *co-naître*.[1] Just so, for a human being 'to know oneself is to produce oneself in correlation'[2] – correlation with other beings, and with God. Only a triune logic, containing a trace of the Trinity, can do justice, Balthasar is saying (more clearly than Claudel) to this universal state of affairs.

But then secondly, and more after the fashion of the greatest of the Western Fathers, Augustine, Balthasar furnishes an account of images of

---

1 P. Claudel, 'Art poétique: Traité de la Co-naissance au monde et de soi-même' (originally 1903–4), in *Oeuvre poétique* (Paris 1967), pp. 147–204. Claudel claimed it was St Thomas who had 'opened to me new horizons and made me start off on a way not opposed [to his] but lateral' – thus *Mémoires improvisés* (Paris 1955; 1969), p. 233 – a claim accepted by D. Millet-Gérard, *Claudel thomiste?* (Paris 1999). But the constellation of influences – Stoicism, Augustine, Leibniz, Bergson, *Naturphilosophie* – make of *Art poétique* a wayward text from the standpoint of Thomistic epistemology: see M. de Gandillac, 'Scission et connaissance d'après l'*Art poétique*', in G. Cattaui and J. Madaule (eds), *Entretiens sur Paul Claudel* (The Hague 1968), pp. 115–30. The same could be said, of course, of the epistemological elements of *Wahrheit der Welt*!
2 Claudel, 'Art poétique', p. 190.

the Trinity in finite being. This he will focus, however, in distinctly *non-*Augustinian fashion, on the necessity whereby to be personal I must be *inter*-personal, not only in enjoying relationship with another subject but in finding the I–Thou relationship in its 'fruit'. By 'fruit' he does not necessarily mean a literal offspring (though it could be that – the child in the family bosom) but something at any rate born of two persons' common love. Here Balthasar is especially indebted to the mediaeval Scots theologian Richard of St Victor – an Augustinian canon – for whom the triune logic of *caritas* presumed a Lover, a Beloved and a Third to enjoy their love.[3] Concerned, it seems, that such a 'social' doctrine of the Trinity might be thought to lead in the direction of tritheism, Balthasar goes out of his way to emphasise that Richard – of all people! – devoted four out of the six volumes of his Triadology to the divine unity.

The notion of the fruitfulness of intersubjectivity, which avoids at once the perils of a monadic individualism and those of an amorphous communality, is to Balthasar's mind the key sought in vain by both 'dialectical' and 'dialogical' thinkers from the early nineteenth-century Hegel to the mid-twentieth-century Jewish philosopher of religion Martin Buber. It may seem a large jump from the mediaeval theologians of the triune God to such modern thinkers. But Balthasar has already shown in the theological dramatics how crucial the twin notions of otherness and difference are *both* for the Trinity *and* for creaturely freedom. The foundation of the inequality between God and the world is the equality of the divine hypostases where the difference between Father and Son is not 'something else than God but, as the Spirit, the Other in God'.[4] What Balthasar particularly emphasises in the context of the theological logic is that while the method of *dialectic* à la Hegel

> is a method of the spirit as knowing and the highest reachable stage we can reach on the basis of this method is that of absolute knowledge, the method of *dialogic* – in which the other is the positive – is a method of love, which ever fulfils itself in its self-stripping. And so all worldly images of this [Trinitarian] Archetype, whether they be put forward in an Augustinian or a Riccardian way always constitute possible approaches, within the world, to the eternal Archetype of the absolute event of Love.[5]

True, a passage on the nature of love, and especially of married love, from Hegel's *Philosophie des Rechts*, shows that philosopher, by whom Balthasar remained perennially fascinated, alert to the significance of the Trinitarian image in man.[6] In fact, for Balthasar the entire journey of Hegelian thought is a traversing of the 'sphere of the Christian *imago*'. But to what end? Balthasar regards such insights in Hegel's corpus as exploited

3 Here Balthasar draws on the interest shown in Richard (and the whole Victorine school) by French historical theologians after the Second World War, and notably F. Guimet, '*Caritas ordinata* et *Amor discretus* dans la théologie trinitaire de Richard de Saint-Victor', *Revue du Moyen-Age latin* 4 (1948), pp. 225–36, and G. Dumeige, *Richard de St. Victor et l'idée chrétienne de l'Amour* (Paris 1952).
4 *TL* II, p. 40.
5 Ibid.
6 G. W. F. Hegel, *Philosophie des Rechts* (1833), § 158.

quite differently in the Berlin thinker's own *dialectical* writing compared with the work of the *dialogical* philosophers who succeeded him. In Hegel's thinking, love as the emerging and yet dissolving of contradiction (unity with another both takes away my autonomous being and restores it wondrously enhanced) finds its place in an all-embracing dialectic which amounts to a *Konstruktion Gottes*, 'a construction of God'. Pure logic, in Hegel's hands, represents God in his eternal essence, prior to creation, while Hegel's logic of nature and historical spirit evoke God's fulfilment as he 'becomes' world and spirit in history. (The parallel with Whiteheadian process thought, where God is ascribed two natures, 'primordial' and 'consequent', is clear.) Among the *dialogical* thinkers, in contrast, the I–Thou relation, as set forth in Hegel's perceptive observations on love and being, is taken as the true starting point of reflection, and the communion of being is understood as a linguistic happening – a notion not a million miles removed from that of the creation of persons through the (divine) Word. Not for nothing, Balthasar thinks, are so many dialogical philosophers either Jews (Hans Rosenzweig, Martin Buber) or Christians (Ferdinand Ebner, Gabriel Marcel), for such philosophising owes much to the prophetic light of the Scriptures. In very different ways, perhaps, these writers make the reciprocity of I and Thou rest ultimately on the Absolute. The trouble with Hegel, in Balthasar's judgment, is that for him the 'other' is always a *negative* moment, even if it is also one by whose mediation (when negation is itself negated) the self attains true positivity. Hegel sees the individual only as opposed to the other, even if via that opposition fuller selfhood can result. The positivity of selfhood makes sense only in terms of the negativity of coming to terms with the other, and vice versa, such that in the last analysis 'love is logicised and at the end disappears completely in absolute knowing'.[7]

The dialogicians, by contrast, are key to Balthasar's project in *Theologik* because, at their hands, the interpersonal reality of speech is in some way led back to the sacrosanct foundation of the divine Logos.

> The dialogicians aim at a theo-logic for which by his gracious self-disclosure God is, within the inter-human realm, truth – because he is the ultimate Ground of the truth that occurs between the I and the Thou (and so in all authentic human speaking).[8]

Human beings need to he addressed before they can address. Hence (in a coining by Balthasar) *Angesprochenwordensein* – our being the sort of creatures that have been aroused by address – is a condition of possibility for any human dialogue at all.

This is not to say, however, that Balthasar is satisfied, as a Catholic theologian, with these predecessors' work. Rosenzweig, the most ambitious speculative thinker among them, founded the I–Thou relation, and the experienced world which emerges as its context, in the 'unspeakable Origin of language'. He incorporated Christianity within his own Judaism by treating it as a sub-class of a tradition that looks to the end of the world

7 *TL* II, p. 44.
8 *TL* II, p. 45.

for the final disclosure of that Origin's 'name' – and indeed rather suspected the Gospel of subverting the eschatology of the Hebrew Bible by continually looking back to the Christ-event as the test of truth. Buber, who saw speaking *to* God as characteristic of Judaism and speaking *about* God as typical of Christianity, regarded the second as a sad declension from the first. Ebner, while acknowledging the Word made flesh as the centre of the God–world relation, and so of any divine-human logic (and surely this estranged Catholic, who was reconciled with the Church on his death-bed, played a major part in helping Balthasar articulate the overall project of *Theologik*) also played off, like Buber, faith against thought – and by his rejection of a speculative theological doctrine of the Trinity sundered the revelation of Christ from an account of the cosmos, and Christ himself from his Church. There is, then, much left for Balthasar to do: with Rosenzweig and Buber he will affirm that the true contours of the world emerge from the foundational religious act of confessing God; with Ebner, he will place Jesus Christ at the heart of that confession – but he will also make good the lacunae in their accounts. With Augustine, he will see Christ as not only the Father's Word but also his 'doctrine', his teaching (thus the *Tractates on John* 29.3); with the great doctors of all the ages he will see Christ as accessible only when he is approached in a *Trinitarian* way.

What the dialogicians have taught Balthasar is what he himself calls 'the fecundity of meeting',[9] for dialogue is what sustains human spirits. But, he believes, one can, in the light of the revelation in Christ of the Trinity, take a further step and say that the encounter which is most fully fruitful is that of *love*. Fertility – not just in organic life but in that of *Geist* likewise – happens in the image of the Trinity.[10]

9 *TL* II, p. 56.
10 As in *Herrlichkeit* I, Balthasar acknowledges his great debt here to the nineteenth-century Rhenish Scholastic Matthias Joseph Scheeben who not only considered natural marriage quasi-sacramental but also compared the Holy Spirit as 'bond of love' between Father and Son to the mother's role as *Liebesband* in the family (without, of course, prejudice to the Filioquist account of the Son's original generation). Thus M. J. Scheeben, *Mysterien des Christenthums* (Cologne 1865), pp. 572–6, 173–81.

12

✢

The Self-expression of the Logos

The foregoing hardly more than begins to explain how the divine Logos might express himself in terms of this world. The Christian writers already discussed were perfectly aware of the inadequacy of their proposals – even in the case of Hegel who identified divine logic with human and considered that a logic theologically thought through was the method needed to clarify the totality of being. The others – Augustine, Richard, Scheeben – were aware that they were just meditating on *menschliche Seinsstrukturen*, 'human ontological structures', for the sake of the further illumination of the divine reality presupposed by faith – even if from within those human 'structures' there could sometimes appear a postulate or two offering fresh insight into the triune God of the historic revelation.[1] As for the Jewish thinkers (and Balthasar groups the Christian Ebner with the other 'dialogicians' for this purpose) they were chiefly interested in throwing light on what human dialogue entails – though, as we have seen, this could lead them to raise the question of address by a divine Thou. What we have found then are ana-logical projection lines. But starting from below what we cannot see is their point of intersection. They were useless tools for Jesus Christ, accordingly, when faced with the task of interpreting that ordering of the divine to the human found in his own person. For us too, something more distinctively *Christo*-logical is needed.[2]

The Invisible made visible

As the opening of *Wahrheit Gottes*, the second volume of the logic, has shown, for theological logic the basic affirmation found in the Church's faith is that Christ is the interpreter of the Invisible. That means, in the first place, *of the Father* – though, thanks to the reciprocally defined relations of origin of the divine Persons and their consequent relations of communion, the Father cannot be revealed without a concomitant self-

---

1 *TL* II, p. 61.
2 Note, however, that at *TL* II, p. 79, Balthasar calls the *imagines Trinitatis* superfluous to the Saviour's needs (not unserviceable for them) – and even then he makes an exception for a (non-philosophical, everyday) version of *Mitmenschlichkeit* (co-humanity) and *Fruchtbarkeit* (fruitfulness) including that of human word, since these appear in, respectively, Jesus' love-command and his parables.

revelation of the Son as the One sent by the Father and of the Spirit in
whom the interpretation of the Father is both made by the Son and understood by ourselves.

The essentially invisible God – whom, as Scripture witnesses (cf. 1
Timothy 6.16), no man has seen for he dwells in light unsearchable – is
sheerly other than the world, his difference from the world infinitely
greater than any difference within it. If he establishes a relation with the
world, and with man, that can only be by grace, or what the Old Testament
terms his 'covenant love'. It is the testimony of Scripture, consolidated by
the holy Fathers, that in his Word God has thus made himself known.
Here Balthasar cites that patristic figure so favoured in his corpus, Irenaeus
of Lyons:

> Conformably to his majesty it is impossible to know God. It is not
> possible, then, that the Father be measured. But according to his
> love – for this love is that which, through his Word, shows us the
> way to God – we ever learn by obedience to him that God is the one
> who is thus great.[3]

Balthasar sets forth his account of the Word as divine self-expression
by contradistinction to Palamism, that fourteenth-century Byzantine
account of the God–world relation called after its originator, St Gregory
Palamas. The idea that the essence of God remains forever unparticipated
in by creatures, forever strange to them, whereas his energies can be and
are participated in – *experienced* – thanks to the saving revelation, strikes
Balthasar as a fair characterisation of what was involved in the biblical
knowledge of God in the *Old* Testament. In Christ, however, the Palamite
theological structure is, in Hegel's famous term, *aufgehoben* – simultaneously cancelled out and yet raised to the highest level of its own
possibilities, subjected to a conceptual version of the maxim *Stirb und
werde!*, 'Die and become'. For now, in the New Testament, as St Irenaeus
stresses so constantly, the Son made man has by his visibility disclosed
the actual substance of the divine life – the communion of the divine
Persons, while the more clearly declaring the invisibility of that substantial communion's ultimate source, the Father. Just so in *Wahrheit*, the
disclosure of the mystery of being in appearance at once unveiled that
mystery yet, by its revelation of being's depth, the more deeply concealed
its origin.

Astounding familiarity

Balthasar was evidently worried, however, that this dismissal of the
Palamite distinction between the revealed divine energies and the hidden
divine essence could expose him to the charge of an excessively cataphatic
– an epistemologically over-confident – view of Christian revelation, not
least at its very heart, in the Word made flesh. He deals with this anticipated objection in two ways: first, through the manner in which he
describes the actual self-expression of the Logos in the man Jesus and,

---

3 Irenaeus, *Adversus Haereses* IV.20, 1, cited *TL* II, p. 63.

secondly, through a novel version of negative theology, now taken as referring above all to the engirding silence of the Word.

First, then, Balthasar stresses that while Jesus possessed a human nature complete in every way he none the less presented himself to his fellow humans as not only the 'same' but also the 'wholly other'. How does Jesus' 'wholly otherness' show itself? By an attitude of superiority joined directly – that is, without any mediation that could offer an explanation of this paradox in human terms and so mitigate its force – to an extreme sense of abasement and obedience. Jesus presented himself as not so much thrown into the midst of human life by that (literally!) consummate chance which is our parents' coming together in generation but as, more fundamentally, entering upon existence in his own freedom as ratifier of the will of the Father. And yet, because he reveals his total otherness in his humble service of others, this is in no way a super-man with whom we have to deal. As the Carmelite patrologist François-Marie Léthel shows in his study of Christ in the Garden of Gethsemane according to Maximus the Confessor, it is a *human* will which must come to full assent to the ways of the Father.[4] And here Balthasar can, for the moderns, cite Schelling to good effect when the latter wrote in 1812 to Eschmayer:

> They say, God absolutely *must* be superhuman. But if, though, he wished to be human, who could object? If he himself comes down from that altitude and makes himself common with his creature, why should *I* wish to insist on maintaining that altitude. Why would I be abasing him with the concept of his humanity if he chose to abase himself?[5]

Yet the biblical account sets clear limits to this translation of the divine into the human. As Balthasar notes, Jesus maintains his transcendence, his 'humble altitude', in never dialoguing about the Father but always, simply, speaking of him. And on that Balthasar comments, in what is presumably a 'dig' at a certain feature of post-conciliar Catholicism, not least in the 'New Curia' (the specifically modern, post-1959, commissions and councils) at Rome:

> A dialogue with unbelievers who do not recognise the theomorphism of Jesus in his anthropomorphism is perfectly impossible.[6]

For this is someone who not only interprets the truth of God's wholly other being in terms of the difference between his divinity and his humanity, but who also lets this difference actually appear in the very 'language' of his humanity itself.

Here Balthasar signals two ways in which to think of Jesus simply as teacher, as prophet, will not suffice. First, in dealing with the Interpreter

4 F.-M. Léthel, *Théologie de l'agonie du Christ: La liberté humaine du Fils de Dieu et son importance sotériologique mises en lumière par Saint Maxime le Confesseur* (Paris 1979); see further my *Byzantine Gospel: Maximus the Confessor in Modern Scholarship* (Edinburgh 1993), pp. 95–102.
5 F. W. J. von Schelling, 'Brief an Eschenmayer' (1812), in *idem, Werke* I.8, pp. 167–8, cited *TL* II, p. 66.
6 *TL* II, p. 67.

of the Interpreted, the One who is Son of the Father, albeit in the form of a servant, we do not just listen to instruction. Prayer and contemplation – *betende Kontemplation* – is a necessary complement to an attitude of listening in *this* situation, for the teaching must be inwardly received and outwardly responded to by discipleship. And secondly, it is not by his words alone but by his total embodiment or incarnation (not excluding his *silence*) that the Son represents the Father: hence the crucial importance for the New Testament and later tradition of calling Jesus the *image* of God. The Old Testament prohibition of images finds its true rationale when God himself provides his own icon in Christ; a consummation far transcending (if also building upon) the symbolic gestures of Israel's prophets. And this divinely given image is simultaneously, so Balthasar explains, the fulfilment or restoration of the image of God-in-the-human lost in Adam. Here we have in nucleus 'the entire Chalcedonian dogma'.[7]

And yet for all that Jesus *does* teach in a humanly comprehensible way, utilising, as Balthasar describes rather well, all the semantic possibilities of the biblical tradition – metaphor, simile, symbol, example, allegory and, above all, *parable*. If the parables were enigmatic, and the post-Easter Church laboured to supply them with explanatory commentary, this is owing to no desire for obfuscation on the part of Jesus himself. The parabolic form challenges his hearers, in the way already familiar from Old Testament wisdom literature; what the parables describe – the essence and advent of the Kingdom – is at the time of Jesus' speaking still future, and thus inevitably *hidden* reality; and if there is talk of their obscurity 'hardening the hearts' of his hearers this is a Semitism for how responsibility is laid upon them. The aim is communication not its opposite, and through the manner of his utterance Jesus makes common cause with a language both generally human and distinctively Israelite. His interpretative action in expressing divine 'logic' in human did not find the latter altogether unprepared. The question, 'To what may we liken the Kingdom of God?' is addressed to an audience that is disposed to expand the limits of a significance already available to them in the direction of the meaning intended by Jesus.

Thanks to what Augustine would call the interior illumination of the mind by divine Truth, and Thomas the first principles of truth and goodness, the natural man already knows what ethics and practical reason are, just as the Jew knows, through the Old Testament revelation, what might count as right relation towards the living God. This is the twofold grammar – the grammar of creation, and the grammar of Israel – in which Jesus can express incisively the divine Word.

Nevertheless, the authentic understanding of his words cannot be had without the subjective enlightenment of the spirit of Father and Son who alone can render their full meaning, a meaning which Jesus himself creates by his own 'practice' as, in his Passion, Death, Resurrection and Ascension, he goes to the Father. The 'humanly familiar existential and ethical situations' which the parables evoke serve as a *starting point* for their proper comprehension. And that comprehension concerns

---

7 *TL* II, p. 68; cf. my *The Art of God Incarnate: Theology and Image in Christian Tradition* (London 1980), pp. 13–48, 119–35, which lays out this argument in fuller form.

the action of God *vis-à-vis* the world through the Son and the Spirit, who thus solicit the human situation to orient itself to the *divine behaviour*.[8]

In all cases it is a matter of learning to take the model of God – the prodigal Father, the good Samaritan – as the norm for human activity, for what God reveals Christologically and Pneumatologically is precisely the ultimate Good, the norm of all norms for man. And this enables Balthasar to return to a disputed theme of contemporary theology – the relation of 'theory' to 'practice' – which he last touched on in the opening volume of the theological dramatics.

> 'Theory', in the case of Christianity, is the understanding of the 'praxis' of God – which is what, in the final analysis, the parables mean us to grasp – and that in such a way that this 'praxis', being as it is the absolutely good and right, becomes as it should the norm for human beings too.[9]

Nowhere more clearly than in the parables, so Balthasar thinks, do we find divine logic expressing itself in human – thanks to what he terms an 'analogy of language' itself based ultimately on an analogy of being, the two brought to their fulfilment in the God-man Jesus Christ.

By 'analogy of language' Balthasar means that the logic of the creature is not in and of itself alien to the logic of the Creator, the logic of God. He has already explained in the concluding volume of *Theodramatik* how this is so. The otherness which the Triune hypostases constitute within the perfect unity of essence of God is the foundation for the otherness of a possible creation. The (Thomistic) 'real distinction' between essence and the act of existence of the creature is a distant echo of the single divine nature existing as it does by way of the Persons. Even the potentiality, as distinct from actuality, which is in different ways a creaturely hallmark is taken by Balthasar to be the faint reflection of the relations both of origin and of communion of divine Persons who *receive* as well as give. God's supervitality is the model for the becoming of creatures; the letting-be of the divine hypostases provides an archetype for what we enjoy as space and time. All of which means that, while the Incarnation of the Logos is certainly a free, unsuspected act of divine grace, the Word none the less, as St John points out in his Prologue, 'came to his own' (John 1.11), not to a strange country (here Balthasar appropriates a saying of Barth) but to a land whose tongue he knew. Balthasar is not speaking of Galilaean Aramaic, but of that language whose logic is furnished by *creaturely being as such*. The being of the world, with its daily round, gave the Logos the diapason by which he could sound out divine music.

Cataphatic and apophatic

Still, it is with Balthasar a sacred principle that whatever the likeness of creature to Creator the unlikeness is greater still. Never does he forget

---

8 *TL* II, p. 74. Italics added.
9 *TL* II, p. 75. Cf. my account in *No Bloodless Myth: A Guide through Balthasar's Dramatics* (Edinburgh 2000), p. 14.

that so important rider to the doctrine of analogy which the Fourth Lateran
Council spelled out in 1215 and which remains, from beginning to end,
an Ariadne's thread to guide us through Balthasar's work.

Applied Christologically: in his transcendence *vis-à-vis* other human
beings and their resources of meaning, the Word incarnate retains both
his mystery and his initiative. He never reduces himself or his teaching to
a level of ordinariness which would render the Word of God ultimately
trivial and boring – the inevitable last end of an excessive cataphaticism
in its obsession with making everything as clear as possible. And so
Balthasar has still to explain that, considered as the expression of divine
logic in human, the Incarnation must never be seen without its proper
context of apophatic – 'negative' – theology.

The original negative theology of Scripture he finds in those Isaianic
oracles which portray the Lord as the only Saviour, he and no other, the
only Lord, who will not yield his glory to a second. The God who cannot
deny himself in his divine singularity by that very fact denies all usurping
would-be gods or idols. But in the second place there is the negative
theology of biblical man as counterposing himself to God, whether
through idolatrous cultus, or through attempting to control God by means
of the Law or, finally, by denying God openly at the supreme point of his
self-revelation, 'You have heard the blasphemy . . . he is deserving of
death' (Matthew 26.65–6). This last is the decisive human negation
which stands at the centre of the theological dramatics, and in recording
the divine answer thereto – the 'word of the Cross' as Paul calls it in
1 Corinthians – Balthasar hints at the character of his own preferred form
of apophaticism. Then, thirdly, there is the philosophically derived
negative theology, originating in the Platonic tradition, and given house
and home by the Church Fathers. To this form of negative theology
Balthasar is largely though not altogether opposed. For a pagan antiquity
lacking the crucial theological concept of personhood for the 'hid Divinity',
it must have seemed that the necessary criticism of the woefully finite
gods of mythology entailed negating all finite concepts in the religious
search for the Absolute. Whereas on occasion, in the Neoplatonism of
such men as Proclus and Plotinus, that search might eventuate in the
experience of a mystical 'touch', once the *via negativa* was made the dead
centre of a philosophy it led, in Balthasar's view, to an equally dead end.
Now no speculation could lead to mysticism, no mystical experience be
translated into speculation. Looking at such a negative way against the
backdrop of human religion at large he finds that, via Mahayana
Buddhism, the inevitable outcome was reached in Zen for which the only
reality is pure experience. Once this path had been trodden the only
alternative was a resigned agnosticism, moving from one refusal to affirm
to another until it gives up seeking altogether. Balthasar does not hesitate
to call such a negativist religious mindset the 'strongest bastion against
Christianity'.[10]

And yet Balthasar is no Harnack. He does not hold that the Fathers
denatured the Gospel in Hellenising it, for example by their introduction
of a pagan negative theology. Their use of the vocabulary and procedures

10 *TL* II, p. 88.

of such a theology was, he points out, strategic. In the struggle against a rationalistic Gnosticism and Arianism, it was a summons to respect the mystery of a God who in his spiritual freedom calls for loving response to his gracious demand. Moreover, once contextualised within the world of the Scriptures, negative theology became a powerful rhetorical tool for exhortation to that ceaseless 'seeking the face of the Lord' which the psalmists and prophets urge on those whom the Lord has already found in his covenant grace. The meaning of the negations of the idols in Scripture is not unrelated to the philosopher's criticisms of ideas of God unworthy of man's last End: these formal negatives are materially positive, for they incite us to seek the One who, in his super-positivity, lies wholly beyond all finite limitation – which is why, in Scripture, the encouragement to search is often associated with words of joy.

And yet Balthasar would wish that the negative theology of the Church be more fully determined by the New Testament itself – by encounter with the Word made flesh. For there is another silence – the silence of adoration elicited by the sheer excess of what has been given in the revealing and saving Word, Jesus Christ. That 'excess' is attested by the reiterated *hyper*, 'super', of Paul's characteristic vocabulary, expressing as this does a sense of 'overwhelmedness', *Überwältigtwerden*, by the God of grace. In one way, Balthasar comments, this renders negative theology superfluous. If negative theology there is to be in Christianity, Balthasar would prefer to see it as a manifestation of the Gospel's special quality of silence. By contrast to both Buddhism and Neoplatonism, where silence has priority over against the word, in the latter's plurality and clamour, Balthasar sees it as typical of the Gospel to *transpose the silence into the Word itself*. As Ignatius of Antioch saw, the actions of the Word incarnate were at the deepest level carried out in silence (*Magnesians* 8.3) since the self-communication of the God who holds back nothing in the gift of the Son goes way beyond what the Word could formulate. Neoplatonist silence is silence before a 'non-word' (*Unwort*) where a philosophy which would ascend into the divine presence abstracts from all that is corporeal, or even spiritual in a finite fashion, to hymn the unspeakable One. Christian silence is silence before a 'super-word' (*Überwort*); it is sustained by a theology which retraces through faith the descent of God himself in the willing humility of his Flesh-taking. And if Balthasar can find evidence of a modern Christian 'theology of silence' in Karl Rahner's 'most beautiful' book *Hearers of the Word* where man must listen out for a possible divine breaking of silence in revelation,[11] and, at greater length in Max Picard's *Die Welt des Schweigens*,[12] it is the author of the Ignatian letters who must carry off the prize – for he alone sees silence and word as co-determining in God, in the Incarnation, in the Church. Has enough been made of the silence of Jesus' hidden life, of his silence in the case of the Woman taken in Adultery, in the scenes of the Passion before Caiphas, Herod, Pilate? Or what about the many situations in the public ministry where he is absent to those who seek him? Or his silent return to the Father's bosom, and equally silent presence under the forms of bread and wine in the

11 K. Rahner, *Hearers of the Word* (Et New York 1969).
12 M. Picard, *Die Welt des Schweigens* (Zurich 1948).

Church? Is it not significant that, as the Word made flesh he speaks more
by gestures than by words? Balthasar is not withdrawing what he has
earlier said about the comprehensibility of Jesus' logic: he is asserting,
rather, that such comprehensibility is perfectly compatible with the unsoundable depths of his words. These are what Paul calls the 'inexhaustible
riches of Christ' (Ephesians 3.9) in whom 'lie hid all the treasures of
wisdom and knowledge' (Colossians 2.3), for the receiving of which, as
the mysticism of Tauler, John of the Cross and the French School knows
well, what must be negated is *our* too insistent sense of our own substance
and centrality.

After all, in grace man is called to respond to God in Christ not only by
words but by the gift of all he has. And here a truly evangelical negative
theology

> at last becomes the place of perfect encounter, not in dialogical
> equivalence between God and man [as though man should ever have
> words equal to the Word of God] but in the metamorphosis of the
> entire human creature in an *ecce ancilla* [an attitude of obedient
> service] before the mystery of God's ungraspable, self-emptying
> love.[13]

13 *TL* II, p. 113.

13

The Place of the Logos in God

We now come to the organic centre of *Theologik* II – the place of the Logos in God, his procession from the Father as the latter's Word, Son, Image and Expression. The logic of the Logos in God can only be discerned Christianly from Jesus' attitude toward Father and Spirit. And these Balthasar has acquainted us with thoroughly enough in the aesthetics and dramatics. It is enough to recall in the context of the logic that in all the scenes where Jesus figures, in all his deeds and his words, we are dealing with the Trinitarian Son, the 'single Lord Jesus Christ' of Chalcedon, and not with his humanity alone. When Jesus calls the Father 'Thou', this expresses an eternal relation; the sense of intimate unity yet difference which emerges from Jesus' references to the Spirit points us 'beyond the sphere of the creaturely to the divine'.[1]

Approaches and limitations

The great variety of New Testament terms for the Son's unique relation to God shows him to us as the 'door' opening up the *mysterium tremendum* of the Father. Only by expressing himself in this Son is God 'Father'. Yet at the same time, he is God since what he expresses is God – as is what proceeds from Father and Son, the Spirit. Here Balthasar raises the question of the *relative priority* to be conceded to, on the one hand, the hypostasis of the Father, and, on the other, the divine nature in its inner fruitfulness, when we are construing the doctrine of the triune God. Where will his accent fall: on a 'personalist' or an 'essentialist' account of the Holy Trinity? This is, evidently, a matter of some moment for any positioning of the divine Logos which is his subject.

Where an orthodox Triadological essentialism is concerned (we are not speaking here of any merely *technically* Trinitarian monotheism), the work of Anselm of Canterbury is perhaps the best example that theological history affords. For Balthasar, St Anselm's development of the Augustinian Triadology he inherited from the Latin tradition makes the Fatherly origin of Son and Spirit virtually coincide with the divine Essence common to all the hypostases'.[2] Such prioritising of the divine Essence is compatible,

1 *TL* II, p. 118.
2 *TL* II, p. 120. He has in mind such Anselmian texts as *Monologion* 63.

Balthasar points out, with seeing the persons as relationships (something we might otherwise consider a sign of advanced personalism in these questions) for 'relation' *can* be an ontologically weak term posing no threat (as essentialists might conceive matters) to the divine unity. A hypostasis which is pure relationship would be, Balthasar suggests, only the (logical) end term of the relation in question. But that is not at all how Augustine's Trinitarianism seems in St Thomas' perspective. For Aquinas, because the relations are one reality with the Essence they are (ontologically) productive, actually bringing forth the persons. In his approach, the persons' relations on the one hand and their processions on the other are only distinct *quoad nos*, to our thought. For a personalist Triadology, then, it is not so much the divine nature that is fecund but the divine Father, as he generates the Son and, with the Son, spirates the Spirit. Nevertheless – and here the Anselmian line of thinking is perfectly justified – it is from out of his substance, the unique divine *ousia*, that the Father is in that fashion productive. Texts from Aquinas – as we might expect from so classically balanced a theologian – give support to that notion too.

Still, the integration of essentialism and personalism in the Christian doctrine of God is not plain sailing. The *aporia* (for the question to whose adjudication Balthasar has summoned Anselm and Thomas – and indeed also Augustine and Bonaventure – can hardly be said to be wholly resolved) will afflict, Balthasar thinks, all theology of the immanent Trinity. The latter, as it tries to think both with and beyond the doctrine of the economic Trinity, tends to give rise to these two counterposed positions whose synthesis is by no means easy.

> If then it is not a matter of letting the one divine Essence be active as such in the personal processions and relations, it is on the other hand clear that in these relations and processions we are dealing with the identical divine being of each hypostasis.[3]

It would seem that, speculatively, we can grasp the mystery in its twofold aspect only in the interplay of the propositions that speak of the Essence on the basis of the persons (personalism) and the Persons on the basis of the Essence (essentialism) – not through any real unification of these judgments in constructive thought. (The same difficulty, so Balthasar notes, recurs in the issue of Trinitarian appropriation – by which, for instance, wisdom, not least on the cue offered by Paul in 1 Corinthians,[4] is especially assigned to the Son, owing to some internal affinity of that attribute to a hypostasis who proceeds in the way the Son does, even when it is recognised that everything essential to God, including, then, wisdom, belongs in common to the three persons.)[5]

A resolution

Though Balthasar will attempt to resolve this *aporia* through what we can call a Triadology of *love*, he first explains, in a lengthy footnote, why he is

3 *TL* II, p. 126.
4 1 Corinthians 1.24: 'Christ the Wisdom of God.'
5 Hence Thomas' incisive definition of appropriation: *manifestatio personarum per essentialia attributa*, *Summa Theologiae* Ia, q. 39, a. 7.

not, however, taking the option of those – and here he has in mind the French philosopher Jean-Luc Marion – who would cut the Gordian knot of such problems by dispensing with ontology altogether. Martin Heidegger's objection to 'onto-theology' – that it thinks the divine being on the model of finite *Dasein*, 'being-there', and so leads to a forgetfulness of Being in its distinctness from beings – has no relevance, so Balthasar avers, to Christian Trinitarianism. The divine being does not, in the persons, subsist in something distinct from itself. Rather does it *subsist in itself*, just as do the 'relative oppositions' of the hypostases. As Marion's colleague and co-national Claude Bruaire has put it, 'being does not differ from the supreme Being; it differs *in* him'.[6] In Balthasar's eyes, Marion has made too many concessions to Heidegger's critique of the ontology subjacent to the doctrinal tradition – and in any case no thinking can dispense with *some* account of being, in the sweeping way Marion would counsel in *L'Idole et la distance* and, more explicitly still, *Dieu sans être*.[7] It is because the divine being is already *der Abgrund aller Liebe*, 'the abyss of all love', that the gracious goodness gifted by God to the world needs no other 'higher' source than that being for its own provenance. Unlike Marion's, Balthasar's theology of gifted love will not attempt to *replace* Trinitarian ontology but to *illuminate* it from within.

For Balthasar, what the Father pours forth on the Son in generating him is the perfect, undivided Godhead which is his, yet he possesses that Godhead only as thus poured forth. And the same is true of Father and Son in spiration of the Holy Ghost. In this formulation, Balthasar thinks, the spectral prospect of the divine Essence as, alongside the Trinity, a 'fourth' in God at last vanishes.

> And if the self-giving of the Father to the Son, and of both to the Spirit, corresponds neither to a free arbitration nor to a necessity, but to God's intimate essence, then this most intimate essence – however we may distinguish between the processions – can itself be in the last analysis only love.[8]

Balthasar concedes that for the New Testament it is the Father's 'economic' giving over of Son and Spirit which counts as the love of God (and indeed the free letting themselves so be given on the part of that Son and that Spirit). But he goes on,

> why should this fundamental statement concerning the order of salvation not have as its presupposition a determination of the Essence of the triune God?[9]

Once this is allowed then all the problems we have encountered in moderating the relations of a personalist and an essentialist triadology begin to fall away.

6 C. Bruaire, *L'Être et l'Esprit* (Paris 1963), n. 190, cited *TL* II, p. 125. Balthasar also presses into service Gustav Siewerth's Thomist critique of Heideggerianism in *Der Thomismus als Identitätssystem* (Düsseldorf 1979).
7 J.-L. Marion, *L'Idole et la distance* (Paris 1979); *Dieu sans être* (Paris 1982).
8 *TL* II, pp. 126–7.
9 *TL* II, p. 127.

The divine Essence, thus considered, would be not only co-extensive with the event of the eternal processions but co-determinate with it by way of the – in each case unique – participation in that Essence of Father, Son and Spirit. In other words, it would exist in a way that is never anything other than *vaterhaft, sohnhaft und geisthaft*, Fatherly, Sonly, Ghostly. And since the persons are all hypostases of the concretely one divine nature, with which each of them is really identical, their unity of Essence can also be described as their coinherence, their 'circumcession', whereby they form all together the single, free, 'personal' Face of God.[10]

Here too the problem of 'appropriation' finds its solution: what is, on grounds of the economy of salvation, appropriated to one hypostasis (in the example earlier chosen, wisdom to the Son), can be re-appropriated by the whole Godhead – the other persons – as their common good.

Let us retain from this account the rôle played by the concept of love: for the particular way in which Balthasar has united personalist and essentialist Trinitarian thinking was made possible by privileging the idea of the *Je-schon-sich-Weggeben*, the 'ever-already-being-given-awayness', of the Father as itself the key to the uniqueness of the divine Essence. It is from the 'primordial mystery of abyssal love' that all the divine properties take their 'coloration'.[11]

Persons and attributes

Balthasar now goes on to show how this is so. What is admirable in his account is the way he sets forth the divine attributes in closest connexion with an evocation of how the divine hypostases determine the divine Essence of which those attributes are the qualities – while all the time referring to the economic manifestation of the hypostases in the divine missions, the salvation-historical sending of Son and Spirit into the world. We have here, evidently, an audacious attempt at a really *integrated* theology of God (not, however, one that stands utterly alone, for Balthasar's project is not the least of the enterprises he approved in Karl Barth).

Jesus as the Trinitarian Son made man discloses a plurality of aspects of the single divine nature: in words of Augustine cited here by Balthasar, God's 'simple multiplicity and multiple simplicity'.[12] In the way Jesus situates himself, he discloses what Balthasar terms the foundational properties that contour the intimate divine Essence. Balthasar singles out for mention seven of these:

first, 'free and yet absolute' *love* – and Balthasar links the gratuity of redemption and love and creation to the Father's imprescriptible generation of the Son and spiration of the Spirit, crucial as that is to all reading of the divine Essence itself;

---

10 *TL* II, p. 127.
11 *TL* II, p. 128.
12 Augustine, *De Trinitate* VI. 4, 6; cited *TL* II, p. 129.

secondly, a *wisdom* that provides ultimate meaning for all knowledge and reason, and orientation for all that 'aims at a sense or a road'[13] – and this wisdom demonstrates that beyond all 'aiming', all finality, lies, once again, the 'whylessness' (*Umsonst*) of love, which explains how wisdom is revealed in the folly of the Cross;

thirdly, *omnipotence*, where what is omnipotent is the divine love, which can do everything that lies within love's 'imaginable realm', thus embracing, as the kenotic self-gift of Father in Son shows, supremely in the *dead* Christ, *both* almightiness *and* impotence as this world would understand them;

fourthly, *justice*, which, once again, Balthasar links to the divine love, since the latter is necessarily exact in its measuring in relation to itself all things – and this is no 'soft' re-writing of the concept of justice, for, as Balthasar explains, nothing is more characteristic of the divine love than to refuse to leave the unjust man in the state in which it found him, hence Christ's expiatory sacrifice can be for Paul the demonstration of the gift of God's *dikaiosunē* – precisely his *justice*;

fifthly, *mercy*, which few would have difficulty, presumably, in seeing as a mode of love, not least in its revelation in Jesus' dealings with sinners and the sick;

and sixthly, *faithfulness*: constancy, not least in his promises to the creation – something whose depths are sounded for Balthasar in, once again, the mystery of the Cross.

Characteristically, Balthasar names the seventh and crowning attribute of God as his *glory* – understood as his distinctively different divineness in all its sublimity, its disproportion to the virtues of the world. This is, in Balthasar's presentation, a complex attribute which embraces Jesus' simultaneous uniqueness and familiarity to others, Thabor and Calvary, the Transfiguration and the Cross. Indeed, Balthasar speaks of it as less a divine attribute than the point at which all the divine properties are 'absorbed into the mystery'.[14] But at the same time, so as to avoid any Nominalistic confusion of the divine glory with that 'absolute power' whereby for Ockham God could do whatever, irrespective of his nature, his choice settled upon, Balthasar insists that this glorious liberty of God's is one thing with his goodness and wisdom. We have here, evidently, a justification, in terms of the theological logic, of the theological aesthetics, though not in such a way as to isolate them from the theological dramatics too.

In the revelation on which Balthasar has thus drawn for his *De Deo*, God gave his uttermost (in Son and Spirit) so that his intrinsic mystery now abides continuously with us. For this reason, Palamism – the Byzantine theological theory that in the economy God manifested his energies but not his essence – cannot be, in its literal sense, true. There is no Essence beyond the Trinity in the way that, in the Latin West likewise, Porretanus was believed to hold (Balthasar does not seem to have known

13 *TL* II, p. 130.
14 *TL* II, p. 136.

of the vindication of Gilbert de la Porrée's reputation by mid-twentieth-century scholarship) and Eckhart actually held. If in the immanent Trinity the Father gives the Son everything save the property of being Father, this is not to *reserve* anything. And similarly, if in the case of creatures, the triune God makes them to participate in the divine nature – a reference to 2 Peter 1.4, it should not be supposed that the language of participation is intended here to deprive creatures of anything save literal apotheosis, the absurdity of the created becoming God.

Placing the Word

But Balthasar's treatise *De Deo*, 'on God' (if that be a fair way to describe pp. 119–38 of *Theologik* II) is intended above all as a preamble to an account of the place, more especially, of the Logos in this always and imprescindibly triune Godhead.

By now it should be clear that, for Balthasar, what becomes visible in the Father's Word is his 'love in all its dimensions, and therefore in all the consequences which arise therefrom for a possible free creation'.[15] If the Logos can be defined as that 'place' in God where a divine logic unfolds, the logic in question can, therefore, only be that of love; the love of its fontal Spring (the Father) set flowing there in all its inner essence-hood. Here Balthasar's discussion of the interrelation of personalist and essentialist theologies of the Trinity comes at last into its own. And since the Logos is no mere objectivisation of a subject but is its reflecting mirror, its living icon, it or rather *he* has to express that movement of 'groundless' loving manifestation of himself that is the Father. The Son's being, accordingly, has not only a provenance, it also has a goal, and here there comes into view the spiration of him whom we call the Holy Spirit. The Logos has not only a 'whence' in the Father. He has a 'whither' in the Spirit as well.

To say as much obliges Balthasar to face the whole issue, so crucial for Catholic–Orthodox dialogue in past and present, of the *Filioque*, the relation to the Son which co-determines the Spirit in his procession from the Father. Balthasar speaks of two 'directions' for the Logos which on the one hand correspond to the positions historically occupied by the Churches of East and West, and, on the other, are to *his* theological mind inseparable. For in the first place, the Word as expression of the Father naturally belongs to the latter's *Zeugerichtung*, his 'generative direction', as the Father pours forth his all – and here we have, according to Balthasar, the Oriental *dia Huion*, the *per Filium*, whereby the Spirit proceeds not so much from (the Father and) the Son as *through* the Son. And in the second place, since the Father from whom the Word springs is sheer love, a love to which the whole being of the Word answers, that Word may also be said to be wholly turned towards the Father, in a direction which is, this time, that of a wondrous meeting – and here we have, again according to Balthasar, the Occidental *Filioque*, whereby the Spirit proceeds from the 'doubling back' of Son to Father as the 'fecund encounter of love that

---

15 *TL* II, p. 140.

gives and love that receives', and so *from* not the Father alone but the Son likewise.[16] Following a cue of St Bonaventure's, were we simply to think in 'static' terms, the Logos is simply the Image of the Father, but it is also possible to think of him as realising after his own fashion the entire dynamism of the Father, in which case we shall see him as the expression of the whole Trinity. And Balthasar paraphrases this Bonaventurian dictum by saying that the Son 'represents the entire Trinitarian love in the form of expression'.[17]

So far Balthasar has been musing on speculative possibilities, but his two interrelated hypotheses turn out to be verified by the facts of Jesus' career – for his mission can and should be understood as the temporal prolongation of his procession.

> The logic of the incarnate Son cannot be reduced to the 'historical Jesus' but includes in itself his 'whence', from the Father, and 'whither', to the Spirit . . .[18]

Just so, earthly logic too has its 'whence' in ontology as a whole – something which cannot, we must add, be neatly separated from the concrete forms it takes in different 'areas' of reality (compared by Balthasar with the way the doctrine of the divine Essence is inseparable from an account of the divine hypostases). Just so, too, earthly logic has its 'whither', its regulative function in those various realms of being. Ordinary logic, like Christological, can claim a special relation to a territory of its own – and yet this 'territory' is itself determined by a wider web of relations, just as it helps to determine that wider web in turn. What Balthasar is saying here is that Christological logic cannot be separated from the being and activity of all three divine persons, and that it none the less governs the particular economy of the Son – that Son who does not, however, define his work save in relation to the Father who sends him and whose reign he inaugurates, and to the Spirit in whom he is sent and whose free gift he releases into the world.

This comparison of the two logics, though interesting in itself and valuable in liberating a Christology of the Gospels from the narrowing limits of a purely historical exegesis closed to the meta-historical realm, does not take Balthasar very far in his aim of 'verifying' the attempted resolution of the Filioque controversy on which he has embarked. And indeed, as he tells us, the whole question of the distinction between the processions of Son and Spirit (at the heart, evidently, of that ecumenical problem) is fraught with difficulty.[19]

After all, for the Old Testament the two concepts of 'Word' and 'Spirit' interweave in the biblical accounts of creation and history; their interrelation becomes particularly obscure, Balthasar reports, in the context of the idea of the Wisdom of God in the sapiential literature. Hence the uncertainty whereby, in the tradition, the Wisdom of God is sometimes identified with the Son, sometimes with the Spirit, whereas, thinks

16 *TL* II, p. 141.
17 *TL* II, p. 142.
18 Ibid.
19 *TL* II, p. 144.

Balthasar, taking the tradition *in globo*, it is best to treat that Wisdom as a property of the divine Essence which 'the Father manifests on the occasion of the Son's works, and dispenses to his children in the Holy Spirit that they may comprehend them'.[20] After all, it is with the New Testament that the distinction between the Word (God's Exegete) and the Spirit (the Interpreter of this Exegete) begins to become less obscure. For the Latin Scholasticism inspired by Augustine's treatise on the Trinity, much confidence was reposed in the possibilities of the famous psychological analogy, distinguishing Word and Spirit in terms of understanding and love – excessively so, in Balthasar's eyes.[21] He would like to see it nudged out of its position of centrality in favour of a distinction between two different processions within that all-embracing Fatherly love which, as we have seen, at the level of the Essence unifies the divine properties in itself.

Expressivity and liberality

In fact, Balthasar aligns himself with Bonaventure who, while not rejecting programmatically the analogy put forward (by no means dogmatically) by Augustine, wished to retain for the procession of the Son (and not just the Spirit) some reference to the Father's love – conformably, after all, to the New Testament witness. Though Thomas speaks, to be sure, of the divine Son in his eternal generation from the Father as his 'Image', he lingers only briefly on the point. It is the Franciscan doctor who dilates on it, drawing out the term's ontological potential in the realm of the Uncreated. For the Bonaventure of the *Commentary on the Sentences*, the Son proceeds from the Father's love *expressively* (he is, comments Balthasar, *der einmalige Ausdruck eines Einmaligen*,[22] the 'unique expression of a unique reality' and the Spirit, in contrast, *liberally*, by the sheer outflow of the divine generosity. Exemplarity and liberality are, then, the best *idées-clefs* for our exploration of the divine Second and Third. Putting the idea of expressiveness in central place does not only enable Balthasar to distinguish between Logos and Pneuma in their distinct processions in love. It also makes it possible for him to recover – without, this time, the slightest trace of subordinationism – the conviction dear to the ante-Nicene Fathers of the

> *disponibilité* of the Logos for every creation–decision of God as of his archetypal expressive form . . .[23]

It is the Logos – and not any other Trinitarian person – who can 'become world', and man the microcosm who, as the image of God, enjoys 'the closest ontic relationship' with the Logos whose nature the Word can and will assume.

---

20 *TL* II, p. 147.
21 He shares Karl Rahner's concern that, as the Father already understands and loves by virtue of the divine Essence, these cannot be formally constitutive of Word and Spirit: see K. Rahner, 'Der dreifaltige Gott als transzendenter Urgrund der Heilsgeschichte', in J. Feiner and M. Löhrer (eds), *Mysterium Salutis: Grundriss heilsgeschichtlicher Dogmatik* II (Einsiedeln 1967), pp. 317–401.
22 *TL* II, p. 154.
23 *TL* II, p. 155.

And this gives Balthasar his marching orders for the rest of *Theologik* II. He will look at the derivability of the world from the Trinity, and then its actual 'descent' (*katabasis*) in the Logos-centred triune act of creating (whence his term for this mode of theologising – 'cata-logic'), and finally, in the concluding section on the Word made flesh, ask how a divinely Trinitarian logic can 'adequately' express itself in a Logos incarnate in the midst of the world – the question to which, indeed, the whole of the second volume of his theological logic is devoted.

14

The Emergence of the World through the Word

Balthasar is certainly not one of those theologians who linger so long in textual interpretation that they never do ontology. He opens his preamble to 'cata-logic' by declaring that it is too constrictive, with Augustine, to think of the Trinity's expression in creation by reference to the human spirit, or, with Barth, by allusion to the spirit–body and male–female unity of man, or, with such mediaeval theologians as Rupert of Deutz and Joachim of Flora, by exclusive appeal to the history of salvation. A starting point generous enough to be congruent with its subject can only be the way God's triune being is reflected in the being of the world: *imago Trinitatis in ente creato*. To Balthasar's mind, a theologian has to be a metaphysician, just as a metaphysics which refused to be a theology would fail in its own proper enterprise.

The transcendentals and the Trinity

The question must be, then, how are the 'transcendentals' – unity, truth, goodness, those most pervasive and yet value-intensive features of all finite being, related to their Trinitarian source? Balthasar begins from Bonaventure's dictum that since the first Cause is also the most perfect, these highest qualities of being must needs be found, above all, in him. In the *Breviloquium*, the Franciscan doctor relates the ordered sequence of the one, the true, the good, in things to the Trinitarian *taxis* of Father, Son and Spirit,[1] and in the *Hexaemeron*, his commentary on the six-day creation, defines the terms of that comparison more sharply. It is because each and every being is placed in existence by an operative cause (is *ex alio*) that it is one (numerable, and inseparable from itself); it is because each and every being is formed according to a model (is *secundum aliud*) that it is true (knowable, and inseparable from its form); and it is because each and every being is ordered to a final end (is *propter aliud*) that it is good (participable, and inseparable from its work). And being thus *ex alio*, *secundum aliud*, and *propter aliud*, the creature, in its share in the transcendentals, mirrors from afar the triune Being of God who exists *ex se* in the Father, *secundum se* in the Son, and *propter se* in the Holy Spirit.[2]

---

1 Bonaventure, *Breviloquium* I. 6, cited *TL* II, pp. 160–1.
2 *Idem, Hexaemeron* I. 13; cf. *Breviloquium* II.1.

But the transcendentals cannot simply be attributed to the divine
Essence as such (not even to an Essence thus active in the divine
hypostases), for in the world's *exitus* from God it is the three Persons who
act – on the basis of their common Essence, of course, yet none the less
according to their hypostatic distinctiveness. Truth cannot be sundered
from God the Image in his expressive exemplarity of all created things,
nor goodness from God the Holy Spirit in the liberality which underpins
their real creation, that 'excess of love' by which all things envisaged in
the Logos are made.

By an aboriginal *kenōsis* – here Balthasar takes over a chief feature of
the daring speculative triadology of the Russian philosopher-theologian
Sergei Bulgakov – the Father empties the entire divine Essence into the
processions of Son and Spirit. The Son springs from love – for to say the
Father generates him so that he might recognise himself as God would be
Hegelianism, while to maintain that he brings him to be so as to know
himself perfectly is, when consistently thought through, Arian. And as to
the issuing of the Spirit, this 'last in execution', as the Scholastics say, is
'first in intention', and the mediaeval doctors whom Balthasar takes as
his sources here are agreed that his name is *Amor*. Why does Balthasar
thus insist that the generation of the Son, like the spiration of the Spirit,
must be considered as a procession of love that goes beyond knowledge?
Aside from the New Testament credentials of this way of seeing the
Father–Son relationship, already mentioned in the last chapter, it is so
that he can identify love, with the Catholic metaphysician Gustav Siewerth,
as the 'absolutely transcendental', recapitulating the reality of being, of
truth, of the good.[3] It is love which is the final truth of being – in the
divine Essence, in the reciprocal self-gift of the Persons, and so, since God
the Trinity is the Creator, in the created world itself which bears his mark.
And if there, then above all in *humankind*. For while Balthasar does not
wish to think the Trinitarian imagehood of finite being solely in terms of
the human spirit, he has no doubt that it is in our spiritual being that the
transcendentals attain their highest intensity this side of the creature–
Creator divide. Do we not see every day how the human essence only
develops itself in a child in the form of a *communion of love*?

I have spoken above of the 'creature–Creator divide' and surely this –
for a theologian of the *maior dissimilitudo* such as Balthasar – must profoundly affect the working of such divinely originated transcendentals in
the workaday world. Scripture speaks everywhere of the gratuity of God
in creating and electing – and the Thomist ontology of the creature, with
its inescapable duality of essence and existence allows us to glimpse
the metaphysical gulf that divides the creating Lord from the works of
his hands. And yet over this abyss – in Balthasar's own metaphor – the
revelation of the Trinity throws a bridge, and of a kind that no one could
imagine until it actually appeared.

If in the identity of God there is the Other, which is moreover the
Image of the Father and in such fashion that it is also the archetype

---

3 G. Siewerth, *Metaphysik der Kindheit* (Einsiedeln 1957), p. 63; *idem, Grundfragen der
Philosophie im Horizont der Seinsdifferenz* (Düsseldorf 1963), p. 112, cited *TL* II, p.
162.

of everything that can be created; and if in this identity there is the Spirit, the free, outflooding love of the One and the Other, then the 'other' of the creation, orientated as this is on the model of the divine Other, and its being in general, owed as *this* is to the intra-divine liberality, is propelled into a positive relation with God which no other non-Christian religion (Judaism and Islam included) could dream of . . .

For, as Balthasar explains:

> where God (also YHWH and Allah) can be only the One, any explanation favourable to the other becomes inaccessible: where the world is thought philosophically as the other and as the many (something which has not happened in a serious way in Judaism and Islam), it can be thought only as a declension from the uniquely blessed One.[4]

So the fact that the God of Christian revelation is the Holy Trinity who alone is the Creator means that the creature is not simply 'from God' but is marked by the inner-Trinitarian hypostatic differences – the Son in his exemplarity, the Spirit in his liberality, the two of course originated by the Father – and this enables an ontologically richer account of its make-up. Both the real distinction between essence and existence (*Seinsdifferenz*) and the imaging of the Trinitarian distinctions (*Trinitarische Differenz*) must be given their proper place in an account of the world made through the Word – and made not least for the embodying, in myriad ways, of the transcendentals.

The Trinity and the 'real distinction'

It was one of the principal lessons of *Herrlichkeit* – notably in its crucial but much-neglected volume on metaphysics – that the glory of God is found in the creation chiefly by the gratuitous self-emptying of being as it pours itself out, unremarked, into the things that are. The seeming poverty of non-subsistent being – so belittled by Anglo-Saxon commentators that they consider the very vocables meaningless – is in fact its wondrous richness, since by its kenosis in favour of actual essences it mirrors the glorious self-sharing love of its own divine Source.[5] It is, says Balthasar, the 'pure and free expression of the divine goodness and liberality'.[6] But the plurality of existing things in which such being comes to subsist (the created order must be a plurality else what subsists thereby would be God himself!) and the task that each, sheerly by existing, is set so as to fulfil its nature, these take their orientation from the divine exemplarity – from the Logos. *Both* divinely subsistent being *and* non-subsistent being are in different fashions the creature's source, and for this reason the created thing (or person) shows a likeness to God as well as a (yet greater)

4 *TL* II, pp. 165–6.
5 See my *The Word Has Been Abroad*, pp. 143–4, 182–6. Also *idem*, 'Von Balthasar's Aims in his Theological Aesthetics', *Heythrop Journal* XL (1999), pp. 409–23.
6 *TL* II, p. 167.

dissimilarity. The transcendentals are in the creature according to this twofold law of its being (since for it, unlike for God, to be what it is can never amount to being *simpliciter*), and in that way they indicate the finitude of their expression in creation, pointing on to the divine reality that is their originator, conserver and goal.

And yet because there is also difference in the *Trinitarian* God himself, this duality – non-identity – in the creature is not to be regarded as a tragedy, the result of some cosmic fall. Otherness is at home in God – as the processions of Son and Spirit show. Evidently, difference does not of itself destroy unity – one need only think of how the diversity of the divine hypostases leaves the divine simplicity intact. The question is, though, When is difference a creatively unifying model of the divine life and when is it, by contrast, alienatingly divisive? It is to the hope for a *reconciled creation* that Balthasar now turns.

15

⁂

Cata-logic: Fulfilment from God

The task of cata-logic

If ana-logic goes up (from the world to God), cata-logic comes down (from God to the world). Even if ana-logic, in the hands of Christian thinkers, presupposed in different ways (contrast the dialogical thinkers with, say, Richard of St Victor) a knowledge of the Word of God, it was essentially a matter of postulation, proposing ways of relating structures of thought or being to the One disclosed in divine revelation so as to suggest how the Incarnation of the Logos – and his further interpretation by the Spirit – might be thinkable. In other words, it was an epistemic affair. In cata-logic, however, we are dealing with a very different kettle of fish. We must recall how in the opening volume of the theological logic, Balthasar has made it perfectly plain that, at his hands, 'logic' will include ontology – since the true is inseparable from the real. Very well, then, now that, in the previous chapter, he has identified how the world comes from the Logos in a form that is polarised – though in no *exclusively* negative sense – we need him to show, on the basis of the Judaeo-Christian revelation, how the tensions that result are provided for in the divine plan, the divine operation. In a world where diversity too often means conflict, to speak in theological ontology of *reconciliation* is virtually to use a synonym for salvation itself.

According to Balthasar's cata-logic, Christ comes to fulfil as the Word Incarnate the work which the Trinity has enterprised from the beginning of the world. He shows himself: first, as the unifier of polar tensions in cosmic being (here Balthasar follows the seventh-century theologian Maximus the Confessor); secondly, as the fulfiller of the arts and sciences (here Balthasar regards the thirteenth-century Franciscan doctor Bonaventure as his model); thirdly, as the key to the Trinitarian structure of history (with the twelfth-century black monk theologian Rupert of Deutz); and fourthly, as the founder of a new relation between the world and God (with the fifteenth-century cardinal Nicholas of Cusa). In all these ways Christ acts as the source of new ontological bonds, and thus fresh logical connexions, between God and the world the Father so loved as to send not only the Son but the Spirit also.

The general rubric under which all this is placed, to repeat, is 'reconciliation'. We have seen how for Balthasar's ontology of the created realm, as for that of Aquinas, the difference between existence and essence is vital. We have seen, moreover, that such difference is not only positive in that it constitutes the creaturely in both its multiplicity and its possible fecundity, it also has an aspect of extreme tension which can ultimately take the form of tragedy.

Four pillars of cata-logical wisdom

Christ as mediator of the reconciled unity of a creation not only differentiated but at times ruptured is very much the chosen theme of Maximus the Confessor – as one of the most influential patristic monographs of recent decades, *Microcosm and Mediator*, by the Swedish Maximian scholar Lars Thunberg, bears witness.[1] For Balthasar, the various dualities Maximus discusses – man and woman, paradise and inhabited earth, earth and heaven, sensuous and spiritual, God and creature, are unified, in the Confessor's thinking, by the setting up of a 'mysterious equilibrium' between the most individual and the most universal aspect of a creature's being. Totalities (*Ganzheiten*) must be nourished by individuals (*Einzelnen*) and individuals indwelt by totalities – and this seems eminently possible to a Chalcedonian Christian like Maximus, for whom the God-man is the concrete Universal. Whereas Hegel so dissolved Christ that he became, in Balthasar's metaphor, a principle of being as fluid as a river without banks, with Maximus the story is very different, as a wonderful passage of the *Ambigua* attests:

> The essential wisdom of God the Father and his prudence is the Lord Jesus Christ, who in the power of his wisdom includes in himself every universal and embraces the parts which compose it in his sapient knowledge, given that he is precisely the Creator and Preserver of all being, leads into unity all that is distorted in existent things, softens every conflict and struggle in the world of being and joins everything in heaven and on earth, as the apostle says, in peace and friendship, in order and concord.[2]

Where man failed, the Logos-made-human took his place, and thus the human being who occupies the midpoint of creation was enabled to unify the cosmos in himself and so present it to God as to join it with God in his grace. Balthasar regrets that Maximus' Latin translator, John Scotus Eriugena, in his own *De divisione naturae*, pressed the Confessor's Chalcedonian vision of a universe restored to unity with God 'without either division or confusion' in a (Neo-)Platonic direction which threatened the integrity of the specifically Christological component in his thought. Yet enough of the original inspiration remains for the Christologically defined hope for a restored, re-united cosmos to endure – rendered possible by the Resurrection which, in raising to glory that human nature which is

---

1 L. Thunberg, *Microcosm and Mediator: The Theological Anthropology of Maximus the Confessor* (Lund 1965); see for an interpretative summary my *Byzantine Gospel*, pp. 158–95.
2 Maximus, *Ambigua*, at PG 91, 1313B, cited *TL* II, p. 174.

the microcosm of the universe at large, signifies the transfiguration of the latter in its totality.

Balthasar speculates about a possible chain of historical influence linking Eriugena, via the Victorines, to Bonaventure, and it is to Bonaventure (in many ways, as *Herrlichkeit* has shown, Balthasar's favourite mediaeval divine) that he turns for the *second* manner in which cata-logic presents the rôle of the Word incarnate: Christ as fulfiller of the *sciences* (*Wissenschaften*). Now Balthasar admits that the opening 'demonstration' in Bonaventure's *Hexaemeron* can easily appear forced – and this is the case even when we recognise that by *scientiae* Bonaventure means all genuine disciplines, including rational philosophy and ethics, as well as natural philosophy (within which we would indeed have to include our 'natural sciences' and so Christ as fulfiller of neuro-physiology, of genetics, of astrophysics!). But Bonaventure, unlike ourselves (so Balthasar explains) approaches the topic of the sciences in a metaphysical-epistemological fashion. He asks what is the ontological and noetic space in which such sciences must develop, and seeks after a principle capable of constituting a unifying centre for their multiplicity, a principle which can order the epistemic space they inhabit. In the first *collatio*, 'conversation', of his commentary on the Genesis creation narrative, Bonaventure explains that all the sciences carry within themselves from their natural environment some 'seal of the archetype' – that archetype which is not just the pre-existent Logos as such, but the Logos made man, first and last idea of the world. However, the sciences cannot discover this 'seal' for themselves. Their only attainable basic principle lies within created nature, and so here they run up against their own limits; and in any case their focus of interest in the domain of the world makes them 'forget' their own origin; and thus the call to self-transcendence of these sciences is lost in oblivion. It is not a question, Balthasar urges, of supernaturalising these studies out of all recognisable existence, but of their 'inner conservation and salvation through orderly incorporation in a comprehensive noetic space'.[3] This is why Christ needed human as well as divine knowledge. Bonaventure lists some telling examples of how the sciences betray their own integrity by excessive, or humanly damaging, claims – to which modern intellectual culture could contribute some instances of its own. But more positively – and more importantly for the project of *Theologik* – he sets out to show how the states of the Logos are crucial to the right location of the sciences – his eternal generation via the notion of origin to metaphysics; his Incarnation via the notion of power-source to physics; his Cross via the notion of centre of gravity to mathematics (mathematical physics as we would now say); his Resurrection via the notion of demonstrative force to logic; his Ascension via the notion of right decision to ethics; his sitting in judgment via the notion of just judgment to law; and his blessedness via the notion of reconciliation to theology. Naturally, the schema of disciplines and key concepts needs rethinking for the modern sciences (and arts), and even in its own time some linkages were, doubtless, more persuasive than others. Yet the entire proposal remains highly stimulating, while Bonaventure's coupling of

3 *TL* II, p. 180.

a Christocentrically practised theology with the theme of reconciliation encourages Balthasar to pursue the 'cata-logic' on which he is embarked.

A Trinitarian cata-logic of history, centred on Jesus Christ, can best be found, Balthasar opines, in the work of Rupert of Deutz, who took further hints in such patristic writers as Gregory Nazianzen and Augustine,[4] or earlier mediaeval divines like Hugh of St Victor and Anselm of Havelberg.[5] In a sympathetic presentation of the *De Trinitate et operibus eius*, Balthasar emphasises the novelty with which Rupert periodises salvation history in terms of the work of the persons while never neglecting their common co-operation at all times. For Rupert, the Logos presides over the entire epoch from Fall to Incarnation, gradually advancing toward his own embodi-ment, showing himself in figures from Adam to Noah, in actions and friendly relationship from Noah to Abraham, in promises from Abraham to David, and then, from David to the deportation to Babylon (an age dominated by the royal institution and its theology) as king, while in the generations that join the return from Exile to the Incarnation (where the cultus of the restored Temple kept Jewish faith alive) as priest. Finally the Logos, now become man, rests in the tomb at the completion of his work, as the Father had himself rested on creation's seventh day. On Rupert's scheme, the Holy Spirit predominates in the time from the Annunciation – which enables him, faithful to the Gospel record, to emphasise the rôle of the Holy Spirit in Christ's baptism and public ministry, his Passion and Resurrection. But whereas the climax of the economy of the Logos takes place at its close, the high point of the Spirit's work is at the inception of 'his' age, with the life of Christ and the foundation of the Church – with, then, Easter and Pentecost. The Spirit's rôle, indeed, is to complete human imagehood of the Trinity by bringing human beings to a condition of likeness to the triune God on the basis of the supreme epiphany of the divine Wisdom in Jesus Christ – something which he does through the Church and her sacraments. Not that such transfiguration of history is smooth: Balthasar finds congenial the conflictual theodramatics of Rupert's *De victoria Verbi Dei* and his commentary on the Apocalypse where justice is done to the anti-God historical powers.[6]

Balthasar's references in this context to the Calabrian abbot Joachim of Fiore – whose speculations, in one way comparable, were finally rejected by Church authority – are largely intended to throw Rupert's theology into relief. Treating more seriously than Henri de Lubac the claim that Joachim's origins and early education were Jewish, Balthasar regards his attempt to render Old and New Testaments concordant, as well as his doctrine of a future Church of the Spirit strongly contrasting with the present Church of the Son, as a downplaying of the specifically Christological structure of historical redemption. Although the 'labyrin-thine' quality of Joachim's typology allowed him to identify anticipations

---

4 See more widely A. Luneau, *L'histoire de salut chez les Pères de l'Eglise: La doctrine des âges du monde* (Paris 1964).

5 On these writers, some materials can be found in B. Smalley, *The Historian and the Middle Ages* (London 1974).

6 Balthasar has made use in this section of L. Scheffczyk, 'Die heilsökonomische Trinitätslehre des Rupert von Deutz und ihre dogmatische Bedeutung', in J. Betz and H. Fries (eds), *Kirche und Überlieferung* (Freiburg 1960), pp. 90–118.

of successive covenants which both complicated and mitigated his basic scheme, the abiding result of his intervention was a recurring tendency in Western intellectual history to propose the supersession of the ecclesial covenant of the Son through political, ethical and speculative messianism. Swedenborg, Hegel and Marx, all these belong to the 'spiritual posterity of Joachim of Fiora', to borrow the title of de Lubac's encyclopaedic study.[7] As Joseph Ratzinger has noted, Bonaventure's correction of Joachimism lay in the provision of an otherwise lacking Christocentricity.

> With his Cross he [Christ] has uncovered the lost centre of the world's circle, thus giving their true dimensions and meaning to the move-ment both of individual lives and of human history as a whole.[8]

Balthasar's cata-logical researches end with the fifteenth-century theologian Nicholas of Cusa whose *De docta ignorantia* he regards as one of the clearest examples of the genre, for Cusanus treats the world as the *explicatio* or unfolding of that perfect *complicatio* or infolding which is the triune Lord's fullness of unity. While by no means underwriting the whole of Nicholas' highly original thinking (his notion that, mathematics apart, all natural human knowledge remains conjectural strikes Balthasar as an anticipation of the contemporary scientific world-view – by no means an unqualified compliment!), Balthasar applauds Cusanus for working out a Christological 'coincidentia oppositorum' where maximal humiliation and maximal exaltation come together on the Cross. Christ is the 'medium' between the 'sheerly absolute' and the 'sheerly concrete'.[9] In the late, and much less well-known, *De visione Dei* (1453), published in the year of Constantinople's fall, the ecclesiastical statesman who had worked to save Byzantine Christendom from such a fate took consolation in the broader view of the vision of God. In that treatise he argued that, since, both as God and as man, the Logos is the one absolutely loved by the Father, all created being inasmuch as it is 'enfolded' by the hypostatic union can be loved thus unconditionally in the Son. The Spirit's task is precisely to conjoin the 'lovable' (the world) to the beloved (the Logos made man) as to an 'absolute mediator'. While Balthasar has his suspicions that Nicholas' 'infinity thinking' is over-motivated by a quasi-Neo-Platonist longing for unconditional unity – in despite of the message of Trinitarian doctrine that there is otherness in God, he is reassured by the detailed and subtle work of the Cusanus scholar Rudolph Haubst.[10] In the *Cribratio Alchoran* (1460), prompted by his visit to a now Islamic Constantinople and written for the purpose of converting Muslims to the faith, Nicholas took fuller stock of the distinctive Christian doctrine of God's oneness: this unity is finally that of love, and 'a love is nothing other than the other'.[11]

---

7 H. de Lubac, *La posterité spirituelle de Joachim de Fiore* (Paris 1979).
8 J. Ratzinger, *The Theology of History in Saint Bonaventure* (Et Chicago 1971), p. 146; for a discussion, see my *The Theology of Joseph Ratzinger: An Introductory Study* (Edinburgh 1988), pp. 51–65.
9 Cited from *De docta ignorantia* at *TL* II, p. 194.
10 R. Haubst, *Das Bild des Einen und Dreieinigen Gottes in der Welt nach Nikolas von Kues*, *Trier theologische Studien* IV (1952).
11 Cited from the folio text of the treatise at *TL* II, p. 198.

16

The Word Is Made Flesh

Conjoining flesh with Word

Throughout *Theologik* II so far, Balthasar has been assuming that the Word *did* become flesh, but he has offered no theology of the hypostatic union – as all orthodox Christologians have felt obliged to do since Cyril and Chalcedon – to legitimise this presupposition. What is peculiarly Balthasarian in his tardy acceptance of this duty is perhaps the extraordinary weight he gives from the outset to the term 'flesh'. Not for nothing is the author of this theological logic the composer of a theological aesthetics as well. In tones reminiscent of the early North African theology of Tertullian, Balthasar declares that the redemption of the flesh is the whole counsel of God.

> The Christian religion is the only religion which, leaving to one side the most evident of all facts – namely, the mortality of the flesh, something which has forced all other religions to regard spiritualisation as the only possible way of salvation – has found the unsurpassable goal of the ways of God in flesh: mortal, eucharistic, mystical flesh, flesh that rises from the dead.[1]

In the Incarnation God has become, and remains, one flesh with man – a daring application to this subject of sayings about the wedding of male and female, Christ and the Church, in Old and New Testaments (Genesis 2.24; Matthew 19.5, and parallels; Ephesians 5.30–2).

Sifting rapidly the biblical uses of 'flesh' – *basar* in Hebrew, *sarx* in Greek, Balthasar concludes that St John brought the Old Testament sense of the word into fine focus when (to judge by the references in his Gospel) he treated it as denoting 'quite neutrally the God-created human being who by his transitoriness and in his gendered condition [the latter reinforcing the former, for this is a being which maintains itself only through generation] stands over against God'.[2] It is at *this* flesh which the Word who was with God and was God set his aim. On this event – the Flesh-taking – there rests, so the Johannine Letters attest, all salvation (cf. 1 John 4.2–3; 2 John 7–11). In the Hebrew Bible, though humankind is made to

---

1 *TL* II, p. 201.
2 *TL* II, p. 203.

God's image and likeness, the body falls foul of death and Sheol where the writ of the covenant of life does not run. For ancient philosophy, despite the anthropological ideals of *harmonia* and good-and-beautiful man, the body is finally if not tomb, prison or chain for the soul then at any rate something to be left behind. It is ultimately only when the Word of God unites itself with flesh that 'a really affirmative light falls on the body', for this union is not that of a 'fugitive and only half-real avatar'; rather, the Logos makes the body 'his dwelling-place for ever'.[3]

The afterlife of classical philosophy meant that the new evangelical view of the body would be constantly impeded – but at the same time, at least one thesis of ancient thought, the notion that man is microcosm to the world's macrocosm, was, by contrast, a facilitating factor. It suggested, after all, why the Logos had elected union with the human being, who in his or her inseparably spiritual and physical existence occupies the mid-point of the created universe, and not with any angel. Though Irenaeus, who once again takes on something of the importance he enjoys in the theological aesthetics and dramatics, does not exploit the microcosm theme he none the less insists that the living artwork of the embodied man, formed by the Word and Spirit (those 'hands' of the Father), occupies the cosmic centre. It is at *this* point that, if God is to save his needy world, he must act. We now know much more than any ancient thinker, pagan or Christian, about the manner in which the life-forms of the cosmos came to culminate in *homo sapiens*, this knowingly-animated body. In a daring excursion into what we might call metaphysical biology, Balthasar speaks of man as, in this way, the end product of a 'sacrificial process' in nature. Other, lower, biological forms, dispositionally apt for assumption into higher forms, died that he might live. But if *homo sapiens* is, as microcosmos thinking would have it, the 'quintessence of the world', then can we not see the human being as itself dispositionally open to that sacrificial Death from love for which the Logos made itself one flesh with man, a 'death that eucharistically fills the cosmos with the Trinitarian life'?[4] Outside a fully developed philosophy of nature (and we might add theological cosmology) these can only be, as Balthasar admits, suggestions. But that they may be ill-founded suggestions he does *not* concede. For first, if the act of being which actualises the essences of all things does not, outside God, subsist in itself but only in them, to the end that the world of intel- lectual as physical existence may arise, a 'chalice-character' is impressed on finite things from the word 'go'. Moreover, in material beings this self- emptying (*Entäusserung*) takes the very concrete shape of that common ground of enablement (*Ermöglichsgrund*) which enters into the constitution of all such beings, thus permitting them to be ever more amply informed. (Even in death, after all, physical things are at the disposal of others; much more are they in exchange with them in life.) Here Balthasar finds a natural basis in man for a divinely relevant disposition: openness to the entry into his life of the 'divine difference' which founds in Trinitarian fashion all positive difference within the world. At the same time, so crucial a position furnishes man with terrible temptations: 'it is impossible that the

3 *TL* II, pp. 204–5.
4 *TL* II, p. 208.

serpent not be in Paradise'.[5] An essentially limited creature, which, thanks to the breath of God which animates it, has concerns that range as universally as the act of being itself, can only be asking for trouble. It is easy for man to forget he is not as God, and all too possible to neglect his debt to the circumambient world of creatures without whose stimulus his mind would never awaken. Drawing on the account of the place of mind in nature that he has laid out at length in *Theologik* I, Balthasar reminds us, with Paul Claudel, that for us *connaissance* is *co-naissance* – knowledge presupposes our 'co-birth' with all other things.

The 'natural communion' whereby creatures in general belong within a web of life whose 'natural gathering-point' is man provides a foundation in the created order for the 'wonders of vicarious substitution' worked on the Cross and in the Holy Eucharist. Balthasar's thinking at this juncture is remarkably reminiscent of the Anglican poet, novelist and mystic Charles Williams – though the interest in *non*-human nature inevitable to a Scholastically-trained mind working at a formal metaphysics is less emphasised in Williams' *oeuvre*.

> *Men* co-inhere in Christ and in one another as part of what Williams calls 'the web' – the criss-cross threads of *human* motive and action forming parts of a divine pattern with Christ at the centre, in which all courteous and selfless actions have their place.[6]

But endemic temptation to revolt against one's place in the co-inherence means that the assumption of flesh by the Word can only precipitate a drama – and quite possibly a tragedy. Here the theological logic, already indebted to the theological aesthetics for the centrality of 'flesh', now finds in the conjunction of flesh with Word a reason for adverting to theological dramatics as well. Though the flesh is *in itself* no 'sinful principle' for the New Testament, *in history* it has turned away from the Light of men which is the Life of God (the capitalised terms come from the Johannine Prologue). Left to its own mercy it is indeed already abandoned to death. And precisely this is why the Word took flesh: to restore flesh to that integrity God had always willed for it. But because – following now Bonaventure's Christocentrism – it was not our misery that compelled the Son to become human but his own merciful love (Christ does not act to our agenda but enables us to act for his), the ultimate foundation of the Incarnation is 'the predestination of the Son to be the centre and fulfilment of the world'.[7]

Contradiction or predictability?

It falls now to Balthasar to consider various aspects of the Flesh-taking of the Word, aspects which enable him to comment on a variety of theological and philosophical positions. First, 'the Word as contradiction'. His own had not received him, and this is putting it mildly. Readers of Balthasar's *Theodramatik* will not be surprised at the facility with which he brings together biblical texts to illustrate his claim that 'he came not to bring an

5 *TL* II, p. 209.
6 G. Cavaliero, *Charles Williams, Poet of Theology* (London 1983), p. 136. Italics added.
7 *TL* II, p. 213.

idle peace but the sword that divides'.[8] If his be a 'benign sword', as Augustine claims in his discourse on Psalm 143, this is because, as the same doctor explains, in cutting away putridity it heals the members of Christ.

> Not only does his simple presence work division and enmity; from his first appearance he speaks with provocation.[9]

Because his Jewish interlocutors will not go beyond the 'popular' level of his discourse, which for Balthasar consists in its coincidence with the Old Testament, to the new, transcendently personal level of his utterance which is that distinctive of the New, and because, in this fashion, these conversation partners will not *listen*, Jesus turns, most manifestly in the Fourth Gospel, to his own distinctive form of dialectic. Nor do the disciples always fare better: whenever a consensus seems to be reached between Jesus and themselves, 'the ever greater Word of God breaks the consensus and passes beyond',[10] and here again it is the Gospel of John which provides the most copious examples. But of course at times Jesus underscores, conversely, the unity of the Testaments: both in St John and St Matthew he speaks in 'perfect syllogisms' which presuppose a common fund of belief. We may think that Jewish hearers could hardly be blamed for not appreciating on the other occasions the novelty of his words. But for Balthasar (following Rupert, whose biblical theology he has already commended in the last chapter) the oracles and actions of the God of the Old Testament were 'steps' taken by the Logos towards this fulfilment: a generous heart could have divined the passage.

And here Balthasar touches on another aspect – or possible aspect – of the Word's Flesh-taking, one associated in particular with a theologian he both admired and opposed, Karl Rahner. How much of the event of Christ can we regard as 'transcendentally' – on the basis of universal structures of intelligibility – capable of anticipation beforehand? Whereas Rahner, in the accounts of resurrection offered in his *Schriften* and the various lexicons he edited,[11] speaks of it as the object of a 'transcendental hope' and thus to a degree a natural postulate (since the destiny of the human person is unthinkable without it), Bernhard Welte, a second Germanophone theologian discussed here by Balthasar, is more circumspect in describing the ambiguities of bodiliness as we know it: thus his *Auf der Spur des Ewigen*.[12] Balthasar finds both projects in differing degrees presumptuous – for the reason that, until the 'depth' of the world's fault has been plumbed to the bitter end on the Cross, the true dimensions of what God must do in redeeming 'the flesh' cannot be known. Balthasar endeavours to show that the actual Resurrection of the real and only Saviour – the

---

8 *TL* II, p. 215.
9 *TL* II, p. 215.
10 *TL* II, p. 216.
11 K. Rahner, 'The Position of Christology in the Church between Exegesis and Dogmatics', *Theological Investigations* XI (Et London 1974), pp. 185–214, and especially pp. 206–14; *idem*, 'Zur Theologie der Auferstehung Christi', *Lexikon für Theologie und Kirche* I (Freiburg 1957, 1986), pp. 1038–9, *idem*, 'Resurrection', *Sacramentum Mundi* 5 (Et New York and London 1970), pp. 323–4, 329–33.
12 B. Welte, *Auf der Spur des Ewigen* (Freiburg 1965), pp. 83–112.

Word made flesh – was beyond all prediction. For here we have ultimate failure of a mission and equally ultimate knowledge of its fulfilment not, as with the Old Testament, one after the other, but inhering *in* one another. Here we have the uttermost alienation from the Father and also, in the fulfilment of the mission, the ultimate journey into his presence – and the second happens *as* the first. From this mystery comes what the Filioque doctrine (in Balthasar's understanding thereof) would have us see: on the Cross the Word made flesh so serenely entrusts his collapsed earthly work to the Father as to let it 'unfold and develop beyond himself, in a sphere that the Spirit administers' – that of the flesh's Resurrection.[13]

The language of the flesh

Now logic cannot dispense with a concern for language – which its own name, indeed, betokens. And so after these sorties into the 'problematic' of the Word–flesh conjunction, Balthasar withdraws to consider the 'language of the flesh' in which the actions and sufferings of the humanised Word were carried out.

This 'language' is, fundamentally, that of man as a spiritual corporeal unity, and hence it should not surprise us that Jesus can use verbal language in many registers playing as it were on different 'keyboards' of an organ. In this, his 'voice' corresponds to that of Scripture as a whole, whose media can range from impassioned metaphor to lucid concept. (Balthasar's comment that no purely 'scientific' theology can encapsulate such richness casts light, incidentally, both on his rejection of a 'standard' Neo-Scholasticism and on the election of the literary style – or rather styles – of his own theological work.) We are dealing here with a spectrum which it would be artificial to sub-divide too nicely. None the less, Balthasar would have us identify three 'main spheres' of Jesus' linguistic activity, and these he describes as, in ascending order of significance, 'general expression', 'image [and imagination]' and 'the free word'.

At this point many of the materials of *Theologik* I come into their own. In a lengthy discussion there, Balthasar has already shown how being naturally expresses itself in appearing – a principle for which he was as much indebted to Thomism as to phenomenology, for, as the English Dominican theologian Cornelius Ernst wrote:

> Thomas's genuine and permanent originality was to display the internal consistency of a view of the world in which the world effort-lessly shows itself for what it is, flowers into the light . . . Ultimately, things show themselves for what they *are*, to *be* is ultimately to *be true*.[14]

But from his Bonaventurian inheritance – marshalled above all in the second volume of *The Glory of the Lord* and in *Theologik* II – Balthasar can go on to make the further statement that the expressive power of things

13 *TL* II, p. 224.
14 C. Ernst, 'Seven Hundred Years of Thomas Aquinas', *The Listener* (10 October 1974), p. 480. Reprinted in idem., *Multiple Echo. Explorations in Theology* (London 1979), p. 11.

follows from their creation in the *Expressio*: the Word who expresses the Father (and the entire Trinity). From Goethe to Claudel the poets have heard the language of the creative Logos in the being of creatures. And if poetry renders such natural expressions into word, so by an 'alphabet of movements' the body can in turn give the word nuanced articulation: Balthasar names the Spanish philosopher Ortega y Gasset as an important precursor of that in origin largely American pastime the study of 'body language'.

And if Balthasar's account of the keyboard of expression at large was implicitly Thomist, he is explicit about his debts to the Thomist Aristotelian theory of the image.[15] Word and concept are not enlivening without *conversio ad phantasmata*, 'turning to the image'. As (once again) the opening volume of the theological logic has shown, it is through the imagistic self-presentation of things to our minds via the senses that we come to an interpretation of them as the *appearing of* this or that existent being. What the implications of that may be for religion, which should not locate the divine reality in images and yet cannot dispense without the sensuous medium of meaning, Balthasar will shortly explore.

First he has to explain how man arrives at language: for he has now reached the topmost 'keyboard', the 'birth of the word'. We have already seen how for Balthasar dialogical thinking has the advantage over the dialectical thought characteristic of philosophical Idealism, and now he discloses the real foundation of this preference. The 'smile of the mother', whereby a 'thou' awakens an 'I' to consciousness in the shape of her child should be, according to Balthasar, the keystone of epistemology. It is from that smile that being at large can appear as a mystery of mediated presence. The existent – the child – finds itself 'called' by being (not of course verbally, for this entire process transpires in 'deepest silence' – though presumably it can be punctuated by gurgles), and discovers the gift character of its existence in the world. Balthasar follows the philosophy of language of his friend Gustav Siewerth in holding that it is in its self-perception as 'spoken' (by being, and ultimately God) that the child learns to speak.[16]

To linguisticians of a more (or is it *less*?) sophisticated bent, this account may seem unilluminating. And in fact Balthasar treats language here as simply the highest instance of (natural) revelatory and communicative expressiveness and it is the latter which he thinks one must chiefly explain in explaining the phenomenon of language. Not inappropriately, then, he deals with the mythic and the iconic before coming to the symbolic and metaphorical, for the former are imaginative modes which may crucially require language yet which language does not alone compose.

Myth and image fulfilled

Balthasar's fascination with the mythical is patent from Volume 4 of *The Glory of the Lord*, where he traces sparks of divine beauty running through

---

15 This is also an area where Balthasar was guided by Romano Guardini – notably in the latter's 1961 study of Rilke and his *Über des Wesens des Kunstwerks* (Tübingen 1965); see J. F. Schmucker von Koch, *Autonomie und Transzendenz, Untersuchungen zur Religionsphilosophie Romano Guardinis* (Mainz 1985).

16 G. Siewerth, *Philosophie der Sprache* (Einsiedeln 1962).

the stubble of Greek myth. Myth treats of the 'powers that carry existence along',[17] of cosmic forces that, so men think, manifest divinity in immediate fashion – a natural presumption, where the historic revelation has not touched their minds, for the child's aboriginal discovery of the 'love of Being' in its parent bonds the sacred with its image in the human mind. Balthasar finds fascinating Schelling's notion that the history of mythology is a necessary preparation for the Incarnation of the Logos, though he cannot regard Schelling's philosophy as evangelically satisfactory (and cites approvingly the French Jesuit Xavier de Tilliette's charge of excessive benignity against Bishop Walter Kasper's fine study of Schelling's later thought).[18] A Logos who, in Tilliette's sharp characterisation, is 'neither God nor man' can hardly be the Word who became flesh. Yet Balthasar warms to the idea of the gospel as the transcendent fulfilment of myth, which he re-interprets, however, in terms drawn from C. S. Lewis, as the surprise sprung on the world when myth – the myth, at any rate, of the dying and rising god – becomes fact.[19] No longer does imagination by means of mythical narration clothe something bodily with deep cosmic significance. Rather does

> the fact itself in its bodiliness entertain this deep, divine significance in itself, and make it apparent to believers in all its manifestations.[20]

In addition to accepting the notion of myth-become-fact from Lewis (who himself took it from G. K. Chesterton's *The Everlasting Man*),[21] Balthasar offers a comment more his own. Myth is the general in the particular – but God is not the general, and Jesus is less the particular than he is the unique. What he represents in his 'free and rigorous obedience unto death' are unsoundable depths, alright, but those depths belong to the 'Fatherly will to salvation'.[22] It is no mythopoetic hermeneutic that can read *this* 'fact', but only Christian faith – for the depths are the depths of the Word and only a responding word of conversion on our side can open up the space for that Word to act in us.

The same determination to identify a peculiarly Christian way of invoking general categories for interpreting Christ can be sensed in Balthasar's discussion of the Word made flesh as expressive *icon* of God. It was a strictly incomparable reality that in Jesus Christ lent itself to the eye. It was only to be expected that the attempt to render as artistic image the unique icon whereby he who saw the Son saw the Father too (John 14.9) would unleash a major theological quarrel – and so it was in the *Bilderstreit*, the struggle over the images, which convulsed the Byzantine empire in the eighth and ninth centuries.

---

17 *TL* II, p. 233.
18 W. Kasper, *Das Absolute in der Geschichte: Philosophie und Theologie in der Spätphilosophie Schellings* (Mainz 1965); X. de Tilliette, *Schelling: Une philosophie en devenir* (Paris 1970), II, pp. 454–65.
19 C. S. Lewis, 'Myth Became Fact', in *idem, God in the Dock: Essays on Theology* (London 1979), pp. 39–45.
20 *TL* II, p. 238.
21 G. K. Chesterton, *The Everlasting Man* (London 1925).
22 *TL* II, p. 239.

His own account of Christ the divine icon is largely indebted to the Dominican patrologist Christoph von Schönborn, at the time of writing archbishop of Vienna, whose own researches took their marching orders, at any rate in significant part, from the Eastern Orthodox historian of theology Georges Florovsky. Origenist prejudices against materiality and Eusebian doubts about the survival of the recognisable human form of Christ in the Resurrection glory – on this view – were overcome by Cyrilline praise of the flesh taken by the Word and Maximus the Confessor's emphasis on the hypostasis of the Saviour as 'composed' since it personalised the two natures simultaneously.[23] The latter's theology, which had fascinated Balthasar since the 1940s, is peculiarly helpful.

> The mode in which Jesus is active in his human freedom is deter-mined by his eternal Sonship and thus at the same time reveals the absolute Good which is the triune God. Maximus, therefore, can define the Incarnate One in downright terms as the symbol of himself.[24]

Balthasar rehearses fairly enough the argument of the Iconoclast theo-logians and, so far as their Iconodule opponents are concerned, places Theodore of Studion at their head. 'In the human features of Jesus his divine Person is "condensed" and made visible in a relational ... presence.'[25] Looking often at the holy icons purifies human representation just as does the frequent hearing of the word of God.

The West knew only a pale reflection of this controversy in certain reservations of the house-theologians of Charlemagne. It was natural to suppose that, with the New Testament, seeing enjoyed a higher status than in the Old. Balthasar could point out – he refers to Franz Mussner's study of the *ocular* element in the Fourth Gospel[26] – that the seeing eye was crucial to Christianity long before there was ever a Christian art. Thanks to that art, however, senses and spirit conspire in the service of faith in the incarnate Word; in the diverse styles which the history of iconography has known artists and sculptors have tried to capture something of the 'intensity of the language of God in the flesh'.[27]

And yet, so Balthasar insists, the dogmatisation of the icon at the Seventh Ecumenical Council (Nicaea II, in 787) should not be taken to mean that art can *never* be for the Gospel less a sacrament than a snare. Where the artist has insufficiently purified his intention, the artwork can absorb rather than pass on beyond itself. And Balthasar suspects that Denys the Areopagite, that attentive discerner of spirits, would have

23 C. Schönborn, *Die Christusikone: Eine theologische Hinführung* (Schaffhausen 1982); *idem*, *Das Geheimnis der Menschwerdung* (Mainz 1983); *idem*, 'Der bizantinische Bilderstreit, ein Testfall für das Verhältnis von Kirche und Kunst', *Internationale Katholische Zeitschrift, Communio* 11 (1982), pp. 518–26. For a summary of the Florovsky–Schönborn analysis, see A. Nichols, *The Art of God Incarnate*, pp. 64–74.
24 *TL* II, p. 241.
25 *TL* II, p. 243.
26 F. Mussner, *Die johannische Sehweise* (Freiburg 1965).
27 *TL* II, p. 244.

preferred the peasant art of a Catholic countryside to that of Michelangelo or Rubens.

Objectively symbolic revelation

What then of *symbol* and *metaphor*? Before offering us his account of these expressive forms – exhaustively (and exhaustingly) discussed as they have been in a variety of modern disciplines concerned with the interpretation of signs, Balthasar summarises his conclusions on the *modus loquendi* of the Word made flesh. Every created nature has some part in the duo of expression and that-which-is-expressed. In the sensuous realm, expression takes the form of the image (in the imagination an integral image); on the level of *Geist*, the intelligent spirit, it becomes word, and manifests a power of referring to things which requires freedom (without, however, ever becoming sundered from natural images). Now in the Logos incarnate *everything* is expression, image, word: expression of the Father in the Holy Spirit; the Invisible imaged in the visible Image; word alluding to the One whose word it is. At all points, Balthasar goes on to stress, there is adequacy of expression without identity between Expressed (the divine Trinity) and expressing (the flesh assumed).

> Christianity is firm on this point: the language of the flesh is not for a divine Word an approximative expression but an adequate one, which, however, does not eliminate distance; neither therefore does it cancel the distinction between idol and image.[28]

It is because the *full* apprehension of the expressive adequacy of revelation belongs, however, only to the Age to Come that here and now symbol and metaphor are needed.

Balthasar's notion of symbol is a pure (in the best sense) derivation from the etymology of the word – and the social practice which gave the word its use. In ancient Greece, the two halves of a *symbolon* enabled one person to recognise the credentials, belonging or affinity of the other. Revelation in Christ is objectively symbolic because 'what is expressed (the Father) is exactly recognised in the expression (the Son)', just as the Son's expression in his visual or verbal self-manifestation *is* the 'legitimation' of his being the Word of God, the probative sign that he is Emmanuel.[29] That objective symbolhood, however, must be subjectively recognised by us – and so it is in faith. But, as Balthasar underlines (for, as theological Modernism showed, getting this right is vital to the integrity of the Gospel), the need for subjective appropriation of such a revelation in no way suggests that the revelation itself is 'merely symbolic', the projection of a prior understanding. It is precisely the objective symbol which gives rise to the whole subsequent process of understanding: here Balthasar makes good use of the French Protestant philosopher Paul Ricoeur's dictum that 'the symbol gives to thought',[30] that is makes thinking subsequently possible.

28 *TL* II, p. 246.
29 *TL* II, p. 247.
30 P. Ricouer, *Le Symbolisme du Mal* (Paris 1963), p. 324.

And on the topic of metaphor it is to Ricoeur that Balthasar turns but this time in the company of his fellow-Protestant Eberhard Jüngel who co-authored with Ricoeur a substantial essay on the truth of metaphor in the Evangelical context.[31] Jüngel, who takes the whole topic further in his superb dogmatic study 'God as Mystery of the World',[32] expects from a philosophical *analogia entis* no more than a negative theology (though this is already an advance towards the Catholic position when compared with Jüngel's master, Barth). What strikes Jüngel as much more interesting, so Balthasar reports, is the 'evangelical analogy' of Jesus' metaphors. The parables of Jesus, on Jüngel's view, 'invert', as Balthasar remarks, the teaching of Lateran IV, by demonstrating an ever greater likeness to man of the God who made himself human in Jesus Christ, a *maior similitudo* which goes against the grain of the *maior dissimilitudo* that is all metaphysics leaves us.

We would not expect Balthasar to agree with this stark contrast and indeed he does not, citing as suitable therapy for those who suffer from phobia about the analogy of being Gottlieb Söhngen's crisp saying, 'Metaphysics without the metaphorical is empty, the metaphorical without metaphysics is blind' – another clever re-writing of Kant's axiom on the necessity of both concepts and perceptions.[33] The Jüngel–Ricoeur view does not do justice, he thinks, to the sense in which the world is (as *Theologik* I has argued) already expression and thus can serve to furnish a pre-under-standing for the 'Word' of New Testament revelation (as indeed the Old Testament shows). If for these Evangelical thinkers the 'event' whereby being becomes language in metaphor is the only ontological reference we need, and divine revelation provides its own key to its own specific metaphoric utterances so that we grasp how in the parables God himself is 'eventfully' turning to us, then do not the Gospel metaphors become somewhat hermetic, a world of significance that is enclosed?

At the same time, Balthasar *also* criticises these writers for not drawing themes of grace and the Spirit into their hermeneutic scheme. If the metaphors Jesus uses are to be grasped in a way that takes us beyond their (inevitable) finitude in the direction of their (inexhaustible) tran-scendent meaning, the inner gracious illumination of hearer or reader is required; without reference to the interpretive function of the Holy Spirit (in the Church), we are, moreover, launched without hope of rescue on a sea of conflicting interpretations.[34] To reach the conclusion that in the parables the divine Love itself appears a Pneumatology is necessary.

The primacy of silent deed

And now Balthasar reminds himself that he is theological aesthetician and dramatologist and not just a student of divinely given language. He

31 E. Jüngel, 'Metaphorische Wahrheit: Erwägung zur theologischen Relevanz der Metapher als Beitrag zur Hermeneutik einer narrativen Theologie', in *idem* (with Paul Ricoeur), *Metapher* (Munich 1974), pp. 71–122.
32 E. Jüngel, *Gott als Geheimnis der Welt* (Tübingen 1978).
33 G. Söhngen, 'Analogie und Metapher', in *Kleine Philosophie und Theologie der Sprache* (Freiburg 1962), p. 87, cited *TL* II, p. 248.
34 A reference to Ricoeur's *Conflit des interprétations* (Paris 1969).

rounds off his account of the linguistic dimensions of the Incarnation with a study of the 'silent deed' of this unique Word. For the 'word of the Lord' made known in Israel's *preparatio evangelica* was never simply discourse: it was always visitation as well. (Hence the dual meaning of the lexically crucial item *dabar* as both word and *thing*.) Jesus himself refers his interlocutors from his words to his deeds (John 10.38). The 'total language' of God and its 'verification' can only be found in the event of Jesus' existence – which must include, then, the death and resurrection to eternal life. 'Verification' of language must mean ultimately – declares Balthasar, leaning on a third Evangelical theologian, Gerhardt Ebeling[35] – the verification of a human life, and so (for this is where Gospel truth-claims terminate) the verification of love. Precisely this 'silent deed will give rise to an explication of the word that can come to no possible end'.[36] Only if what is given is infinite, after all, can it be the true God who is given, and none other. Thus vast spaces of silence are entrusted to the never-ending interpretative work of the Holy Spirit in the Church's history, as he deepens and clarifies the tacit dimension in Jesus' self-expression – though never to so highly wrought a finish that the mystery is laid bare.

The Flesh-taking

The Word become flesh is a happening. Balthasar must now disengage further the significance of that temporal conjunction between the Logos and the flesh: *egeneto, factum est,* 'became'. In its sheer 'facticity', this *factum* must be accounted the true starting point for all theology, and so has to be studied in the Christological volume of a theological logic – even if the question of the 'forms and conditions' for accepting the *factum* belong to Pneumatology and so are deferred to the closing book of the work.[37] Balthasar does anticipate that sufficiently, however, to mention that we are not likely to believe in the 'happening' in its full dimensions simply by regarding it as its own self-evidence, or on the basis of 'religious experience', or by appealing – a typically Positivist trick, he thinks – to the future, eschatological verification of its claims. We will believe in it, if at all, because of Christ's gift of his own truth through the word of witness, the Eucharist and the gift of the Holy Spirit as interpreted by the Church's apostolic magisterium for 'He who hears you hears me' (Luke 10.16). Only a truly *catholic* reading of the Christ-event enables us to see the 'fact' which is Christianity's basis.

Prior to considering various 'dimensions' of the 'fact' that is the Incarnation of the Word, Balthasar tries to get it into slightly sharper focus. It is a unique fact with which we have to do for it has its foundation only in itself (and thereby in the determination of the Holy Trinity). To see it in a *well-founded* way means apprehending its own *foundation* – the free act of the eternal Logos for humanity's sake. And so as to rub in his conviction that from no starting point in comparative religion can we grasp this 'fact',

35 G. Ebeling, *Einführung in die theologische Sprachlehre* (Tübingen 1971), p. 191.
36 *TL* II, p. 254.
37 *TL* II, p. 256.

Balthasar adds that the goal of the Logos in giving himself in and as the human nature of Jesus is the precise opposite to that of the mystical religiosity of pagans: it is nothing other than the 'everlasting fixing of man in his finite carnality'.[38] Otherwise what Balthasar has to say on the eternal origin of the *factum* is pure Rahner – a rather rare instance of a copious citation of the erstwhile Jesuit colleague with whom he has so many bones to pick. Like Rahner, Balthasar wants to stress how while what Jesus humanly is – someone in human nature – makes him totally in solidarity with ourselves, this 'what' that in his case and his alone is *also* the self-expression of the Logos creates an 'abyss of difference' between us and him.[39] And with Rahner he wants to say that the *kenōsis* of the divine Love, not the *assumptio* of the human nature, is the *primary* message of the Incarnation.[40] Not that God has ceased to be what he was, but (so it turns out) he enjoys in his divine freedom the 'primordial possibility' (*Urmöghlichkeit*, a term of Rahner's) to become that which has issued from him by way of creation. The exaltation of our nature, taken up as it is in union with such a God by Incarnation, follows from that.

Those Christologies which have understood the Flesh-taking by God as simply a rhetorically stronger statement of the *assumptio* of man have generally done so because they feared to compromise the divine changelessness. Does not the *factum est* (in the Greek original of the Creed, the *egeneto*) otherwise imply a 'becoming' incongruent with the divine being? Balthasar – in this text, at any rate – brushes aside such anxieties, citing Rahner (again) with approval. Here ontology must learn from the gospel, not vice versa. In point of fact, however, Balthasar hardly pauses to discuss the fundamental issue – the divine immutability, preferring instead to render what the gospel says in narrative rather than speculative mode. Relying this time on Adrienne von Speyr, Balthasar writes that the Logos now knows himself as incarnate – this is the 'change' in God, and in so doing discovers the Father in a new way, and not only the Father but also human creatureliness, human innocence and – thanks to his solidarity of nature with fallen humanity – human sin. Balthasar especially emphasises the Word's *Geschehenlassen*, his new experience of what it is to 'let be' in the sense of 'let happen' – as the Son lets the Spirit bring about his human conception in the womb of Mary, and lets the Father dispose of him, throughout his life and ministry, as he wills – something which comes to its climax, of course, in the death on the Cross.

There is a question, evidently, about how much of this 'experience' belongs to the Logos specifically *as man*, and it is to the limitations of the human mind and will of the Word that Balthasar now turns.

He takes the intellectual first, and then the volitional. It has often been noted that, to affirm the unique being of the single Word incarnate in his

38 *TL* II, p. 258.
39 Cf. K. Rahner, 'Theology of the Incarnation', *Theological Investigations* 4 (Et London 1966), pp. 105–20.
40 There is a good statement of this in J. Saward, *The Mysteries of March: Hans Urs von Balthasar on the Incarnation and Easter* (London 1990).

dual natures it is not required to imagine what the consciousness of such a One might be like. And yet the question of Christ's intellectual powers – most notably *vis-à-vis* his Father – seems an irrepressible one. Balthasar's footnotes become entirely tributary to the writings of von Speyr as he struggles with this topic. On this one, Adrienne wants to have her cake and eat it: she speaks of the Saviour's 'seeing faith' (*schauende Glaube*) as the vision of the Father he ever enjoys is adapted to the faith proper to man of which he is to be, in the words of the Letter to the Hebrews, the 'pioneer and perfecter' (12.2). The incarnate Word looks at the Father, in Adrienne's phrase, 'together with men' – thus her chapter on this subject in *Objektive Mystik* – and, in his mission to become the visibility of the Father (an ancient theme this, going back to Irenaeus and St John), chooses less to *look* than to be *looked at* as the Father's living icon.[41] In *Die Welt des Gebetes*, in contrast, Adrienne von Speyr tries a different tack.[42] She holds that what in the Lord's enjoyment of the vision of his Father appears incompatible with the execution of the obedience which is the heart of his earthly mission (and the earthly expression, indeed, of his relation to the Father as Word) is 'deposited' with the Father until he can claim it back in the mystery of the Ascension. This is a strange metaphor – taken, one supposes, from the Helvetic equivalent of the Cloakroom at Victoria Station or – perhaps more likely – the vault of a Swiss bank. Already exploited in the theological dramatics, it serves here to essay a *via media* between kenoticism and its opposite. On the one hand, the Word does not empty himself of an attribute of his divine personhood which would otherwise affect – nay, inundate – the human intelligence of the nature assumed. Nor, on the other hand, does he activate that aspect of divinity which the attribute involves. Rather, while still possessing it in principle he allows the Father to keep it on his behalf. One sees what Balthasar (and Adrienne before him) wishes to avoid; one is less sure of how much this metaphor really explains. Still, the basic idea that what we say about the Saviour's vision of his Father should be measured by our account – Scripturally and tradition-ally based, of course – of his mission is a good one. By itself, however, it does not tell us why we should reject the more generous account of the Word's human knowledge of the Father which in such classical theologians as Thomas is taken to exclude the faith of a 'wayfarer', a simple pilgrim to the Father's house.

What then of the volitional aspect of the Saviour's constitution, where the motifs of freedom and temptation come into play? Specifically human rationality implies a will: a desiring animal cannot be conformed to the order of reason *except* by rational will. Owing to the Monothelite con-troversy of the seventh century it became the Church's settled conviction that the humanity of the Lord did not lack this essential feature of its own integrity: thus the teaching of the Sixth Ecumenical Council on the two wills, not just divine but human too, of the Word incarnate. As Balthasar puts the problem of articulation this creates:

41 A. von Speyr, 'Schauen und Glauben', in *idem*, *Objektive Mystik* (Einsiedeln 1970), pp. 155–6.
42 *Idem*, *Die Welt des Gebetes* (Einsiedeln 1951), pp. 70–4.

> But how can this freedom [the *human*], assumed and guided by a
> divine Person, still maintain its own zone of activity, if the Son has
> come not to do his own will but the will of the Father who sent him
> (John 6.38)?[43]

Can Jesus choose something which is outside the will of the Logos –
who himself has always chosen the will of the Father with which he
is perfectly, ontologically one? In Aquinas' version, that space of free
decision for the human will at the level of the order of human reason
concerns only 'secondary' matters, since in the primary concerns of the
Saviour his human freedom is already pre-determined by the eternal
freedom of the Word. Balthasar feels that Thomas overlooked two
points. First – and this is religiously the meatier – surely the salvation of
the world, of humankind, appeared to Jesus in his human rational will
as of all goods the most superlative. The salvation of the world was
the object of his utterly free choosing, even though he knew that his
human liberty could and should unfold only within his 'absolute' or
divine will, one as this was with the will of the Father. In the Agony in
the Garden we see the tension, as his rational human will is conformed to
his divine will, united with the Father's – all for the sake of bringing our
rebarbatively ungodly fallen humanity into his own wondrous obedience.
But then secondly, there was surely in the Word incarnate a free exercise
of human imagination. It was by creative imagination that he discovered,
not least in prayer, how to be humanly face to face with the Father and
centre his human deportment on the divine good pleasure. The rôle of his
human freedom in that mental undertaking is clear if we consider how,
on the basis of sharing our humanity, the Saviour must have been
imaginatively affected by the decisions and attitudes of sinners – for no
man is an island. In that sense, the Temptations of Jesus did not simply
compose one episode in his life; temptation was the continuing 'place' of
the Incarnation. Why else does the Lucan Christ call the disciples those
who have 'continued with me in my trials [= temptations]' (Luke 12.28)?
The Spirit makes the Word sink down into 'carnal' reality, the reality of
fallen flesh, so that he may know from the inside the situation he has to
redeem.

Dimensions of the embodied Word

It is in this section that Balthasar offers us his ontological Christology –
one interested not only in the metaphysical make-up of the God-man but
also in his Trinitarian, cosmic and ecclesial character. In case we are
wondering whether Balthasar has loosed his hold on the Cicerone
supposed to guide him through the Christian mystery in this work – the
idea of theological logic, he will round off his remarks with some reflections
on analogy-thinking and the Word who became flesh.

The Word made flesh is, in the first 'dimension' Balthasar considers, a
Triune Word. Looking at the Word incarnate in Trinitarian guise enables
Balthasar to sum up, in the context of the logic, the elaborate Trinitarian
Christology, adumbrated in the opening volume of the theological

---

43 *TL* II, p. 265.

aesthetics but expounded on majestic scale in the dramatics. The key to all three discussions is given with the following words:

> The Trinitarian God is . . . no subsequently excogitated dogma, but manifests himself in immediate fashion in the fact of the Word made flesh.[44]

And the particular perspective in which this datum is viewed in the theological logic opens out as he adds:

> And so this fact [i.e. Jesus Christ] as a fact simply of the world and of history is already transcendent in all its aspects. By virtue of a logic that is not limited to the creation its very facticity can only be grasped and interpreted on the basis of a Trinitarian logic.[45]

Balthasar finds that logic displayed to good advantage in the *prooemium* of the Letter to the Ephesians. The Father initiates the saving plan; the Son executes it in his blood; the Spirit is the guarantor of our share in that inheritance until we acquire possession of it – and all this (for the Letter to Ephesus) is to the praise of the Trinitarian grace, to the praise of God's glory. Of course Balthasar does not simply paraphrase the Pauline text; he also illuminates it, notably by emphasising how the Father's act of giving the Son is not just the presupposition of the Son's work but is actually co-extensive with the Son's humanity. If the Cross is the climax (within history, at any rate) of the Father's gift, then the Resurrection is the supreme manifestation of the 'working of his great might' (Ephesians 1.19) – to all of which the Spirit forms the 'eschatological fulfilment'.[46]

This Trinitarian approach to the God-Man is the best way, Balthasar thinks, to approach his next 'dimension', his *unity*. Jesus speaks a multiplicity of words (so the Gospels have it, even if the radical exegete delights in whittling them down), and he inhabits a multiplicity of states (so must any human being that survives infancy, but the spiritual theologians, meditating on the events of the life of Christ, have gone deeper here). Where then is his unity? Palpable, answers Balthasar, once we realise that all of these are modulations of the unique Word, the Father's single self-expression – which means for humans, who never previously encountered it (or rather, *him*), God's 'new commandment', a reference, evidently, to the Last Supper Discourse of the Christ of St John's Gospel.

When Balthasar thinks of unity in this context what comes first to mind is the way the Saviour draws into a unity the 'many and various ways' whereby, in the Old Testament, God 'spoke to our fathers by the prophets' (Hebrews 1.1). In what sense? In the sense, as he explains, that

> repeating – certainly – these words and making them comprehensible to his hearers, at the same time he condenses them, simplifies them, brings them to life, interprets them and sends them further on their way – by making them point to the 'new commandment' which he himself is.[47]

44 *TL* II, p. 272.
45 Ibid.
46 *TL* II, p. 270.
47 *TL* II, p. 273.

Jesus embodies the new commandment of charity by living out the charity which the triune God is in his life, death and resurrection – three syllables, says Balthasar, of a single word. Only when we take those three syllables together – the life of the 'pre-Paschal' Jesus; the Calvary Christ; and the Easter Lord – do we get that 'word's' meaning. And, once again, the meaning in question is Trinitarian from start to finish.

The Word made flesh is not only Triune, and one in all the variety of his earthly manifestation. He is also, Balthasar goes on, 'human universally'. Ingredients of the evidence for that third dimension – the marvellous exchange between the divine Son and humanity in Incarnation and the vicarious representative substitution effected on the Cross – went into the rich brew of *Theodramatik*. Here Balthasar concentrates on the (to non-Christian logics, scandalous) rôle of Christ's flesh in establishing his universal bonding with all men and women. He scans the writings of the Fathers – chiefly Greek, but giving an honoured place in this connexion to the Latin Hilary – for evidence of how they saw the unity between the Logos-in-the-flesh and the rest of humankind. Is the decisive principle in our salvation the life-giving Logos, or is it the unity between the flesh assumed and the flesh of all other persons who are in the body? For the patristic witnesses he summons it is *both* indivisibly, since if the former is the agent of our redemption the latter is the condition of possibility for its efficacy. However, Balthasar shows his hand as a *Catholic* theologian (rather than a neo-patristic writer in the Orthodox or Anglican tradition) when he adds that to those considerations we must conjoin a third factor, the insight of Scholastic metaphysics into the foundation of communion in the flesh: the conviction, dear to Thomas and his modern disciples, that 'common matter' is where forms are rooted.

From here it is but a short step to the fourth dimension of the enfleshed Word Balthasar explores, one that is conjointly *ecclesial* and *cosmic*. For the New Testament, and notably for the Pauline 'Captivity Epistles', Christ is Head both of the cosmos and of the Church.[48] True, yet the world is never called Christ's Body, as the Church is. The reason is not far to seek. Only the Church enjoys, through, above all, Baptism and the Eucharist, an intimate share in Christ's life, death and resurrection; only in her is the life of believing discipleship lived. Still, the Church is not self-enclosed but turned toward the cosmic realm which the salvific energies implanted in her must penetrate and transform. So there must be an intrinsic relationship between Christ's Lordship of the one and of the other. Balthasar draws on the distinguished exegete-convert to Catholicism of the 1950s, Heinrich Schlier, to establish just what that connexion might be. In Schlier's words:

> In the Lord of the Church the One who holds sway is also the Lord of the powers. In the Lord of the powers the whole world has before its eyes the Lord of the Church . . .[49]

---

48 For the conjunction of themes in Ephesians (but the Colossians hymn must also be taken into account), see F. Mussner, *Christus, das All und die Kirche: Studien zur Theologie des Epheserbriefes* (Trier 1968²).

49 H. Schlier, *Epheser* (Düsseldorf 1957), p. 206. Cited in *TL* II, p. 282.

The 'powers' here are those elemental structuring agencies of which, for 1 Corinthians, Christ is also sovereign Master.

The Fathers have their own ways of expressing the interrelation of cosmos and Church through the *pre-incarnate* as well as the *redemptively enfleshed* Word: the same dominion is exercised in two intensities, through creation and salvation. But Balthasar defers his own version till the end – not so far distant now – of *Wahrheit Gottes*, his study of the Truth of the Word.

Though we have been dealing with the Logos, we have otherwise heard little of late of the language of logic. In a few dense pages of high originality Balthasar makes good this defect. A Chalcedonian Christologic will sub-sume other logics – other general laws which measure truth – under itself, not submit to their tutelage, for, in this unique event of Incarnation, the One who is Truth itself has at last expressed himself in adequate – in 'super-adequate' – form. Where then might *analogy-thinking* – the primary noetic mode of Catholicism *in divinis* – enter, since after all analogy is a way of judging truth and who could judge One who remarked that he *was* truth itself?

Analogy was developed by the Pythagorean philosophers, heavily mathematical as their interests were. They utilised it for the purpose of treating different magnitudes related diversely to each other. Plato turned it to the service of ontology, for in regarding the relation of the Ideas to the Form of the Good as comparable with that of sensate life to the light of the sun that wise master came within a hair's breadth of the notion of the causal dependence of all things on the Good which the Judaeo-Christian doctrine of creation in fact delivered. Compared and contrasted with the absolute divine being, the being of all other realities is for Christian Platonists analogous being. In Christology, however, we are not dealing with analogy–thinking as a way of relating those two diverse magnitudes that are God and the world. Rather are we considering:

> the relation of the Logos, who is himself God and self-identical, to the human nature assumed in uttermost liberty with which he has made himself equally identical [bearing in mind, moreover that] . . . he who is God does not in his humanity explain himself but the Father in the Holy Spirit – with whom he is identical as to his divine nature but not as hypostasis. It is this explanation he characterises as 'the truth'.[50]

Balthasar's Christological application of analogy-thinking would be difficult to understand unless we had seen – in chapters 11 and 15, respectively, of the present book – something of the way he has been practising an 'ana-logic' ('Tracing the Trinity', I called it) and a 'cata-logic' (which I described under the heading 'Fulfilment from God'). 'Ana-logic' proceeds from below, not without some assistance from divine revelation; cata-logic requires accepting a departure point from above, in strict dependence on the divine being and action. Apprehension of the divine in Christ from below (ana-logic) will of itself teach us that true inter-pretation of the same can only come from above (by cata-logic). Only so

50 *TL* II, p. 285.

can this *given* – in both senses of that word, for here the datum *is* the divine Self-gift! – be grasped.

That this is correct epistemology follows from Balthasar's elucidation of the dogmatic content of Christological analogy cited immediately above. In the flesh we recognise the Logos, but the Word is not his own word – he is the Father's. The man Jesus is the expression of the Logos who is himself the unsurpassable affirmation of the Father. 'Whoever sees the flesh of Jesus in the Holy Spirit sees the Father.'[51]

The 'analogy' thus verified in Christology is to be taken – here theological logic reaches its apogee – as the measuring rod for all other analogy-thinking, be that philosophical or theological in nature. In a pair of untranslatable Greco-German puns, Balthasar proposes that all things must be read 'in' the Word made flesh, who is the Alpha and Omega of the divine creative plan. Every existent finds its form within this universally relevant analogy: so the Father willed before the world's foundation in predestining human beings in Christ; so the Son worked; so the Spirit acted. And revisiting that question of how Church and cosmos relate to the recapitulation of all things in the redeeming Christ, Balthasar reveals that his vision is ultimately one of the cosmos become Church, not the Church at the service of the cosmos. The cosmic powers are submitted to the Easter Lord, but his Church-spouse gives him joyful obedience. One day, when the Kingdom comes in its fullness, and the Son renders it in homage to the Father, powers, even submitted ones (one thinks, for example, of the Christendom State) will no longer be. Creation, Balthasar is saying, will receive in that transfiguration the spousal form which now belongs only to the Church.

Of course, the analogy between the world's being and God's, and (chief lesson of pondering that analogy, in Balthasar's eyes, the infinite difference as well as communion between Being himself and beings) is not abolished by Christologic. Balthasar's aim is, as always, to integrate with a Christocentrism rivalling Karl Barth's the traditional ontological cosmology of Catholicism. Still, in real terms, in salvation history in all it has achieved of the divine aim, that infinite distance between God and the world now exists only within Christ's recapitulation of all things in himself. The 'distance' involved thus loses its bitterness. It now becomes that spacious ground where the children of wisdom can play, caught up in the inner relations of Father, Son and Holy Spirit to which the way of the Lord Jesus has led them.

---

51 *TL* II, p. 287. Compare John 8.19; 12.45; 14.7.

17

And Made Sin:
The Logic of Contradiction

Grace needed no fall to be rich. Yet owing to sin, grace the more abounded. All soteriology – even within the Christological volume of a theological logic – is *chiaroscuro*, light and shade. Before ending, Balthasar must fill in the darker brushstrokes. As we shall see, more is involved than simply depicting the recipients of the bounty of the Redeemer (ourselves). For in a riddling saying of St Paul's, God made Christ to be sin, he who knew no sin. Writing in the German language and so in the cultural (and ecumenical) world of Germanophone Protestantism, Balthasar feels the need to do better than Luther in understanding this text so vital to Luther's theology of the Cross. Here, as at so many points in the trilogy, Adrienne von Speyr is summoned to his side.

Contradiction

When the Word comes to his own, they do not receive him, indeed they contradict his assertions, a mystery of iniquity which the Gospel of John, in particular, seeks to explore. That the speech of the Word made flesh should suffer contradiction (the German terms used – *Spruch* and *Widerspruch* – suggest a head-on collision, so perhaps one should speak of the contradiction of the Word's *diction*) is theologically extra-ordinary. For if the Word is truth, then all counter-assertion to his words is the sheerest lie. The dialectic of word and counter-word is not something spiritually neutral, to be resolved in a higher synthesis of insights. Where the truth denied is the personal truth of the Word that God is love, demonstrated in the gift of the Son, dialectic can only exist in the unlovely form of sin.

> *Vis-à-vis* the Logos, in whom dwells all meaning and foundation, the hatred of the lie can only be ground-less and meaning-less.[1]

Such senseless hatred, explicable only inasmuch as, faced with the Light, men preferred darkness (but what can be the explanation of *that*?) finds 'logical' expression when the lie affirms itself as the truth, claim-ing that in the very presence of the Word incarnate. The Truth who is

---

1 *TL* II, p. 289.

the Father's Word and so the interpreter of God is not a form of words or a state of affairs but the disclosure of absolute Love. (No student of the theological aesthetics and dramatics who has gone thus far into the theological logic can demur.) So here the non-acceptance of Jesus' testimony, unbelief, takes on the character of the 'immediately anti-divine', the 'anti-Christic'.

Here the graphics are not so much *chiaroscuro* as black-and-white. The Old Testament had already explored the darkness: one thinks of the terms in which the Psalmist describes the enemies of the just man, or the pure antitheses of true and false prophecy. And of course there is the emergence in the Hebrew Bible of an angelology of sheer negativity, in the form of the evil Angels, the Satanic power. In the Bible the demonic principle bears no comparison with the benign 'labour' of the negative known to Hegelianism, the grit in the oyster that brings forth the pearl of achieved truth. Balthasar notes how in the days of his flesh Jesus shows no interest in the Devil's personality, in the mode of his creaturehood. It is enough to know that he is essentially *pseustēs*, the one who contradicts the Truth (John 8.44).

Sinful flesh, negative theology

Diabolic contradiction is simply not assimilable by divine logic. But what of human sin? That the Saviour came in the likeness of sinful flesh, accepting solidarity with sinners and taking their sin onto himself so as to bear it redemptively into the furnace of the Father's love and in this wise (as the theological dramatics has shown) to bring the divine creative work to its completion – does not this tell us that sin can be the instrument of the Truth of God (*O felix culpa!*) and thus find a positive place in theological logic? When the problem is cast in terms germane to the latter, what we are faced with is a more terrible form of 'negative theology' than any Balthasar has spoken of in *Wahrheit Gottes* so far. That contradictoriness to God could be assumed by the Word in obedience to God – this is not simply a conundrum, it takes us to the deepest, darkest places of the Cross, and our relation thereto.

> On the Cross the contradiction that is sin, its mendacity and illogi-cality, is assumed within the logic of Trinitarian love, not indeed there to find space for itself, but in all truth to be condemned . . . in the flesh of the Son.[2]

Flesh that is the enemy of God, incompatible with him, is thrown into the outer darkness – a phrase taken from Jesus' parables but referred by Balthasar to that 'Hell' which is outside the cosmos, God's beautiful creation, because it lies beyond the sphere of meaning and logic, in-expressible, then, in ontological categories and capturable, if at all, only in dreadful images of which he offers us examples, from Origen and von Speyr. And re-iterating the statement he made in *Mysterium Paschale* – his meditation on the 'three days' of the Redemption, from Holy Thursday to Easter – to the effect that the Descent into Hell is the true centre of Christian

2 *TL* II, p. 297.

theology, Balthasar insists that here – in the Son-made-sin who undermines the contradiction of sin by sustaining it in himself – is the only 'dialectic' that Christianity can finally recognise. Yet because this dialectic passes through the Logos who himself remains perseveringly obedient to God it is not *mere* dialectic – an engagement of contrary forces – but is overcome in the victorious Christ.

All this talk of dialectic and the contradiction of the Cross may alert us to the fact that Balthasar is about to engage with Luther, Lutheranism and Lutheran theology at large for which these themes are all pervasive. Finding, as he thinks, a better answer than Luther's to the questions Luther raised will be, actually, his last task in the Christological volume of the logic.

Balthasar rejects as misinterpretation of both John and Paul the famous Lutheran formulation by which those redeemed through the Cross are said to be 'at the same time righteous and sinners'. The *simul justus et peccator* fails to recognise how in the Johannine letters 'no longer being able to sin' does not sit alongside the confession of continuing sin but functions by excluding the contradiction that would hold good (or rather ill!) if divine regeneration in the Son were to be combined with a life in hatred and darkness, mendacity and death. Again, the Letter to the Romans (source *par excellence* for the distinctively Lutheran doctrine of the relation of law, sin, grace) is misunderstood if its analysis of the glory yet misery of the Law, considered as gift of the God of all salvation, be transferred, lock, stock and barrel, to the Christian's case. The situation of pre-Christians, whether Jews or Gentiles, tempted as these are in the absence of faith-knowledge of *the* saving Gift, Jesus Christ, to construct a flawed religiosity of their own, is hardly isomorphic with that of the baptised. Of course the latter are constantly tempted (here the topic of continuing concupiscence raises its head). Paul's correspondence with the churches of Galatia and Corinth makes that clear enough. But 'these descriptions are far removed from the disruption (*Zerrissenheit*) of the pre-Christian man'.[3]

If we can exculpate John and Paul from the charge of introducing internal contradiction into Christian existence, we can and must ascribe to Luther the insertion of the same into the very heart of the gospel. (Not that Luther would deny this – far from it! The issue between Lutherans and Catholics here is its exegetical wellfoundedness.) In his classic study, Paul Althaus considered that Luther's was a Christology of paradox, cancelling itself out if seen in metaphysical terms.[4] Balthasar sees the same subject more simply: it is neither more nor less than the 'elimination of the principle of non-contradiction' – that maxim, basic to all rational discourse, whereby a thing cannot be described as both X and not-X at the same time and in the same way. To be able to describe a Christian as evil and a son of God, precisely because one can describe Christ as the supremely blessed and the supremely damned, this is not only per-plexing to the logician, it is disconcerting – to put it no more strongly – to the orthodox believer. Whatever, in Balthasar's opinion, is going on? The

3 *TL* II, p. 304.
4 P. Althaus, *Paulus und Luther über den Menschen* (Gütersloh 1952).

simultaneity of being just and sinful, as Luther sees it, is made possible by Christ's work of reconciliation on the Cross whereby in an exchange which, as Luther presents it, *sounds like* the patristic *admirabile commercium* of divinity and humanity in Christ, combines two formally presented contradictions: God's eternal decision to justify sinners (thus the *justus*) and his exposing of Christ to wrath (thus the 'definitive situation of the unredeemed sinner', the *peccator*). The refusal of any 'mediatory passage' (*vermittelnde Übergang*)[5] between these two 'identities' of the Redeemer (who is not only Saviour but also object of wrath), the insistence (therefore) on his uniting of contradictory extremes, this removes Luther from the patristic tradition to which his language would otherwise align him. Not always consistently (thank goodness!), Luther suppresses all the motifs which could soften this contradiction – the single hypostasis of the Lord, his humanity as the image of God, the 'theandric' working of his divine and human natures, his mission of obedience whose climax comes in the cry of abandonment. And of course this reflects on Luther's concept of God: the deity has for him, it would appear, two faces, one loving, the other dreadful. And this is in turn reflected in the form he gives to the idea of double predestination – to heaven, to hell.

On the one hand, Balthasar is utterly hostile to Luther's project. He even goes so far as to remark in a footnote that 'an ecumenical dialogue with the original Luther is impossible'.[6] On the other hand, he has already admitted that dialectic – *some* version of contradictoriness – is both verified and overcome on the Cross.[7] It is owing to the latter conviction that he takes seriously the 'abyss' that Luther's Christology has opened. For the same reason, he seeks a way to close this gaping hole. In both respects Adrienne von Speyr's *Kreuz und Hölle* comes to his aid.[8] Take Luther's comments; apply them not to the Cross but to the Descent into Hell; remove the incubus of Luther's refusal of all 'mediating passage' and one has – compatibly now with the staurology of the Tradition, not to mention its soteriology and doctrine of God – the von Speyrian/Balthasarian theology of Holy Saturday. The dead Christ, the sin-bearer, passes through the 'second chaos' of Hell, passes through it as one has 'not the least to do with the Father as good Creator'[9] – and yet just this dread journey, *objectively* seen, *is* his Easter victory. Here if you will are Luther-type contradictions on every side. The Son goes towards Paradise with the good thief, and towards the pit with the bad. In his deadness he is no longer the active Word, yet just this silence is the most eloquent expression of the Father he has ever produced. But because it is the loving obedience of the Son to the Father's initiating love – love of the Son and of the world made through the Son and now to be his crown – that sends him on this journey, here is no mere contradiction. In all these contradictions he is perfectly identical with himself – and in this way he overcomes them from within. Or to put it another way which better befits the theological logic, what is

5 *TL* II, p. 309.
6 *TL* II, p. 314, n. 47.
7 See above, pp. 120–1.
8 A. von Speyr, *Kreuz und Hölle* (Einsiedeln 1966); also cited are *Objektive Mystik* and *Tagabücher* I–III, published at Einsiedeln in 1970 and 1975–6 respectively.
9 *TL* II, p. 318.

seen from within creation as contradiction is overcome by the logic of the Trinity.

Though Balthasar is eirenic in suggesting an element of experiential truth in the *simul justus et peccator* (one can have fresh joy over the forgiveness of a sin long ago pardoned), the conclusions he draws from Adrienne's writings are profoundly antithetical to classical Lutheranism: Purgatory; post-baptismal concupiscence as the means of a deeper hold on grace; the Christian mystic, with his or her dark nights, as a *partial* participant (again, by grace) in the state of mind and heart of the Lord on the Cross. Nowhere is this robust re-affirmation of distinctively Latin Catholic themes more manifest than in his penultimate words on the Virgin of Calvary whom he sees as 'opening herself vicariously for sinners', and her Son forgiving them not least for her sake.[10]

---

10 *TL* II, p. 329: the words are borrowed from von Speyr.

PART 3

TRUTH OF THE SPIRIT

18

The Spirit's 'Entry' into Logic

The preceding volume of the logic may have been, so Balthasar concedes in concluding it, methodologically messy, the opposite of what a *logic* – however theological – might be expected to be. But really there was no alternative. A method, after all, if its etymology can be trusted, is a matter of following a way (*met' hodos*), and the way the Logos chose to declare himself as absolute Truth was an utterly strange one, which ended on a Cross. Humanly speaking his work was a failure (*ein Scheitern*) – which just shows how much was left to the Holy Spirit to do.[1] Faith, hope, love; justification and Christian courage; the 'mysterious organism' we call the Church; Scripture, Tradition, the apostolic ministry; the fantastically varied mediation of the truth of the Son in holiness and theology: all this it will be the Spirit's task to achieve. This will not happen without the Son, as though the latter had entered a well-earned retirement. It is in the Holy Spirit that the Son continues to work until the end of time. And so if, within a theological logic, a Pneumatology appears to be a conclusion, it is really only a beginning.

Plenitude of truth

Balthasar's problem, in this final volume of the trilogy, is to draw within the confines of the concept of 'logic', however much, *in divinis*, this may be analogically stretched, the superabundance of what there is to say on the Holy Spirit. He is, after all, in the words of Jesus, the leader into 'all truth'. So as not to lose oneself in these multiple truths it is all the more necessary to give a high profile to the fundamental Trinitarian affirmations about the Spirit – and these occur in the Gospel of John when Jesus tells the disciples that the Spirit will not speak of himself but will 'take from what is mine', which means 'all that the Father possesses' (John 16.13). This Balthasar understands as a reference to what is inseparably the Father's and the Son's – namely, the unity of the Trinity's saving work in the Church and cosmos, which expresses the inner personal riches of the indivisibly one and only God. A better way to round off the entire trilogy than such a 'logic of the Spirit' could hardly be found.

1 *TL* II, p. 329.

Balthasar opens with some reflections, partly about content, but mostly to do with method, setting out for the reader the way a theology of the Spirit of Christ, the Spirit of the Father, fits into a theological logic. Shorn of its questionable context, a remarkable comment of Hegel's in his history of philosophy provides Balthasar with his *Leit-motiv*. Before Pentecost, the disciples had believed in Christ, but not as yet in him as *infinite Truth* – and this is the necessary completion which the Holy Spirit brings.[2] And to show that this contribution from German Idealism is in no way alien to Tradition, Balthasar at once adds that precisely so the Fathers (at the time of the late fourth-century Pneumatochian controversy) concluded that the Spirit must be personally God. For how can One who expounds the truth found in the Son's revelation of the Father not himself be divine? This truth, moreover – and here the Spirit's Godhead becomes peculiarly plain – does not consist simply in doctrinal statements about the relation of Jesus to the Father, any more than the Son's own revelation of the Father took place in words alone. Just as that revelation is found embodied in all the phases of the Son's fleshly existence so now too the Spirit will introduce believers into what Balthasar terms the 'living depths' of the event which joins Father and Son in all their hypostatic relatedness. We are not to know the Son as clients of a tour operator, as mere observers like speliologists noting some interesting rock formation (Balthasar's similes!), but as ourselves 'sons' of the Father in the everlasting Son. And in this sense Balthasar can say that, if the Spirit is – as Filioquist Pneumatology would insist – the substantial Love of Father and Son, and if he is also – as Balthasarian theology in its specificity further maintains – the fruit of that paternal and filial love, then what he 'introduces' us into is in a sense *himself*.

And this goes on primarily in the Church but not only there. Whether with the Greeks we think of 'ecclesial man' as man purified, enlightened, united to God and thus 'divinised', or with the Latins as man incorporated into Christ's body which the Saviour loves as he loves himself, makes no difference here. Just as for an Oriental like Cyril of Alexandria it is the *pneumatic* flesh of Christ which is life-giving, and makes divine, so for a Westerner such as Augustine to know Christ according to the Spirit is impossible without receiving the Spirit – which is why Jesus told his apostles that the Paraclete must come to them if Jesus himself were to be with them in a wholly new way. But the Spirit is that Spirit of the Lord whom the Old Testament described as already shed abroad in the creation, such that Balthasar can speak of a *Pneuma spermatikon*, a Spirit who sows seeds of divine life beyond the Church's visible confines, just as the Christian apologists in their turn had said the same of the *Logos spermatikos*, the *Word's* anonymous action. And Balthasar will ask in the penultimate section of *Geist der Wahrheit* how we may distinguish (if at all) these hidden economies of Spirit and Son.

But since such speculations are situated on the periphery of revelation (and so of Christian theology – here Balthasar once again distances himself

---

2 G. F. W. Hegel, *Geschichte der Philosophie* III (Berlin 1836), p. 134, cited in H. U. von Balthasar, *Theologik* III *Der Geist der Wahrheit* (Einsiedeln 1987), p. 13. This work will be referred to below as *TL* III.

from the shade of Rahner), we shall do better, in expounding a logic of the Spirit, to concentrate on what is centrally evangelical – but also simultaneously Catholic. And this is Balthasar's opportunity to indicate (again) his version of the idea of the dialectic between doctrinal 'development', in the term made famous by Newman, and the once-for-all gift of saving divine truth. The infinite truth of Christ necessarily needs time for its own endless explication. Yet this for Balthasar does not so much work by the Spirit first (in the Councils) clarifying the essentials and then gradually polishing off the more partial corollaries, but by his illuminating unexpectedly, as he wills (and so not in any straightforward progress) ever new aspects of a truth which is not, however, a vague thing but what Balthasar terms a 'defined totality'. And this is not just an intellectual gift of fresh insight, but a loving gift which elicits fresh forms of loving behaviour. Characteristic of Balthasar's exposition of this important theme of fundamental theology is the way he stresses how the Spirit is, so to speak, not interested in partial aspects of revelation for their own sake but in the way these can bring to light (and life) for us the revealed totality.

> A theology that lost itself in particulars, a praxis which brought into prominence in a unilateral way one aspect of Christianity could not be considered as animated by the Spirit.[3]

And thus emphasising the qualitative catholicity of the Spirit's action, Balthasar makes it a condition of all quantitative catholicity worth the name: the Church can only go rightly to the 'ends of the earth' in a generous sweep of missionary enlargement that takes in everything and everybody if by a simultaneous movement of concentration she takes ever better account of the 'goods' – the treasures of wisdom and knowledge given with Christ – she has to display. (This is Balthasar's answer to the question raised by the German Lutheran theologian Jürgen Moltmann as to how the Church can become 'relevant' without losing her 'identity'.) The Spirit leads the Church towards a future which is not itself a humanly realisable project (here Balthasar differentiates himself from what he sees as a 'fatal tendency' of liberation theology in this direction), but the definitive stage of God's covenant relation with the world. And in this, as in all the functions he carries out in the service of Trinitarian truth, the Spirit is the final object of Christian theology.

Divine disinterestedness

Balthasar rounds off his methodological considerations by asking after the why and the wherefore of a theology of the Holy Spirit *in general*. Though some would regard the Spirit (defectively) as, in Scripture, simply an objectification of the divine power, and therefore a pseudo-subject, a pseudo-person, for Balthasar the key lies, as with the help of Basil the Great's treatise *On the Holy Spirit* he now shows, in the Spirit's rôle as midwife of the realities of revelation and salvation. Quoting from his own earlier essay collection *Spiritus Creator*, the Holy Spirit does not want to

3 *TL* III, p. 17.

be seen *by* us, but to be *in* us as an eye that sees.[4] His light is visible only as lighting up objects – and supremely as enabling us to descry the Father–Son relation in Jesus Christ. But this means then (and the second volume of *Theologik* has already drawn our attention to the point) that Christ is himself only available as an object *through* the Spirit. The Son 'transcends' or points beyond himself not only to the Father but to the Spirit likewise. And thus Christology and Pneumatology are mutually conditioning: neither can be had without the other. The Spirit's rôle in making possible our grasp of the divine–human Object who is the Word made flesh renders him peculiarly anonymous. His 'facelessness', however, does not reflect his lack of subjecthood, an absence of personal specificity, but rather his *disinterestedness*. He is above all the subject, rather than the object, of theology as of the Christian life at large. But as those great hymns to the Spirit the *Veni Sancte Spiritus* and *Veni Creator Spiritus* show, this does not mean that the voice of the Church – and especially her praying voice, the discourse of doxology, falls silent where the Spirit himself is concerned.

We have to do, then, with an interpreter who can none the less be praised for what he is. His work of interpretation provides the model for all Christian theology as such; and the One whose work this is can himself be theologically evoked – so long as we remember that here the Person is our medium of expression (Pneumatology must proceed in terms proper to itself). And these two aspects of our enquiry are, as Balthasar now explains, internally related. The Spirit interprets the incarnate Son in both his difference from and his identity with the Father, thus manifesting at once what is comprehensible (including up to a certain point the 'naturally' comprehensible, the Jesus of liberal Christology) and the incomprehensible which only the 'allegory' (*allos-agorein*, the 'diverse speaking') of a fully ecclesial exegesis can furnish. In interpreting the Father, the Spirit likewise brings us knowledge – including that knowledge which liberal theology can claim, but, unlike such deficient theology, the knowledge of the Father in the Spirit is self-confessedly a knowledge that *surpasses understanding*. Here we are dealing with an 'excess' of knowledge for which neither apophatic theology, the language of negation, nor cataphatic theology, the language of affirmation, will serve our turn. And the ultimate explanation for *that* lies in the mystery of the Spirit himself, who expresses what Balthasar calls, following Adrienne von Speyr, the way the essence of the Trinitarian life is somehow in excess even of itself in the fruitful love which bears forward the relation of Father to Son, Son to Father. Thus reflection on the kind of authentic Christian understanding which the Spirit provides can give us an inkling of who the Spirit himself actually is.

4 *Spiritus Creator* (Einsiedeln 1967), pp. 100–7.

19

※

Christ and the Spirit

Christology, for Balthasar – and doubtless many theologians and exegetes of various schools would agree – should always fall within the wider framework of Pneumatology. Towards the end of his life Karl Barth wondered whether he might not have learnt a thing or two from the very father of liberal Protestant systematics, Schleiermacher, and presented the materials of all theology from the starting point of the Holy Spirit. At any rate, comments Balthasar, a Catholic 'Christology of the Spirit', without for a moment displacing the Word incarnate from his central position, will want to ask after that 'conceived by the Holy Ghost' so little attended to in Barth, and see the Spirit at work not only in the Incarnation but even (as he who 'has spoken through the prophets') well before. For the Canon of Scripture as a whole, the God who acts is, from the first moment of creation, the Trinitarian God, while, so Balthasar thinks, the Spirit's rôle not just in creation but also in Incarnation does not come to a temporary halt, as it were, with the assumption of humanity by the Logos – even though the Creed, in confining the pneumatic reference of its Christological section to the conception of Jesus, *might* give that impression.

The question of the continuing rôle of the Spirit in the life of Christ – his outpouring of graces on the man Jesus via that pre-eminent sanctification which is the hypostatic union – will occupy Balthasar later. Meanwhile, he offers a rapid survey of 'Christologies of the Spirit' before rising even higher to give a bird's-eye view of the development of pneumatological understanding in Scripture and Tradition – the essential prelude, this, to his own attempt to formulate a 'logic' of the Spirit as theological Interpreter of Jesus Christ, the Word.

Though the ancient Church knew somewhat naïve 'Christologies of the Spirit' – especially where, as in the Apostolic Fathers, the entire sphere of the divine could be called (understandably against the background of the Hebrew Bible) 'Spirit', accounts of Christ which begin from the presence of the Holy Spirit in the Saviour have a tendency to end up in Adoptionism: here Balthasar agrees with a summary judgment passed by Pannenberg.[1] Actually, with all its deficiencies, Hegel's version of a Spirit-

---

1 W. Pannenberg, *Jesus – God and Man* (Et Philadelphia and London 1968), pp. 116–21.

Christology – his 'speculative Pentecost' as Balthasar calls it – sets out correctly what such theology should aim, at least, to do. For in his 'theological philosophy' the Spirit (understood, evidently, in Hegel's idiosyncratic sense) embraces all reality from beginning to end, yet the centre from which alone this is graspable consists in (an equally curious) Christology. And here then Balthasar pauses, conscious that much of the most ambitious contemporary theology not only Protestant, as with Pannenberg and Jüngel, but also Catholic, as in Claude Bruaire of the Sorbonne and André Leonard of Louvain (bishop of Namur at the time of writing), is indebted to some at any rate of Hegel's categories. At the heart of Hegel's Triadology lies for Balthasar the error that the distinction of the Persons (which the tradition, certainly, has spoken of as their – *purely formal* – 'opposition') should be regarded as a contradiction constantly to be eliminated, rather than, as Balthasar would have it, the condition of their fruitfulness. So we cannot follow Hegel – but we can try to emulate, with more faithfully biblical categories, that Trinitarian interpretation of all reality he set out to give.

For his part Balthasar will find the starting point for a biblical Christology of the Spirit in the Holy Ghost's task of rendering the humanity assumed by the Word 'obedient in *a priori* fashion' to the mission the Son receives from the Father. Concretely, the Son made man carries out that mission only through abandonment to the Spirit. That reverses what one might well expect on the basis of the Catholic teaching that the Spirit is eternally from the Son but, so Balthasar insists, that teaching in fact remains unimpaired for this special state of affairs, which crowns the Spirit's pre-Christological acting in Israel's prophets, is the peculiar dispensation of the economic, not the immanent or absolute, Trinity. From the first moment of his human conception, the Son allows the Spirit to carry him forward on his project of redemption.

Here Balthasar makes his own a conclusion of the Tübingen theologian Walter Kasper at the end of the latter's *Jesus the Christ*. It is in the union in God of sovereign freedom with self-donative love (a point missed by Hegel) that we see aright the relation of Christology to the Spirit. As the 'medium' in which the Father both sends the Son via the Spirit-borne hypostatic union of Jesus with the Logos, and finds in him, through the Spirit's sanctifying work, the 'incarnate response to the divine self-communication',[2] the Holy Spirit renders Jesus in his own person the divine-human Mediator and (even more importantly for Balthasar's purposes here) enables him to communicate a truly *universal* salvation.

> Only such a Spirit Christology can combine Jesus' uniqueness and incomparability with the universality of his claim and rule.[3]

2 W. Kasper, *Jesus der Christus* (Mainz 1974), p. 298. It should be noted that Bishop Kasper's Christology is situated at the far Antiochene end of the spectrum in its willingness to accept a twofold personality in the Word Incarnate – understood, however, in relation to a metaphysical account of the dependence of human freedom on the absolute freedom of God which saves it from the anti-Nestorian strictures of Ephesus.
3 *TL* III, pp. 52–3.

And if Kasper was able to articulate that insight thanks to his deployment of Schelling's philosophical doctrine of God as freedom, his Christology of the Spirit converges at this point (so Balthasar thinks) with the speculations of another twentieth-century Catholic theologian who has drawn on the same philosophical resource – the French Oratorian Louis Bouyer. In describing the way that the Spirit immanent as the Wisdom of God in creation rejoins through that *ascending* movement of the world (under grace) towards God the *descending* movement of the Word of God into the world, Bouyer showed how the divine–human Fruit of Mary's womb must also be the eschatological fullness of God's plan. Here too the Spirit mediates the universal significance of the uniquely particular Jesus Christ to the Church and the world.[4]

---

4 L. Bouyer, *Le Consolateur: Esprit Saint et vie de grâce* (Paris 1980), pp. 444, 448. Balthasar is more circumspect *vis-à-vis* F. X. Durrwell's *L 'Esprit Saint de Dieu* (Paris 1983) which, despite some consonances with the pneumatology of Marius Victorinus, he finds somewhat Hegelian in its insistence that the Spirit is, in the Trinity, 'in the end as at the beginning'. Durrwell would have done better, he thinks, had he heard Adrienne von Speyr's words of warning, in *Die Welt des Gebetes*, against excessive use of temporal categories when construing the Trinitarian 'equilibrium'. The French theologian exposes himself to her strictures when he writes of the Holy Spirit as so much the 'personalising Person' by whom the divine nature becomes personal communion for the first time that the Spirit must be said to enjoy an anteriority to Father and Son in their mutually constitutive relations.

20

The Holy Spirit, the Interpreter

These, then, were theological straws-in-the-wind which gave Balthasar confidence that what he was attempting in *Theologik* III was on the right lines. But of course Catholic theology does not consist in a conversation of contemporary *savants*: its deliverance must prove themselves by the yardstick of Scripture and Tradition. Without more ado, therefore, Balthasar offers us his own overview of the course of reflection on the Holy Spirit from biblical to modern times, with the aim of answering the question, Who *is* this 'Expounder' or 'Exegete' of the Truth of the Son?

On the basis of Balthasar's deliberations so far a brief formulaic definition can help in taking us through the labyrinth of the books of Scripture and their successive unfoldings in the theologies of the Church. It runs as follows: the Spirit is he by whom God makes himself known as God to whatever (or whomever) is not divine. It is by the Spirit of the Lord that Israel, or particular Israelites, can in the Old Testament speak or act for God in ways otherwise beyond their capacity. And while physical nature depends on this Breath of the Lord for its very life (the Psalms), in the post-Exilic period the Spirit is made the source of Israel's Godly institutions in the past and of their messianic future (the later prophets) as well as being found in the form of the Wisdom of God in the texture of creation itself (the Sapiential books). The Apocalypses of the inter-Testamental period are written by those rapt in the Spirit, while the rabbis come to ascribe all Scripture to the Spirit of God. In the New Testament, Jesus is experienced as having worked in the Spirit, and the Paschal dawn of his Resurrection opens a time when his young community enjoys a many-sided experience of the Spirit which Paul will attempt to generalise in his doctrine of the Church as Christ's 'Body' where all the members receive from the Spirit some gift useful for the greater whole.

Yet Balthasar is curiously negative about both the capacity of the Old Testament materials to carry us any distance towards the specifically Christian doctrine of the Holy Spirit and the extent to which the Spirit figured in Jesus' own discourse. For him, a just account of the Paraclete is the gift of that inspired biblical theologian in whom that word for the Spirit ('Paraclete') occurs : the evangelist John. Only here (and this fits of course with the strongly marked Johannine character of Balthasar's thought, as of Von Speyr's exegesis) do we find 'openness to the supreme fullness'.[1] And if this leaves the Fourth Evangelist somewhat perilously exposed within the biblical corpus, Balthasar compensates him by the quality of the attention he brings to John's words.[2]

Even before the Lord's death and Resurrection John had presented him as possessing the Spirit 'beyond measure' (John 3.34). The One who in his own being is filled with the Spirit is the source of the Spirit for others (cf. John 7.37), and this explains how during the public ministry the disciples could already see something of his glory and, within certain limits, believe in him. And yet, according to the Last Supper discourse, the Spirit cannot come unless Jesus go, a puzzle whose Balthasarian solution is crucial for the last volume of the trilogy:

> The incarnate Word of God can be expounded in his totality only when he has been spoken out to the end – in his death and Resurrection.[3]

Those climactic events of salvation history are the 'things to come' of which Jesus promises the Spirit will speak (John 16.13), for the fact that the Saviour has 'many things' to tell the disciples which they 'cannot bear now' (16.12) does not at all mean that his self-revelation is to be truncated. On the contrary, it is the full eschatological import of the happenings, the end of the ages, which the Paraclete will pronounce. 'All the truth' – the limitless dimensions of the task assigned to the Spirit in completing the disciples' initiation – does not mean that he is, however, to introduce them, first and foremost, to an indefinite number of individual truths. Rather, it means that he will induct them into the 'single truth of the exposition of God through the Son in the inexhaustible fullness of his concrete universality'.[4] This will happen, moreover, through the testimony of the Holy Spirit in the disciples (15.26): it will be a lesson taught through the Spirit's very being, by way of intimate participation. And speaking with those anti-Palamite accents that might be expected from a perusal of *Theologik* II, we shall then be

> introduced not only into the 'energies' of God but into the incomprehensibility of his Essence – which is that which passes understanding in his very being revealed and shared.[5]

Intimacy with the Spirit means entry into the divine 'space' of the Son's relation with the Father. If the Spirit is to lead into all truth in this pregnant sense, he must also be, as the New Testament tradition attests, the Sanctifier.

1 *TL* III, p. 58.
2 Not without aid from the more dogmatically alert modern exegetes: notably Heinrich Schlier, 'Zum Begriff des Geistes nach dem Johannesevangelium', in *idem, Besinnung auf das Neue Testament* (Freiburg 1964), pp. 264–71; Ignace de la Potterie, 'Le Paraclet', in *idem, La vie selon l'Esprit* (Paris 1965), pp. 85–105; and Felix Porsch, *Pneuma und Wort: Ein exegetischer Beitrag zur Pneumatologie des Johannesevangeliums* (Frankfurt 1974).
3 *TL* III, p. 64.
4 *TL* III, p. 65.
5 *TL* III, p. 66.

But whatever nuances can be found hidden within the term *parakleitos* (and Balthasar leaves aside the mystery of whence exactly the evangelist took the term), the connotations of Comforter, Advocate, Witness and others cannot and do not detract from the central denotation (for Balthasar) of *Expositor*. The value of the other rôles hinted at in the word – and brought out more fully elsewhere in the Johannine corpus – consists in the way they manifest the full weight and implications of the Spirit's interpretative activity.

Only retrospectively, according to Balthasar, that is, from the vantage point of the pneumatological vision of the Gospel of John, can one rightly assess (as he now proceeds to do) the contributions of Paul, the Synoptics and the Old Testament itself to an account of the Spirit of truth. Just so, the Johannine mountaintop is also the best place from which to view prospectively the trail that runs down and away to the far horizon in the subsequent tradition of the Church.

The Canon is there to fill out whatever a theologian may wish to say on the basis of elective affinity with some single book within it. The inability to let that happen would be, for a theological reputation, a bad sign. *Paul's* contribution to a theology of the Spirit as Interpreter is found in the way he speaks of him as transferring the Christian from the realm of fallen flesh to a sphere of living where true understanding of the Revealer is possible because the disciple united to the Lord becomes one Spirit with him (1 Corinthians 6.17: given Balthasar's exegesis here, 'Spirit' must be capitalised, something unusual in English translations). Union with Christ in his mission and person deepens and broadens its scope as the Spirit acts to justify and sanctify, bearing his fruits and distributing his charisms as he wills in the body of the Church – potent means of his 'exposition' of the truth of the Word. For *Luke*, to give an account of the experience of the Spirit in the Church of the apostles was surely a major motive for the writing of Acts. The Pentecost descent of the Spirit in wind and flame launches the apostles on their ministry of preaching and of witness before governors and kings, of teaching collegially at the 'Council' of Jerusalem and rendering individuals prophets and doctors of the New Covenant – all of which shows the Johannine Paraclete, the Expositor of Christ, in action. For *Matthew and Mark*, the theophany at the Baptism implies a definitive endowment of Jesus with the Spirit of prophecy – so the Spirit's descent marks out the Word made flesh in his uniqueness. The blasphemy against the Holy Spirit which, so these evangelists report, can never be forgiven, not only implies Jesus' awareness of speaking and acting in the Spirit but also indicates the infernal prospects of those who, recognising the Spirit's interpretation of the Son to be true, none the less despise or reject it. And finally these writers also report how the Saviour predicted that the Spirit would bring appropriate speech to the lips of persecuted disciples throughout the proclamation of the Gospel to the Gentiles: thus the so-called Little Apocalypse (at Mark 13.10–11; cf. Matthew 10.19–20).

So, to sum up: the Word incarnate has the Spirit as his Expositor in many ways. The reciprocal co-determination of the missions of Son and Spirit in the New Testament brings to fulfilment, if in unpredictable fashion, the unity of the Word and Breath of the Almighty in the Old.

Not surprisingly, then, the Fathers of the Church grasped the Spirit's rôle as Introducer into the mystery of Christ and Expositor of the content of that mystery before they explicitly affirmed the Spirit's divinity and personhood. Faced with the difficulty of drawing a coherent doctrine of the Spirit from the materials provided by the New Testament in its ascription to him of a wide diversity of rôles as well as its intimate conjoining of the Spirit's work with Christ's, the Church Fathers did – Balthasar believed – exactly what he himself is doing in the logic. They took the Johannine affirmation of the Spirit's task as Interpreter to be the focus – though not of course the final outcome – of their reflections. For Irenaeus, the Spirit prepares man for the Son; for Tertullian, he is the expositor of the Economy; for Hermas, he is the master of the truth of Scripture; for Hippolytus, while the Father commands and the Son obeys, the Spirit grants understanding; for Novatian, he communicates the truth of eternal life; for Clement of Alexandria, he introduces disciples to the true – the Christian – *gnōsis*; for Cyril of Jerusalem, and here Balthasar breaks off, for we are entering the epoch where the Church defines her faith in the Spirit's Godhead and personality, he descends to bear witness to Christ.

21

The Spirit as Personal Being

We now know what – at any rate in the perspective of theological logic – the Holy Ghost does. We have not yet asked, however, who he is. The fact that the Spirit acts focally as he who makes Christian subjectivity possible might discourage us from taking him as an object of enquiry in this way. But the legitimate patristic principle – increasingly invoked in the debates of the fourth- and fifth-century Church – that 'he who leads to God must be himself divine' (not to mention the resultant dogma) leaves us no option.

A biblical conundrum

Balthasar offers us a selective overview of patristic, mediaeval and modern discussion before giving us his own answer to that question, Who is the Holy Spirit? Naturally, he takes his overall bearings from Scripture – the 'soul' of theology. The New Testament sources suggest (with varying degrees of plausibility, one might add) three possibilities. Is the divine Spirit the expression of God's undivided fullness (his Essence)? Is it (it would be begging the question at this stage for write 'he') neither the Father nor the Son but a third reality? Or is it *both* a 'third' *and* the re-capitulation of the other two (rather after the fashion indicated in modern times by the French Redemptorist theologian François-Xavier Durrwell).[1] Some would object: but what about a fourth possibility, namely, that the 'spirit' is impersonal divine power? Balthasar's response is robust:

> In no way can YHWH's Spirit and power be named impersonally; he himself is always their subject.[2]

New Testament references to the Spirit – even when they fail to connote distinctness of personality *vis-à-vis* Father and Son – can never be reduced to mere impersonality. Balthasar thinks it beyond question that the witness of the Christian Scriptures as a whole establishes two points: first, the Spirit is a divine reality situated 'between' Father and Son; second, about

1 See above, p. 133, n. 4.
2 *TL* II, p. 100.

this reality there is something peculiarly elusive (as John 3.8 puts it, 'The wind blows where it wills, and you hear the sound of it, but you do know whence it comes or whither it goes'). What this tells us is, in the words of the mid-twentieth-century German dogmatician Heribert Mühlen, 'the absolute inscrutability of the personal particularity of the Holy Spirit'.[3] True, there may be at times a functional identification of the glorified Christ and the Holy Spirit (notably in the Pauline letters – but that is explained by Paul's conviction that the Risen One has been transfigured precisely by his complete sharing in the Spirit of God). None the less, the frequent occurrence of triadic (rather than dyadic) formulae makes it clear that the unity in question (between the Spirit and the Son) is of a differentiated kind. Beyond this, what more can we say? The New Testament authors give no speculative answer to our question. They circle round the topic, absorbed as they are in the depiction of the Spirit's many-sided gifts, in Christians and the Church. Yet in so doing they let us know of the Spirit's freedom, of the Spirit's enabling the redeemed to be adopted sons in the Son, of the Spirit as the sanctifier – all pointers to his personhood. In any case, a mere 'binity' would make nonsense of the *imagines Trinitatis* found in the created realm in the 'ana-logic' of *Wahrheit Gottes*. And after all if the One who lets the glory of God shine out in the face of Jesus Christ, and transforms us who have faces into his likeness, is himself 'faceless', we do not need to suppose that Father, Son and Spirit are 'Persons' in precisely the same sense. ('Person' in God is not a univocal concept.) In such a tumble of considerations, Balthasar brings us to the edge of the patristic age.

The Fathers

In the course of a part-chapter in the third volume of a theological logic, Balthasar can hardly present a conspectus of patristic Pneumatology at large. He must, if not quite 'cherry pick', at least be choosy. While Cyril of Jerusalem is content with advocating an apophatic silence on the Spirit's identity, Athanasius confesses his *homoousion* with the Father and Son, though holding back from any more detailed statement. The Cappadocians affirm his Godhead but declare his way of being God, within the divine unity, to be indescribable. It is the distinction between the Son's generation and the Spirit's procession that evades them, though distinction there must be (there are not two Sons). The Latin Fathers are 'no less eloquent', remarks Balthasar, on the point[4] – though for them the difficulty is softened by the increasing conviction that the Spirit is from the Father *and the Son* (Balthasar will have much more to say about this later). All of which confirms Balthasar in his view (shared with St Thomas) that what it means to be a divine *Person* varies with each of the three: that seems indicated if the *tropos tēs hyparxeōs* – the divine way of personal being – is altogether proper to each one, and not altogether theologically 'scrutable'. The Trinity, after all, is the deepest mystery: it is what explains, not what is explained.

3 H. Mühlen, *Der Heilige Geist als Person* (Münster 1966[2]), p. 166.
4 *TL* III, p. 108.

Such lacunae in our understanding are inevitable – even or *especially* when pressing the claims of theological logic. More perplexing is the reluctance of the Fathers to allow that the Trinitarian Persons can be counted, a brake on positive thinking which Basil compares, in the course of his treatise *On the Holy Spirit*, to the Jewish reluctance to utter the divine Name. Both are ways of asserting the transcendence of God in regard to beings. All that Basil will allow within the divine unity is a plurality of an arithmetically non-expressible kind. Probably he had in mind that feature of Plato's late philosophy – reported by Aristotle – whereby the Ideas of sensuous particulars can be themselves numbered but only in the special sense that in them absolute unity is conjoined with the indeterminate.[5] A stream of Greek theologians will follow this, as it were, concessionist line, at least as regards the enumeration of the order of the processions (Father, then Son, then Spirit): in Greek, the *taxis*.

If Basil accepted the possibility of ideal numbers – *arithmoi eidetikoi* – in Trinitarian counting, a second acceptable tack was that of Aquinas (it is presumably only for reasons of pedagogical convenience that Balthasar treats this here). What Thomas called 'transcendental' number, as distinct from 'quantitative', is reserved for a plurality which knows no division. The divine personal relationships 'belong to the plurality of the divine unity yet deny all separateness'.[6] Hegel will take this further, contrasting the 'exteriority' of arithmetical number with Trinitarian 'vitality'. It is a topic that has engaged contemporary Francophone philosophical theologians of differing types.[7]

The mediaevals

So far Balthasar has been even-handed in the praise he accords to sources of theological illumination East and West. But before entering into the question of how the mediaeval Latin doctors can help with our enquiry, he shows out of the door, rather peremptorily, their principal Greek counterpart. The Palamite doctrine of the divine energies (God in his active expression of his Essence) may be dressed in Trinitarian clothing (the energies are hypostatised by the divine Persons, and so are always those of Father, Son and Spirit). In fact, however, this theologoumenon of the Byzantine tradition seems to render the economic Trinity theologically superfluous, while at the same time giving the impression that the immanent Trinity is not the absolutely last word about God. The three epochs in which, for Palamas, the divine energies are revealed in the Persons of the triune God:

> do not [on the one hand] stamp the divine action in a Trinitarian way, while on the other Trinity and energies are so closely bound up with one another that one is reminded, none too pleasurably, of Eckhart: the Trinity as that face of God which is turned to the world

---

5 See Julius Stenzel's *Zahl und Gestalt bei Platon und Aristoteles* (Darmstadt 1959³).
6 *TL* III, p. 113, with reference to *Summa Theologiae* Ia, q. 11, 2, and q. 30, a. 3.
7 Balthasar mentions the 'metamathematical' approach of A. Manaranche, *Le Monothéisme chrétien* (Paris 1985), and the more Hegelianising approach of S. Breton, *Unicité et monothéisme* (Paris 1981).

beyond which the unknowable abyss of the divine unity remains concealed.[8]

The mystery of the Person, in his Essence, coming forth in freedom, by his energies, strikes a chord, on first hearing, with modern personalism in the anthropological domain. But when more rigorously analysed, Balthasar thinks, the impression evaporates: to bestow oneself on others while in oneself remaining unbestowed is *ein Sophisma*, 'a piece of sophistry', which if man is the image of the Trinity must be barred from theological discourse. Moreover, and returning to the Spirit who is the subject of the logic's last volume: as the everlasting *Donum* in the Godhead, he needs no energetic *donatum* to be what he is and how he acts – *the* Gift, the archetype of all giving.

The contribution of the mediaeval Westerners is happier. Though the mediaevals reflected on the anthropology of the (human) person, their thought was essentially governed by the patristic prosopology (theology of personhood) issuing from Nicaea and Chalcedon. A really brilliant page of historical summary synthesises the most important features of research into the origins of the language of 'Persons'.[9] As to an evaluation of what the Middle Ages did with this inheritance, Balthasar awards the laurels to Richard of St Victor and St Thomas – at least as the latter is interpreted (and perhaps over-interpreted) by Heribert Mühlen. Richard's celebrated definition of Triune personhood – *divinae naturae incommunicabilis existentia* – has the merit of underlining relationality (in this case, derivation, *ex-istentia*) as the key to hypostatic being. 'Each Person is called such on the basis of a different relationality.'[10] That the Father is 'from' no one was, however, a dissuasive to the general adoption of this scheme as was its failure to present the divine Persons as *towards* each other as well as *from* each other (the Father's *agennesia*, or unbegottenness, being saved). Thomas' more 'neutral' concept of Person avoided this, but it is his account of the intersection between the idea of divine personhood and divine nature which inspired Mühlen's presentation of Thomasian Triadology.[11] What Thomas offers is at once a doctrine of Trinitarian personhood as the maximum conceivable diversity (the *modus existendi* of Father, Son and Spirit can only be determined relationally) and a teaching about the nature of the divine Trinity as the maximum intensity of unity (each of the Three is identical with the divine nature itself).

As yet, however, this is but general background to a fuller determination of the personhood of the Spirit. In *Theologik* II, Balthasar has already

---

8 *TL* III, p. 117. Balthasar follows the anti-Palamite reasoning of Dorothea Wendebourg, in her *Geist oder Energie? Zur Frage der innergöttlichen Verankerung des christlichen Lebens in der byzantinischen Theologie* (Munich 1980), and, correspondingly, rejects the more eirenic interpretation by Louis Bouyer published the same year as *Esprit Saint et vie de grâce* (Paris 1980).

9 *TL* III, pp. 121–2. Special indebtedness to C. Andresen, 'Zur Entstehung und Geschichte des trinitarischen Personbegriffs', *Zeitschrift für neutestamentliche Wissenschaft und Kultur der älteren Kirche* 52 (1961), pp. 1–39; M.-J. Rondeau, *Exégèse prosopologique et théologique* (Rome 1985, = *Les Commentaires patristique du Psautier* III).

10 *TL* III, p. 124. The Riccardian definition appears originally in *De Trinitate* III.18.

11 H. Mühlen, *Der Heilige Geist als Person*, pp. 107–8.

indicated his reservations about using the Augustinian psychological analogy (*imago Trinitatis in mente*) as a basis for a less agnostic account of the Holy Spirit's procession than the one the Fathers left behind. The increasing mediaeval recourse to this analogy intensifies his jitters. The Son is the unsurpassable *Donum* of the Father's love – so why appropriate that term to the Spirit? The Spirit as Comprehender of what the Father has given in Christ is peculiarly linked with understanding – so why appropriate that term to the Son? The Cistercian school knew perfectly well that knowledge terms – *sapere, sentire, praegustare* – belong to the heart of who the Spirit is and what he does, but the (otherwise admirable) mediaeval preoccupation with the gifts of the Spirit, themselves ordered to such fuller comprehension and 'tasting', left no energy for the further investigation of his personal mystery. For Balthasar the Spirit proceeds as the 'Love-fruit' of Father and Son, at once the Expression of the intersubjective aspect of their love (which in its objective aspect is the divine nature itself) and the 'objective' Witness to the intersubjective love between them. After Richard and Thomas, the Middle Ages had all the building blocks for such a house of triune thinking; but they failed to put them together.

The moderns

This is not to say, however, that no one between Aquinas and Balthasar is worth reading on this topic. Balthasar locates three notable halting places on the way to his 'final' answer to the question about who the Spirit is: Calvin, the Personalists and Hegel. Although Calvin ties the Holy Spirit too restrictedly (in Balthasar's opinion) to the canonical Scriptures and the sacraments, he has got hold of the Spirit-as-Witness idea. Without the Holy Spirit the Bible would be a 'Pope of paper'. But no: the Spirit renders present the living Christ by his internal testimony, so withdrawing as by a sort of kenosis to give prominence to Father and Son, so deflecting attention from himself (the opposite, adds Balthasar wryly, to what Montanus and Pentecostalism suppose) that he points to Christ, rather than inviting us to introspection.[12] The best of the modern Personalists is Maurice Nédoncelle who avoids the mistake of defining the personal over against the ontic, since the personal ever needs its substructure of being.[13] Here are foundations for an account of the triune God as personal communion (an accent, that, typical of a strongly pneumatological Triadology) which will not reject the ontological demands of thinking about God. But Hegel is the real discovery. Though Hegel's thought must be turned inside out in order to be serviceable for Catholic theology, the task can be done, and is worth the candle. (Indeed, much of what Balthasar will have to say later in *Theologik* III about the Spirit and the Church aims to show how that is so.) Within that overall context in which Hegel's thoughts moved – the desire to reconcile the finite and the infinite – the Christian doctrine of

12 T. Preiss, *Das innere Zeugnis des Heiligen Geistes* (Zurich 1947).
13 J. Lacroix, 'L'ontologie personnaliste de M. Nédoncelle', in *La Pensée philosophique et religieuse de Maurice Nédoncelle. Actes du colloque Strasbourg 1979* (Paris 1981), pp. 99–112.

the Holy Spirit came to him as an opportunity. Here is the divine as found 'in' us, yet searching the depths of God. At Pentecost, the God-man shows that in the defeat of his death he has none the less conserved his super-natural truth, and does so by sending the Spirit of love – to be found henceforth in two forms: subjective spirit, discovering its own freedom in gradual fashion through all the ethical configurations of society, and objective or objectivised spirit, which is none other than these institutional arrangements themselves, essential as they are to subjective spirit's appropriation of its own liberty. Catholicised, and transposed into a theological key, we get the following result:

> the Scriptural word, sacrament, Tradition, the ministry, are nothing other than forms shaped by the Holy Spirit of Christ so as to lead the subjective spirit of the faithful in a journey through self-dedication (*Hingabe*) to that purity and universality of outreach it already intended.[14]

The transposal is not perfect. It does not do full justice, for instance, to the assured fact that the Holy Spirit never becomes identical with the Christian spirit (in the fashion Hegel maintained for 'absolute spirit'), since one is uncreated, the other created, gift. Just so, the spiritual individual never becomes the Spirit as soul of the Church (though with Origen we can recognise in the *vir catholicus* an *anima ecclesiastica*). There is also the little matter of what we are to make theologically of Hegel's statement that the Spirit is to be found objectified in nature as a whole – which will lead Balthasar to offer a short meditation not only on the Spirit and the *Church* but also on the Spirit and the *world*. Still, the analysis is serviceable, and chimes with Balthasar's characterisation of the Spirit as both the supreme *subjective* unity of Father and Son and the amplest *objective* fruit of their love.

Pneumatology in miniature

For his own part – in a tiny précis of the Trinitarian theology to be found most amply in the closing volume of the theological dramatics – Balthasar likes best to speak of the Spirit's identity as that of an 'excess' (*Überschwang*) of love, of the variety, he hastens to add, that belongs with *das absolute Sein*, 'absolute Being'. In the distinctively Balthasarian Triadology, the Father does not give his substance to the Word for the sake of his own self-expression, his own self-knowledge, but by an act of inconceivable love – which does, however, itself conceive, does generate, enabling the Son to receive that love not passively but as a co-lover in return. Such reciprocity of absolute love possesses an exuberance (*Überschwang* again) of such a kind that it produces another divine reality, beyond our grasping yet hallmarked by the utter freedom of giving of Father and Son. In this way the Holy Ghost is the vertex of the absolute loving that has its origin in the Father's being. Not, Balthasar must add, in a Dionysian divine frenzy, but in 'sober intoxication' (a favoured term of the Fathers for

14 *TL* III, p. 141.

mystical love) for the Spirit enjoys with the divine Essence all the divine properties in serene unity.

It will readily be seen that Balthasar is a thoroughgoingly Filioquist theologian: the alternative, Monopatrist, picture (where Spirit, like Son, issues from the Father alone) he considers 'Plotinian', and thus philosophical in its derivation, whereas the Filioque is so pure an effluence of Christian theology that he can call it (with the Anglican divine H. B. Swete, writing on Augustine)[15] virtually an inference from the *homoousion* of Nicaea. Balthasar seeks a recognition that the best way of naming the Spirit is to call him not (with Augustine and many others) *Donum*, 'the Gift', for that he considers to be injustice to the Son, but *Donum Doni*, 'the Giving of the Gift'.

> The love given by the Father in the Son is 'poured into our hearts' through the gift of love as Spirit . . . Precisely in that way . . . is the Spirit shown to be the bestowed Interpreter of the divine Gift (which the Father makes to us by his Son) . . .[16]

Such an 'economic' way of answering the question, Who is the Spirit? fits perfectly with what we can say about the inner-Trinitarian life (and so 'immanently' or 'absolutely'). As the terminus of the reciprocal giving of Father and Son he is from all eternity *substantiierte Geschenk*, 'substantiated Gift' – at once then the 'extreme point' of the divine being and its 'most intimate centre'. (This is why, to revert for a moment to the economic perspective, when the Spirit is given to a creature it undergoes salvific 'divinisation'.) In this limited sense, the thesis of F. X. Durrwell, already alluded to, whereby it is in the Spirit that the divine Essence is, so to say, rounded off in its being as love, meets with Balthasar's acceptance.

None the less, Balthasar is against any wider notion of the Spirit's procession 'completing' that of the Son – whether absolutely or economically. When the dying Christ cries, 'It is finished' (John 19.30), he means what he says. The work he always carried out in the Spirit has been brought, on the Cross, to its fulfilment. And that fulfilment is exactly what the Spirit passes on. The theme of the indivisibility of the Spirit's activity from that of the Son will occupy Balthasar in the next section of the theo-logic.

---

15 H. B. Swete, *The Holy Spirit in the Ancient Church* (London 1919), p. 353; cited *TL* III, p. 147.
16 *TL* III, p. 149.

22

Dyad in the Triad:
The Father's 'Two Hands'

For Balthasar it is impossible to isolate the work of the Son from that of the Spirit. The two act together if distinctly as, in Irenaeus' metaphor, the Father's two hands. They do so not only in the central events of the theo-drama but also in the outworking of those events as human beings are simultaneously incorporated into the Son (the Latin stress) and divinised by the Spirit (the Greek emphasis). And of course – as Irenaeus, with his anti-Gnostic message that creation and redemption go together, cannot fail to emphasise – the two hands collaborate in the work of creation itself: God's Logos, the Son, with God's Wisdom, the Spirit.[1] Nor is this an isolated flash in the pan. The Russian Orthodox dogmatician Sergei Bulgakov – drawn on by Balthasar in his account of the Incarnation in the theological dramatics – put together quite a dossier of texts from Athanasius the Great on the same theme: the complementarity, in the Father's prosecution of his plan for the world, of the 'Dyad', the Son and the Spirit. It can hardly be a coincidence, after all, that 'Christ' means 'anointed with the Spirit'. This is how Bulgakov summed up his conclusions in *Uteshitel*, 'The Paraclete'.

> *Vis-à-vis* the first hypostasis [the Father], the other two hypostases are his dy-hypostatic revelation. There is here a determinate hierarchy, that of voluntary loving renunciation, a renunciation proper to each hypostasis of the Holy Trinity in its own way, since each has his concrete *tropos tēs hyparxeōs* ... The centre of revelation is the Father, the revelatory hypostases find their orientation in him. Both Word and Spirit are distinguished as differing modes of this revelation, but are conjoined as the two-in-one image of the Fatherly self-manifestation. They form a dyad of such a sort that it is not possible to grasp one hypostasis without co-thinking the other ...[2]

Balthasar certainly makes this conclusion his own, but he uses it for a different purpose from Bulgakov's. The latter sought an eirenic theology

---

1 Irenaeus, *Adversus Haereses* IV. 7, 4; cited *TL* III, p. 153.
2 Cited from the French translation, *Le Paraclet* (Paris 1946), pp. 141–3. For a summary of the main lines of this work, see A. Nichols, *Light from the East: Authors and Themes in Orthodox Theology* (London 1995), pp. 62–5.

147

of the Filioque; Balthasar is more concerned to show that not in every sense can the Son be regarded as prior to the Spirit in the Trinity – not in every sense in the Incarnation, and not in every sense in the Spirit's inhabiting of the Church and the soul by grace.

Evidence of Spirit–Son interaction

In his survey of biblical materials for the dyad Balthasar stresses the frequent interchangeability of the Old Testament divine 'Word' and 'Spirit' as well as their convergence (the Sinai revelation, *par excellence* a revelation in the 'Word', requires interpretation by prophets – above all, Moses – originally conceived as bearers of ecstasy-making 'Spirit'; the 'Spirit', as found in primitive prophecy in Israel, becomes ever more a matter of the 'Word', as in the great 'writing' prophets of the Canon). In the New Testament, the event of the Incarnation of the Word means that never again could there be confusion between Son and Spirit. But it in no sense signifies – and this way lies Balthasar's chief preoccupation in this section of the theological logic – that their tendency to combine and even exchange rôles comes to an end. On the contrary, it comes to a climax. When we look at how Scripture presents the interacting work of Spirit and Son in the Annunciation, the Baptism, the Temptations, the Atonement (cf. Hebrews 9.14, it was by the 'eternal Spirit' that Christ offered himself), the Resurrection and Pentecost, and at the biblical evidence for Jesus' awareness that the Spirit in a unique way dwelt and acted in him, it seems hard to reach any other conclusion – *especially* in what regards the post-Paschal epoch, the time of the Church. The mission of the Spirit is not now uncoupled from that of the Son. Rather,

> the two missions have entered upon a new stage, in which is revealed the infinite riches of their relations in a different fashion from hitherto.[3]

Summarising the biblical data – with aid from figures as diverse as contemporary exegetes and the Cappadocian Fathers, Adrienne and that papally-patronised German Jesuit theologian of the mid-twentieth-century Roman school Sebastian Tromp, Balthasar has been straining at the leash, anxious to get at the speculative-dogmatic meat of his subject. He has already suggested (and these are no obvious inferences from the biblical text) that the salvation-anticipating action of the Spirit in the Incarnation of the Son is a better explanation for the universal resonance of the Incarnation in humankind at large than is the reason more customarily met with (and associated with such patristic figures as Gregory Nazianzen and Cyril of Alexandria), namely, that it follows from the concrete unity of all men in the human nature assumed by the Word. He has already asserted (in words taken from Von Speyr) that in the Passion of the Lord the Spirit gives to the hypostatic union such a form that it now expresses in an extreme manner the *distinction* between God and man – and yet that, in that same moment, the Spirit maintains the unity of Father and

---

3 *TL* III, p. 161.

Son in the paradoxical (again) form of abandonment – thus the last cry from the Cross in Mark. And he has already argued that when in John the risen Christ sends the Spirit onto the disciples by means of physical gestures the unity of Son and Spirit becomes visible in a new form, uniting body and spirit. Having 'given back' the Spirit to the Father (the reference is to the notoriously ambiguous wording of John 19.30: 'and he gave up his spirit'), the Father now gives the Spirit to human beings only through Jesus Christ.

A speculative reflection

But Balthasar wants to integrate these points – which concern, it will be seen, the 'forms' the redemptive relation between the triune God and the world receives at crucial points in the salvational narrative – into a fuller speculative synthesis. He holds – and this is certainly coherent with the decision to treat Pneumatology, in the context of theological logic, as an account of the conditions (epistemic and ontic, both) of the truth of the incarnate Word – that the central theme of a theology of the Spirit is the mystery of the Incarnation. The Fathers, by their lack of consensus, have left us a problem. Is the sanctifying union of the Word with human nature 'logological' (the result of actions by the Word) or pneumatological (the result of actions by the Spirit), or is it a combination of the two? The latter would be the case if we ought to think of the Spirit as so elevating the humanity assumed that it could be personalised directly by the Word or, again, if the hypostatic union simply sanctified the human nature of Christ at its root, allowing space for the Spirit to bestow further sanctifying grace on Jesus in the actions he carried out or underwent at others' hands.

In nuce this is a quandary left us by Paul (or the author of the hymn embedded in the text of Colossians) and Luke (in his infancy narrative). Was it he, the Logos, taking the form of a servant who brought about the Incarnation (Paul); or was it the Spirit overshadowing the womb of Mary (Luke)? Actually, Balthasar proposes to marry the two by taking a leaf from the book of Bonaventure: the Incarnation of the Word is an action of the entire Trinity, each Person participating according to his proper 'mode of existing'. Balthasar cannot allow that the Spirit's contribution can be restricted to keeping up a flow of 'accidental' sanctifying grace, making such grace (that is) 'happen to' a humanity already 'substantially' hallowed by the Word. Instead, he maintains that, since the Word's action is found in obedience to the Father, the Son acts by obediently letting the Spirit carry out the Father's loving plan. Such an 'economic inversion' (of the 'normal' interrelation of Son and Spirit) 'changes nothing of the intra-divine *taxis*'.[4] According to the needs of the Economy, either the Spirit can come first (to render the Son incarnate and accompany him to his human dying) or the Son can come first, once again to dispose of the Spirit by sending him (with the Father) to the world. These are *propria* of the Son and Spirit as they act in the divine unity, just as it is proper to the Father to be at work through his 'two hands'.

4 *TL* III, p. 166.

Further implications

If Spirit and Son act with and through each other, to what end is this, and what further implications does it hold?

1. It belongs to a theological logic to consider the intelligible structure of our salvation (as distinct from its attracting radiance, the task of the aesthetics, or its dramatic power, that of the dramatics). Balthasar treats the value for us of the dyadic action of Son and Spirit under the rubric of 'divinisation and incorporation'.

   The Spirit 'shows and expounds' the twofold movement of Father to Son (Incarnation) and Son to Father (Resurrection) but in so doing what he lays out for us is the definitive revelation of the Father in the first, and the endless glory of the Son in the second, and therewith the perfection of their mutual love. When we are enfolded in this movement and disclosure we encounter what the Greeks call 'divinisation' and the Latin's 'incorporation in Christ' – both inescapably Trinitarian events or processes. A catena of passages – twice as long for the Greeks as for the Latins – displays to us these perfectly complementary schemes. The Greek witnesses reach their culmination in Cyril of Alexandria's commentary on John, where the Logos is said to divinise Christians – to make them sons of God – through the Eucharist and the Holy Spirit.[5] But these are exactly the divine 'ingredients' (if the word may be allowed) which, among the Latins, Augustine typically identifies as the agents of our concorporation in Christ's body so as to participate in the life of the triune God.[6] That the Western tradition is no stranger to the divinisation schema is Balthasar's last word on the topic as he recalls how for Albert the Great 'created grace' (neuralgic point for many modern Orthodox) is no 'medium' between God and ourselves (it is, insists the Cologne master, 'deiform') and how for his confrère Thomas even in this life the grace of the Spirit 'confers something divine on the soul', and 'constitutes man in divine being'.[7]

2. A further – and far less obvious – aspect of the coinherent action of Son and Spirit is what Balthasar terms 'the indivisibility in the sphere of revelation of theory and praxis':[8] 'orthodoxy' and 'orthopraxy'. A controverted theme in modern Catholic theology where it threatens to dislodge divine revelation from its primacy in the construction of Christian discourse, Balthasar finds a neat way of doing justice to both dimensions: right faith and right action. He begins from two deceptively simply observations, one (periphrastically) Johannine, the other of his own devising. First, the Son, looking to the Father,

---

5 *In Joannem* 11, 11, = *Patrologia Graeca*, 74, 560–1
6 See J. Ratzinger, 'Der Heilige Geist als *communio*: Zum Verhältnis von Pneumatologie und Spiritualität bei Augustinus', in C. Heitmann and H. Mühlen (eds), *Erfahrung und Theologie des Heiligen Geistes* (Hamburg 1974), pp. 223–38.
7 References to Thomas' Commentary on the Books of the Sentences of Peter Lombard, II. dist. 26, 1, 4 and 27, 1, 5, ad iii.
8 *TL* III, p. 175.

works according to him. Second, the Father, sending Son and Spirit makes both act in his gaze.

What Balthasar will attempt, then, is a Trinitarian resolution of the question of the theory and practice relationship, and he will do so (I might add) in a way that helpfully situates that wider and less technical preoccupation of many late twentieth- (or early twenty-first)-century Christians, 'experience'.

In effect, Balthasar's 'solution' is to grant priority to orthopraxy *insofar it is the divine praxis that we are speaking of.* As he writes:

> the Spirit directs our gaze to the Son inasmuch as he, the Son, lives in the sheer deed of revealing the Father. He opens our eyes to a primary *theoria* whose content is the praxis of the Son in living, dying and returning to the Father. This 'theoria' is only possible thanks to the 'eye-salve' (Apocalypse 3.18) of faith which has been given to us. Through that faith – as was shown in *Herrlichkeit* – we come to see the truth of Christ consisting as that does in his 'adequate translation' of the Father (compare *Theologik* II) and in the Trinitarian life he lives in a human existence.

Duly pondered, this passage makes clear that no human praxis could be divinely *orthos* (right) unless it began with a view (theory) of this truth. By the same token, however, like the eye-salve of which the Lord spoke to the church at Laodicea faith must so be acquired that we apply it in our own action (praxis) – notwithstanding the fact that it is itself pure gift. Contemplation of the Son must be lived out as the 'unity of a gift and a decision', by a 'primary inclusion of deed in theory' [*eine primäre Einborgenheit von Tat in Theoria*].[9]

But if the Spirit is not only Interpreter of the Son's truth but our Introducer into his life, we cannot stop there. He cannot explain to us the action of the Son as the 'opening of the space of love between Father and Son', without introducing us into that space where one loves not with words only but in 'deed and truth' (1 John 3.18). Christian theory, because it entails – in the words of the Saviour to prospective disciples in the Fourth Gospel – 'coming and seeing' Jesus (cf. John 1.39), arrives at true vision only by

> an immediate co-living, co-dying, co-rising by means of which entry into the Son's exposition space (*Auslegungsraum*) is for the first time guaranteed.[10]

And here the Spirit acts as no outsider. It is he, after all, who is (on the view Balthasar has earlier established) the author of the Incarnation, and the inspirer of the Son's continued exposition of the Father. In this sense, the first to go along with Christ in the way that Johannine interpretation implies is the Holy Spirit himself. It is with the Spirit that disciples who had persevered in Jesus' trials to the end will give their witness (John 15.27).

9 Ibid.
10 *TL* III, p. 176.

So theory must go to the bitter (yet glorious) end by practice if it is really to share in the theological truth of the Son. The Spirit accompanied the Son right to the last consequences of the Incarnation in the death on the Tree where the ultimate in Incarnation becomes the ultimate in spiritualisation (penetration by the Spirit). Breathing out the Spirit, Jesus becomes the Spirit's Lord such that he can breathe him forth onto his own (John 20.22). The perfect obedience to the Father consummated on the Cross justifies the subsequent words of Paul to the Church in Corinth 'the Lord is the Spirit', inasmuch as the Holy Ghost can now be called the 'Spirit of the Lord' (2 Corinthians 3.17), the Spirit, that is, of Jesus. On that basis Balthasar feels able to formulate a law of Christian living verified in the saints and in the experience of Christian prayer: pneumaticisation increases in direct relation to incarnation.

Experience is a 'much abused word', remarks Balthasar who has already devoted much effort in the first volume of the theological aesthetics to save it from the perils both of Scylla (modernism) and Charybdis (dogmatism). It serves Balthasar's turn that the German word for experience, *Erfahren*, can be given an etymology which suggests a learning through wayfaring – which, where Christian experience is concerned, must entail receiving the *exposition* the Spirit gives and the *introduction* to the Trinitarian reality he provides as he propels believers along the way of Christ. Christian theory, meditation, contemplation, explore the inexhaustible depths to the Gospel events – as Ignatius' *Exercises* exemplify, but behind them, says Balthasar, conscious of the *Exercises'* mediaeval and patristic roots, lie a thousand years of – precisely – experience.

3. The third issue (after differing soteriological schemata and the theory-praxis question) which Balthasar hopes to illuminate by reflection on the Dyad in the Triad is the matter of Christianity's historical concreteness yet claims to universal validity. No doubt because it is in the twentieth century (and has been since the eighteenth) the chief challenge to the gospel's credibility, it is a topic to which Balthasar found himself returning time and again. We encounter it in *A Theology of History* (German original 1959), *Man in History* (German original 1963), *In the Fullness of Faith* (German original 1975), *New Elucidations* (German original 1979) and now in *Geist der Wahrheit*, as late as 1983. After a quarter century of reflection Balthasar offers us his last thoughts on the issue, summed up in the words

> How can an historical person claim universal validity? ...
> This dilemma is only soluble Trinitarianly, and to be more precise pneumatologically. The Father works not with one hand alone, but with two.[11]

Since Balthasar interprets the Synoptic formula 'But I say to you' as eschatological, he has no difficulty in establishing that, even in the days of his flesh, Jesus did in fact put forward a boundless claim to enjoy authority. All other missions (of a prophetic sort) are

11 *TL* III, p. 180.

included and transcended in his. It is as Bearer of the Spirit that the
Saviour demands general allegiance to his words, posits decisiveness
for his actions – and this is true above all of that 'action' that is his
Passion, where he takes upon himself the sin of the world and effects
universal reconciliation with God. Anticipating the consequence of
his death in the institution of the Mass he declares his body to be at
the disposition of the multitude (thus the Synoptic Last Supper
accounts) and indispensable for them (the Discourse on the Bread of
Life in John).

Still, it remains the case that without the Spirit of Easter and
Pentecost the universality already hiddenly enclosed in the concrete
form of Jesus' earthly life and death could not be rendered effective.
At the same time it is not a mere question of one divine mission
(the Spirit's) succeeding another (the Son's). Enough has now been
said about the Spirit's role from Incarnation to Cross to demonstrate
his engagement in the time of the Son, while the Son is hardly
passively present in the time of the Spirit (compare the promises to
be with the disciples embedded in the text of the Great Missionary
Command in Matthew). What is specific to the Spirit, however,
is his task of drawing out the 'treasures' hidden in Christ, and to
do so with the freedom and power which is his. In a major statement
of his position on the 'development of doctrine' notion, Balthasar
writes:

> If the revelation of Christ is 'closed with the death of the last
> apostle' as historic witness, the revelation of the Spirit is never
> closed. And if the Spirit never holds back anything from any
> generation but always holds open the entire treasury of truth
> – of the exposition of the divine love in Christ – he yet remains
> free to throw ever new lights on this totality and precisely on
> its innermost centre, with the result that not only does the
> whole as such bear the character of something novel, but it
> receives that character in ever new ways thanks to these ever
> new illuminations.[12]

Balthasar's tendency is to argue that for the glorified Son made
man to 'reign' is primarily for him to 'let happen' all that is proper
to the Spirit. And yet that does not exclude the active co-working
of both, as the example of the Holy Eucharist shows. There, the
Saviour's bodily presence is made available wherever the Mass
is celebrated – thanks to the twofold economy of the Word at the
Institution narrative, the Spirit at the epiclesis: two coinvolving
moments of consecration. More fundamentally, the universalising
of the work of Jesus by the Spirit is not to be misrepresented as
something 'external' to the action of the Son

> As Spirit of the Father it is always he who transmits the Father's
> will to the Son; as Spirit of the Son he has exercised the latter in
> the practice of obedience as the 'Servant of the Lord'. So the

---

12 *TL* III, p. 182.

universality that he demonstrates as the Paraclete is of course his own, or, better, that of the Trinity. The fact that he carries out this work by way of mission and therefore by way of service does not contradict this affirmation.[13]

Three conclusions follow from this intercalation of Son and Spirit as the Father's two hands: two of them rather particular, but the third furnishing a vantage point for an overview of the entire Balthasarian trilogy of aesthetics, dramatics, logic. First, the further the reign of the Son extends over the creation, the more ample the realm of the Spirit likewise. The early Apologists spoke of seeds of the Logos beyond the sacramental life of the Church; Balthasar goes one better in speaking of 'seeds of the Spirit' (*spermata pneumatika*) – something that accounts for the invisible aggregation to the Church of the unbaptised (by 'baptism of desire') and the efficacy of 'spiritual communion' for those who cannot receive the Eucharistic sacrament (or who for well-founded reasons of a regime of reception, prefer not to do so).[14] Secondly, if in the theological dramatics Balthasar has argued that an individual becomes a person (that is, one with a rôle – persona – in the drama of salvation) only through receiving a mission related to that of the Son, he can now take a further step by ascribing such dramatic personality, in the context of theological logic, to the gift of the Holy Spirit. (A corollary is that no putative 'charism' which fails to lead to the Son can be authentically pneumatic.) But that third and most important inference Balthasar draws from his final reflections on the Dyad in the Triad opens before our eyes a prospect as wide as the trilogy itself.

In the theological aesthetics, 'seeing the form' was itself a dyadic activity – the gracious product of the interaction of the missions of Son and Spirit. There, Balthasar showed how in the perfect integrity of Christ's form – the pattern of his being – the incarnate Son made himself worthy of belief on earth. But he also described how the believer needs the Holy Spirit to enhance his vision, with a view to seeing that form in its complex unity and with all its attractive power. In the theological dramatics – a work more Pauline than Johannine – it became clear for the first time why the rupturing of the form on the gibbet of Golgotha could none the less be the centre of that form in its divine beauty. Without his destiny as the Atoner, which the dramatics pointed up, the form of Christ would lose its significance, for his pertinence to us as our Risen Saviour can only be scanned from the standpoint of his Passion, death and Descent into Hell. It is because the Spirit mediates the concentrated meaning of the form of the Son from this midpoint that the trilogy's final segment – the theological logic – can present the form of Christ as truth. In other words, it is when the *beauty* of Christ yields up its content in terms of *goodness* and we see

---

13 *TL* III, p. 184.
14 Naturally, that is without prejudice to the intrinsic relation of spiritual communion to sacramental which is always in the Son. See H. R. Schlette, *Die Lehre von der geistlichen Communion bei Bonaventura, Albert dem Grossen und Thomas von Aquin* (Munich 1959); *idem, Kommunikation und Sakrament: Theologische Deutung der geistlichen Kommunion, = Quaestiones disputatae* 8 (Freiburg 1960).

what is as stake – the 'historical and cosmic' struggle of God in his infinite Freedom for the re-making of man in his finite liberty – that we can establish the co-extensiveness of Christ's form with *truth*, with (that is) the full range of reality in its infinite and finite dimensions.

Such a synthetic statement suggests, perhaps, Balthasar's awareness that, in the writing of the trilogy, he was by now within sight of journey's end. One large topic still awaited him – the relation of the Spirit and the Church whom the Johannine Christ presents as co-witnesses to himself (see John 15.26–7: 'he will bear witness to me; and you also are witnesses'). But before then there are one or two things to tidy away. The first is that stumbling block to the unity of Catholics and Orthodox in a single Church, the *Filioque*.

The Filioque

Balthasar's unrepentant Filioquism has already been mentioned. He was by no means one of those eirenic Catholic figures who in the latter part of the twentieth century sought ways to soften the dividing force of the (as is sometimes said, peculiarly Latin) claim that the Spirit issues eternally not from the Father alone but from the Son also.[15]

At first sight, his enthusiasm for the Filioque doctrine is surprising. The Irenaean image of 'the Father's two hands' which means so much to him might well be thought to lend itself far more readily to a Monopatrist account of the interrelation of the Son's generation with the Spirit's procession. And would not Balthasar's idea that, in the economic Trinity, the rôles of Son and Spirit undergo an 'inversion' between the moments of the Annunciation and the Glorification of Jesus be easier to defend in that same anti-Filioquist context? As we shall see, he wants so to present the Filioque that it allows for a reciprocal 'conditioning' (my term) of Son and Spirit – an emphasis to which the idea of Trinitarian inversion has surely led him. But by dint of that very concern for the mutuality of the last two divine Persons, he cannot accept a Monopatrist account of their origin which in emphasising the independence of their origination from the Father disables us from speaking of Trinitarian existence as *love*.

After a brief and unremarkable historical prelude, Balthasar plays for us a sonata with four movements. First of all, he shows how each 'side' (Monopatrist, Filioquist) mirrors the other in the way that it makes (illegitimate) inferences from the economic Trinity to the immanent. If the Latins go too fast in supposing that the temporal sending of the Spirit by the risen Christ implies his eternal spiration by the Word, the Greeks mimic this mistake when they point to the theophany at the Jordan as the economic expression of the absolute truth that, in the Godhead, the Spirit, proceeding from the Father alone, 'rests' on the Son (a formulation found in some patristic, and more middle Byzantine, authors). Balthasar simply

---

15 For an account at once historical and theological, see A. Nichols, *Rome and the Eastern Churches: A Study in Schism* (Edinburgh 1992), pp. 188–229. For a spirited defence of the claim that before 431 the Eastern tradition was as Filioquist as the Western, see A. Patfoort, 'Le Filioque avant le concile d'Ephèse', *Sedes Sapientiae* 69 (1999), pp. 35–47.

does not accept, as it stands, the axiom, associated in modern theology with Karl Rahner, that 'the economic Trinity *is* the absolute Trinity', because the obedience required of the incarnate Son in his mission has implications that disrupt that smooth flow of thought. The 'Trinitarian inversion' concept is not introduced into Balthasar's theology as a device for making sense of the gospel narrative against a background of un-thinking Filioquism. It is introduced there so as to show the momentous difference the mission of the Son to a world not only finite but fallen makes *even for the Trinity itself* in the unfolding of salvation. What in a less innovative Latin theology would be called the relations of communion between the persons, following as these relations do from their relations of origin, allow – according to Balthasar – a far ampler space for *modulations* that too wooden a reading of God's changelessness would let us think.

Secondly, Balthasar does not feel that philology alone, as some have suggested, can get us out of this impasse.[16] Simply distinguishing between two Greek verbs, *ekporeuomai* and *prochorein*, and arguing that, with its more general sense and lack of any specifying causal emphasis, only the latter corresponds to what the Latins call the Spirit's *procedere* (where-upon the problem of the Filioque disappears) is too convenient to be plausible – and in any case suffers shipwreck on the rock of what exegesis has to tell us about the key text (purely *economic*) of John 15.27, where the 'paradigmatic' use of *ekporeuomai* is said to occur. At the genesis of the debate lie not words alone, but what Balthasar terms two 'biunities', themselves, he thinks, insufficiently co-ordinated, on the Eastern side.

These 'biunities' are: on the one hand, the Irenaean 'mutual' priority and compenetration of Son and Spirit in the 'two hands' metaphor, and, on the other, the Nicene affirmation of unity of Essence between Father and Son.[17] When these two biunities are compared it springs to the eye that an integration of the Father's relation with the Spirit is lacking. While this is notionally achieved by the confession of the ecumenical Creed of Constantinople I that both are 'adored', only some version of Athanasius' fuller affirmation that the Spirit is conjoined with the Father as the Father with the Son can really secure the Spirit's *homoousion* – his share in the consubstantial Trinity.[18] From here it is but a short step to the assertion that the Spirit proceeds from the Father passing in some sense – yet to be determined – by the Son (without whom the Father would not be Father). That 'in some sense' could be interpreted minimally – in which case one would say that the Spirit comes from the Father as Father of the Son, but one might also determine it maximally – in which case one would maintain that in the Spirit's procession the Son truly collaborates with the Father. (An intermediate position would have the Spirit receive *something* from the Son, falling short of his mode of existence as such.)

Before explaining (in a fourth move) the grounds of his preference (with the Catholic Church!) for the 'maximal' interpretation, Balthasar pauses to (thirdly) remove a possible misunderstanding. It is a crude solecism in historical theology for Westerners to argue that the concern of Greek

16 Contrast J.–M. Garrigues, *L'Esprit qui dit 'Père' et le problème du Filioque* (Paris 1981).
17 The Athanasius reference is to *Epistola* II *ad Serapionem* 1 (*Patrologia Graeca* 26, 608A).
18 *TL* III, p. 194.

Christians with the Father's 'monarchy' – his being the fount of the Son and Spirit alike – is but a reflection of philosophical Hellenism and its fascination with the Monad, the One. (We can note, however, that Balthasar has himself said just this of Monopatrism!) And the same cap fits when Easterners accuse Latin Christians like Augustine and his followers of 'essentialism' in Trinitarian theology, for how could any theologian who takes Scripture seriously *not* begin from the one God prior to reflecting on the internal riches – triune riches – to be found within this unity?

Various expressions of eirenicism notwithstanding, Balthasar's final move is decisively in favour of the Latin tradition. That the Spirit proceeds from Father and Son as the love that unifies these two is an indispensable credal conclusion from the New Testament record. 'That the Spirit is at the same time content and fruit of the love eternal [of Father and Son] is an idea of which the New Testament is full.'[19] That the most Eastern of Byzantine theologians Gregory Palamas should have gravitated to this solution (the Spirit as expression of the common love) while at the same time (inconsistently) maintaining the common later Byzantine rejection of Filioquism makes Balthasar suspect that to this conclusion all evangelically-minded theologians will, *ceteris paribus*, finally be drawn.

Words for the Spirit

One last task remains before those (lexically) Hegelianising expositions of 'subjective' and 'objective' Spirit and Church, Spirit and world, can be undertaken, and that is an enquiry into three keywords for the Spirit's mission in Bible and Tradition: Gift, Freedom and Witness. Meditation on these three titles will help Balthasar to grasp the distinctive contribution of the Holy Spirit to that biunitarian mission received from the Father – and so position him aright for an investigation of the Spirit's role *vis-à-vis* Church and world. In the East, he points out, the great pneumatological treatises of the Fathers take as their aim a demonstration of the Spirit's Godhead, not the displaying of his hypostatic properties (*idiotētes*). In the West, Augustine's insistence that the Word's generation is achieved by the Father as 'knowledge with love' [*cum amore notitia*] entails that the Word enters the world as Revealer of the Father on a mission already filled with love – and so where then is the need for the Holy Spirit? Reflecting on what are perhaps the three words (or word clusters) most commonly linked to the Spirit in Scripture should enable him to fill some gaps in patristic Pneumatology as well as preparing him for an application of the Truth of the Spirit to analysis of the Church and, beyond the Church, the 'world'.

We know already that Balthasar prefers to call the Holy Spirit *Donum Doni*: the Giving of a Gift, the Gift that is the Son. He reminds us that true gifts are not commercial transactions: in making them, 'he who gives wants to give himself in a transparent symbol'.[20] In all love there must be a separation (*Trennung*) of giver and gift if the giver is really to give himself *away* in the gift, thus – paradoxically – becoming present by means of it. If

19 *TL* III, p. 199.
20 *TL* III, p. 207.

the Father–Son relation is dimly shadowed forth in that analysis, we must say of *this* Gift (the divine Word) that it receives and transmits all its Giver is, placing itself unreservedly at the service of his all-bestowing, in the sovereign freedom of its own divine origin. The richness of the personal love of Father and Son is intimately bound up with the poverty of their self-renunciation in each other's favour. Writes Balthasar in a gracious Latin pun, 'the *bonum* of the communion of love is, for the lovers, *donum*'.[21] Both Persons are given in that communion – by a gift that is neither their sum total nor simply the identity that results from their love but (and here is where the Spirit enters the picture) something inconceivably *more*. The sheer exuberance of this 'more' is the ultimate face of the Godhead, its final *prosōpon*, the third Person, the Spirit. It is from this angle that the nature of the Holy Spirit's gift-character becomes plain – and with it the justification for taking the word 'gift' (despite its appropriateness for the Son) as a pneumatological *Kennwort* or tell-tale term. The Spirit is the 'groundlessness' of the inner-divine Love in personal form, its quality as sheer gift from Father to Son, Son to Father, in a hypostatic reality. When the aboriginal self-renunciation of the Father makes itself known in the self-emptying of the Son as Jesus, it is necessarily accompanied by the 'absolute Gift', the 'God who has become simply gift', the Holy Spirit.[22] By the same token, in the pre-Christian dispensation, when the Word is not yet poured out, neither is the Spirit bestowed in this heightened sense as gift – even if in judges, prophets and the poor of the Lord the Spirit of promise was already operative. More far-reaching and more intimate is the Giving of the Gift that follows on Incarnation and Atonement. Here belong the teachings of Catholic divinity on Uncreated grace and the (as Balthasar thinks, poorly named) 'created grace' – the divine indwelling and that effect of the indwelling upon us which lies beyond created categories, whether 'physical-ontic' in the language of substance and accident, or 'personal' in the language of divine I and human thou, for in it the 'otherness of the God-creature relation is "super-formed" (*Überformt*) by the otherness of Father and Son in the Spirit and hidden there, but not destroyed'.[23]

What about the name 'Liberty' or 'Freedom'? Balthasar finds that the unpredictability of the way the Spirit announces and interprets the incarnate Son – no law or prognosis can capture it – indicates the divine origin of his freedom. The Father and the Son share liberty too, of course, yet there is an altogether special affinity of the Spirit with freedom – thanks to his relations of origin with them. That is because, in the Pneumatology inherited from the theological dramatics, the Spirit is spirated in 'surprise' (*Überraschung*), as Father and Son discover that divinely personal 'more' (and its fruitfulness) unfolding from their love even in the moment of its greatest selflessness. And what – or rather *who* – could better express the liberty of love than that (or rather *him*)? It is in perfect liberty that the

21 *TL* III, p. 208.
22 *TL* III, p. 210.
23 *TL* III, p. 216. Pp. 213–17 here offer an excellent brief survey of how Balthasar understood the principal terms used by Catholic theologians in the theology of grace.

Spirit will witness (the third and last of Balthasar's *Kennworte*) to the truth of the Word.

Though that 'exposition' will only start with Jesus' cry *Consummatum est!*, the divine plan which it serves is already stamped and sealed with the spiration of the Spirit in God. In the Holy Spirit, the design foreknown from everlasting by the Father is entertained at the level of the highest possible representation and ripest realisation of the love which the Trinity is. This for Balthasar is the deepest reason why we take the Spirit (and not the Son, or the Father) to be the actualiser of the mysteries of salvation in the stewardship of the Church.

Such a divinely tremendous wind of freedom – does it not blow mere human autonomy away? Here Balthasar can hardly avoid touching on the issue of God's grace and *human* freedom. The grace of the Spirit liberates the human being into due possession of his own freedom of choice, giving him the ability to opt for God not constraining him so to do – as the Jansenist divines of the seventeenth and eighteenth centuries caricatured Augustine as saying. (The 'classic' Augustine, adds Balthasar carefully, for there are certain 'harshnesses' in the North African doctor's last writings.) All this has been sufficiently described in *Theodramatik*, though here, in the theological logic, Balthasar stresses the 'Greek' side of Augustine's thought – how grace not only frees the will from negative constraints but also offers it positive suasions, the Spirit giving to men and women 'sweetness in consenting to and believing the truth',[24] as he enlightens the mind and stirs up the will.

But who won for us this spacious delight? The immolated Lamb, on whom 'all the freedom of creation is founded',[25] thus warranting in an extraordinary fashion the insights of philosophers into the near relatedness of love and death.

There remains the word 'Witness'. The salvific function of the Paraclete to be the Son's decisive witness – and therewith, and this is sometimes forgotten, that of the Father – cannot be separated from his inner-Trinitarian origin.

> As the innermost conflagration of the love of Father and Son, he is Love's absolute knowledge from within. Yet as the product or fruit of that love he is – as Love – at the same time the objective Witness that this love eternally takes place . . . And inasmuch as the Spirit is both of these at the same time, he can count as the eternal enkindler of the divine love which, precisely because the lovers ever recognise the fruit that lies before them, can never be exhausted in the way a love purely among human beings is always exposed to such exhaustion.[26]

This passage – with its re-affirmation that the Spirit is both the love of Father and Son become Person and the fruit of that love – will open the way to the theology of the Spirit in the Church as at once 'subjective' and

24 Cited at *TL* III, p. 221.
25 *TL* III, p. 223.
26 *TL* III, p. 224.

'objective' Spirit that is going to occupy most of the final pages of *Theologik* III.

First, though, one thing must be made clear. When we broach the topic of the Church – the Spirit's homeland in this world – the 'Truth of the Spirit' will not be dispensing with the 'Truth of the Word'. The mutual love of Father and Son takes the economic form of the Incarnation of the Word. The Spirit's witness must be approached, accordingly, in those terms above all.

> By this you know the Spirit of God: every spirit which confesses that Jesus Christ has come in the flesh is of God, and every spirit which does not confess Jesus is not of God.
>
> (1 John 4.3)

Were this not the case, the Spirit would fall into internal contradiction: for he is one reality with the testimony the Father gives in favour of his Son. From this Balthasar draws the conclusion that the witness of the Holy Ghost is always 'incarnatory' (*inkarnatorisch*). 'All disincarnatory, idealistic spiritualisation is anti-Christian.'[27] That claim is highly relevant to a Church that is not only organism but also institution.

Of course, the work of the Holy Spirit in realising the Incarnation brings about the objective humanity in flesh and blood of the divine Son. Yet the flesh of the Incarnate One is pervaded (compare the Transfiguration, compare the Resurrection appearances) with the Spirit who never discarnalises the Word. A Church that was only exclusively subjective–spiritual and not at all objective–corporeal *could not be, therefore, the Spirit-borne presence of Jesus Christ*. Moreover, since the Spirit is the fruit of the love of Father and Son as well as being that love itself, what he constructs, on the basis of dominical foundation, in the Church institution is as much the expression of divine love as is the subjective sanctity which the pattern of life of the Church makes possible. 'He will testify to me; and you shall be my witnesses' (John 15.26b–7a): these are now the 'keywords' for what follows.

---

27 *TL* III, p. 227.

23

◦❧◦

The Spirit and the Church:
Logical Preliminaries

Introduction

Poured out into the world through the Sacrifice of Christ, the Spirit's fruits are never found save in some connexion to the obedience of the Cross, for this is the Spirit *of the Father and the Son* about whom we are speaking. His gifts to the Church-body of Christ – and this reflects more his own hypostatic particularity – are scattered in glorious profusion as and how he wills, yet not anarchically, since he is 'in' as well as 'above' the order of the Church.[1]

We must remind ourselves of the fundamental bipolarity in Balthasar's Pneumatology. First the Spirit is the transmitter of the inner divine relationship of Father and Son – what Balthasar calls, in a calculatedly ironic use of Hegelian language, 'subjective Spirit'. For this mode of the Spirit's gifts he would look to the Holy Ghost's activity in the inner lives, the personal holiness, of Christians, and notably in prayer, in pardon of others, in mystical and charismatic gifts and, above all, in what he terms 'testimony of life', pneumatic effusiveness.

Secondly, the Spirit is the distinct fruit of the interrelation of Father and Son – and thus, continuing the comparison with Hegel's thought, 'objective Spirit', the Spirit who inspires such outer forms and insti-tutional mediations of the saving revelation as Tradition, Scripture, Church office, preaching, the Liturgy and sacraments, and even canon law and theology, all of which partake to various degrees and in differ-ing ways in the Spirit's holiness. Pneumatic effusiveness does not mean sheer confusion.

Just as for Hegel we should never 'play off' subjective and objective *Geist* in personal and social life, for each needs the other in order to be itself, so too here. In Christian living, subjective and objective Holy Spirit – the realm of Christian interiority and that of the corporate Church covenanted by Christ, have absolute need of each other if they are to fulfil their allotted tasks in the divine scheme.

---

1 Cf. *TL* III, p. 229.

Church and World

Are we not, however, going too fast in this concentration on the Church? Surely, the Scriptures speak of the divine plan to save not the Church but the *world*! Indeed, and Balthasar pauses on the threshold of his pneumatic ecclesiology to take stock of the implications of that. To the universality of the Son's promise to draw all to himself (John 12.32) there corresponds at Pentecost a second universality: that whereby the Spirit is to be poured out on all flesh (Acts 2.17). However, the matter is not so simply disposed of. For the Letter to the Ephesians

> the unity of the cosmic dominion of Christ is communicated via the unity of the Church, which itself is owed to the cosmos-encompassing crucified body of Christ.[2]

The cosmic totality bears an intrinsic reference, in the plan of salvation, to the Church-body of Christ. There is a pneumatological reflection of this: the Spirit, when he gives new birth from above to whomsoever he will, is not bound by the baptismal sacrament of the Church, and yet what he gives to those outside the Church is precisely the grace found in Baptism. In other words, the 'diastasis' – the differentiating separation – of Church and/or world is preveniently overcome in Christ and his Holy Spirit. Balthasar finds signs of the Catholic Church's 'inchoatively cosmic' rôle in both the non-Catholic Christian communities which, though sadly outside her visible unity, have sprung up on the basis of the gospel she carries (and the baptismal sacrament), and also in the irradiation of aspects of her message in other religions and world-views and as a leaven working in the lump of culture at large.

Essentially, as Balthasar sees it, the life of the Church is exercised in a twofold movement. First, the Church must go out to the nations in the spirit of the Great Missionary Command at the end of Matthew's Gospel (28.19–20) in proclamation and teaching adapted to the genius of each. But secondly, so as to guard the truth in its 'pleromatic' unity (its fullness), she must 'baptise' those already existing elements in the cultures beyond her that are *either* congruent with the gospel *or* historically derivative from it yet estranged by the play of historical factors from her own life. (The recognition of 'human rights' is perhaps the most obvious example of the latter.)

The two aspects together constitute a ticklish business. 'Inculturation' presents 'wellnigh insoluble questions', while trying to baptise gospel-friendly cultural features will arouse resistance, since these 'seeds of the Spirit' have been assimilated into human totalities that define themselves as other than what is Catholicly Christian. After all, Christ's demands, however much they were a blessed continuation of the plan of creation, brought about his death, and persecution is the predicted lot of disciples – so trouble on the way is to be expected. Still, Paul's letter to the Church at Philippi shows what can and should be done: the range of virtues the apostle commends to his converts is a good example of the twofold

2 *TL* III, p. 235.

imperative to 'transpose whatever is present of the natural law onto a Christian level' and 'render explicit what was implicitly Christian outside the Church'.[3] Balthasar tries to move steadily across a tightrope. On the one hand, the human soul is abidingly situated between the corporeal and the supernaturally spiritual: that is the message of the tripartite anthropology of body, soul and spirit found in a galaxy of Christian authors from the sub-apostolic period to the modern age.[4] On the other hand, that permanent, universal possibility of choosing for (and against!) the God of salvation should not, Balthasar thinks, actively be taught by the Church. It should remain in the background as goad and encouragement. The reason for such discretion is plain: nothing should be done which plays down the difference between the concrete form of the saving revelation – in Jesus Christ as revealer of the Father and the Spirit as the disclosure of their mutual love – and the way seeds of the Spirit may be sown in the moral and religious ideas and ideologies of non-Christians. There is a reflection of all of this in how to do Christology with pagans. One can *begin*, in the spirit of Karl Rahner, with a 'Christology from below' and indeed any cosmological, ethical or existential question that raises the issue of transcendence. But sooner or later space must be made for a 'Christology from above' or there will be no room for the act of faith, the moment of conversion.[5]

On the basis of these principles, Balthasar offers some advice to missionaries engaged in dialogue. They should seek partners of preference among unbelievers who have a sense of theonomous rather than humanly autonomous liberty. They should seek out, in other words, those who consider the power of human decision making to be itself underpinned by an absolute freedom and intended to co-exist harmoniously with such (historically, Stoicism makes a good example). Pneumatologically, there may be hope of success in establishing common ground even where Christologically there is little. In the religions native to Southern Asia ideas of incarnation and particularity are far removed from those of Scripture. Yet ethically there may be consonances between notions of selflessness in, say, Buddhism and Christianity, even though the former knows nothing Christologically of the (literal!) selflessness of the Trinitarian life it is human destiny to image. Again, missionaries should shun the temptation to place on the periphery the pre-history of the gospel in Israel. A current instance, not mentioned by Balthasar, is to treat the Hindu culture as an alternative *praeparatio evangelica* to that of Israel for people south of the Himalayas. He considers this will always issue in some form or other of deCatholicised nationalism of which the *Deutsche Christen* movement sponsored by Hitler is the ghastly exemplar. He seems to consider the social encyclicals of Pope John Paul II to be model cases of dialogue (as he would understand it), which rise up from a philosophical

3 *TL* III, p. 240.
4 H. de Lubac, 'Antropologia tripartita', in *idem, Mistica e Mistero cristiano* (Milan 1979), pp. 59–117. (This essay of de Lubac's was originally published in Italian.)
5 Balthasar cites the Gregorian Jesuit John McDermott as remarking of Rahner's thought in this respect, 'His Christologies from above and from below do not ultimately coalesce . . . his bifocular vision was incapable of attaining a true unity', 'The Christologies of Karl Rahner', *Gregorianum* 67 (1986), pp. 87–123; 297–327.

anthropology (in itself shareable with many) to a theo-logical and Christian crowning of the same. They leave in place thereby the, to Balthasar, all-important distinction between the peace of the world and the peace that is not as the world gives because it is of Christ alone. Liberation theologians, like theorists of a Christian society, do not, in his opinion, leave a sufficient latitude between these two. Unless they are exceedingly punctilious in practising the discernment of spirits they may find themselves not on the side of God but of human parties. The fascination for Balthasar of the German dramatist Reinhold Schneider lay precisely in the fact that his plays deal so often with the tragic incompatibility or at least tension between the holder of power (even one such impelled by the best of motives) and the powerless saint.[6]

Spirit of the Church and freedom

In the course of the threefold commentary the present author has essayed (*The Word Has Been Abroad* on the aesthetics; *No Bloodless Myth* on the dramatics; *Say It Is Pentecost* on the logic), the interrelation of the three parts of Balthasar's trilogy has been, by introductory statements at least, underlined. We recall that the dramatics lays out the content of the aesthetics, while the logic – as well as providing, in its first volume, a repertoire of root philosophical concepts for the other works – also constitutes, in its second and third parts, a reflection on the theological dramatics in the light of the theological aesthetics. Given that the dramatics explores the good which is the content of the beauty of form laid out in the theological aesthetics, what – this is the question of the theological logic – must truth actually be? The centrality of the dramatics in the overall scheme is unavoidable, and affects the dogmatic presentation of the closing volume of the logic not least in a way we must now register.

Prior to entering upon the substance of his pneumatic ecclesiology Balthasar turns to consider the question – a lively one in the context of the Lutheran-Catholic dialogue of the post-Conciliar decades – how justification, sanctification (foundational activities of the Spirit of grace) and *freedom* are interrelated. Clearly, an ecclesiology of the Spirit which arises as a reflexion on the study of the interplay of divine and human freedom in *Theodramatik* will have to say more than a little about the Holy Spirit as the Spirit, precisely, of freedom. Perhaps, as Balthasar explains, the justification motif is more strictly Christological, the sanctification theme more naturally pneumatological in its location among the theological tractates, but the intrinsic connexion of justification with sanctification and both with that 'Christian freedom' motif so important to the ecclesiology of the New Testament writers warrants his *démarche*.

6 See H. U. von Balthasar, *Tragedy under Grace: Reinhold Schneider on the Experience of the West* (Et San Fransisco 1997), and notably the posthumously published 'Preface to the New Edition' at p. 11: 'What most fascinated me in [Schneider's] work was the omnipresent drama of the encounter between two missions that are equally original and yet stand in a deadly mutual conflict: the mission of the one who is entrusted with the task of administering the earthly realm and the mission of the saint as the real symbol of the kingdom of God that descends into the world.'

Justification flows from the sacrifice of Christ carried out as that was 'by the movement and instinct of the Holy Spirit that is, by Christ's charity towards God and neighbour'.[7] Those are words of St Thomas on a text of the Letter to the Hebrews rarely used in the theology of the Atonement. But Balthasar's own comment on them is that, since the fount of justification is the action of Christ *pro nobis* – that refrain of the dramatics – and the *pro nobis* establishes the fullest co-humanity before God there can be, it follows that 'no personal justification is private'.[8] The liberating grace which pertains to redeemed man on the basis of the Son's self-offering by the Spirit takes away the narrowing constriction of original sin, alienating one from God and others as this did, and so bears a necessary relation to the covenant existence of that corporate divine community that is the Church. Justified by grace we are not only free from our egoistic drives and passions, we are also free for our mission in aid of that totality which is the Church of God. Indeed, Balthasar goes so far as to say that in Pauline theology freedom is identical with *disponibilité* in the service of the universal. Such *disponibilité is* faith: 'the letting be true of the divine freedom of love for us and in us'[9] in a way that is intimately interior, yes, but not indeterminate or formless, otherwise its connexion with our readiness for mission would be lost.

The highest case of created freedom needing uncreated freedom for its own liberation is sanctification, whose internal bonding with justification shows, for Balthasar, that the latter has a history and a goal. Only God is holy. No creature possesses 'substantial holiness'. Only the Spirit of holiness can 'anoint' finite spirit with the holiness of God. One can be 'fundamentally freed' and still get behind with one's task, the development of one's 'person' (inescapable as that is for Balthasar from one's mission) – and in that fashion behind, too, in participation in God's holiness. *Pace* the not always perspicuous meanderings of the Lutheran-Catholic accord on justification Balthasar did not live to see (1999: the accord, in four overlapping documents, is said to concern the foundations of the doctrine, but not the doctrine itself), the only sense the Swiss Catholic can give Luther's formula *simul justus et peccator* is that *fruits* of the Spirit can be lacking to one who is justified and in that manner sanctified. No Christian can say that he has as yet fully arrived: he may have been overtaken by grace; he has not yet taken over in his life all that grace means.

There is an exception to that, without which the people of the New Covenant would be as straightforwardly a pilgrim people as the people of the Old.

> In Mary the Church is 'spotless' (Ephesians 5.27) and so she must be, not only for the sake of the Incarnation but for that of the taking up of the Incarnate One into his 'body', which is the Church.[10]

To be in principle body of such a Head, bride of such a Bridegroom, the Church's response to grace must be 'utterly, utterly' at one point at least.

7 Thomas Aquinas, *In epistolam sancti Pauli ad Hebraeos*, 9, lect. 3.
8 *TL* III, p. 247.
9 *TL* III, p. 249.
10 *TL* III, p. 251.

The City of God

We have spoken above, echoing Balthasar, of the Church's 'totality' as a 'universality'. But for many people – most people – the Church is a highly particular entity. How can she claim, then, catholicity which means universality and so particularity's contrary, its contradiction?

Historically, various ways have been found to negotiate the particular/ universal relationship which draws the sting of that word 'contradiction'. There is, first the Hebraic vision, inherited by the Church, in which all peoples are to be blessed through their sharing in the covenant with Abraham – realised in principle in the community founded by Abraham's seed, Jesus Christ. Then again, early ecclesiastical writers like Tertullian and the author of the Letter to Diognetus, perhaps under a certain Stoic influence, see the Church as bearer of the universal claims of Christ which extend to the whole cosmos (Tertullian) or see Christians as forming the soul of the earthly city wherever the latter is found (the Writer to Diognetus). Thirdly, these may be combined as in the more complex theology of the Church in its relation to the human city (and the city of God insofar as this is to be distinguished from the Church) embodied in Augustine's *De civitate Dei*. Just because Augustine's project is more complex it can also be – and, Balthasar thinks, is – less integrated. The predestination of the elect (and the non-efficacious will to salvation of others) blurs the boundary between the earthly *polis* and the ecclesial city inasmuch as these cities represent the *civitas diaboli*, 'united' by cupidity, and the *civitas Dei*, home of true unity and peace, whose members are bonded by love. Though Augustine speaks of the 'Church from [the time of] Abel', the first just man, he does not fully work out the theme of the invisible aggregation to the Church of the just of all ages, leaving his book open to the dissonant interpretations of Catholic and Protestant readers with their respectively higher and lower ecclesiologies.

Perhaps the New Testament theologies can better serve our turn? For the Pauline letters (and notably Romans) the wild stock of the pagans is to be grafted onto the noble olive tree of Israel: thus the *Ecclesia ex Gentibus* and the *Ecclesia ex circumcisione* will grow together. That conception is mirrored in the symbolism of the heavenly, eschatological Church in the Johannine Apocalypse, where the worship of the twenty-four 'elders' embraces the twelve tribal heads of the Elder Covenant and the twelve apostolic leaders of the New.

In any case, Balthasar sees the Church's coming to be as a slow affair, beginning in Israel, its genesis intensifying as the forms of immanence of the Holy Spirit in salvation history become more focused and concrete. The Church was already in formation in the days of Jesus' flesh – where, as Balthasar's Spirit-Christology shows, the Spirit who will be the Church's soul was already intimately involved. Mary's motherhood, which was 'of the Holy Spirit' (Matthew 1.18), carried the Church *in potentia* in itself just as the incarnate Son, acting in the Holy Spirit, carried in himself as Head – once again, *potentially* – his entire Church-body. On the Cross, where Spirit, water and blood give concordant testimony to the death of the Saviour, the Church is born, with the *Mater dolorosa* as its personal centre, even though it is only at Pentecost, with the manifest descent of the Spirit, that this birth will be fulfilled or completed ('manifested' might be a better word) in a way that can be universally experienced. All Old Testament bestowals of the Spirit aimed ultimately at this.

Of course the Church has only entered inchoatively on this mission and its divine promises. At the end of the ages it is not so much that the Church will be dissolved into the new creation as that 'the redeemed creation will enter into her who *de jure* is always and so already universal and catholic'.[11] That affirmation is an index of how Balthasar sees the mystery of the Church as integrally constitutive of the supernaturally enhanced creation – indispensable, then, to a Christian ontology (the topic of the theological logic) even when its practitioners are thinking of the End of all.

Son and Spirit in the Church

Where Son and Spirit are concerned, it is vital, in a pneumatic ecclesiology, not to present the action of the Spirit in animating the Church in such a fashion that one eliminates the rôle of the glorified incarnate Son in ceaselessly constituting her. An anxiety on this score (together with doubts about the hyper-ecumenism manifest in a second edition) dissuaded Balthasar from making common cause with the Paderborn theologian Heribert Mühlen whose ecclesiological masterwork, *Una mystica Persona*,[12] he found otherwise attractive. For Mühlen, the 'Gross-Ich' of Old Testament corporate personality, where the individual finds his or her identity only through a relation with a central (and ultimately divine) person could not throw any directly Christological light on the Church of the New Testament – despite St Paul's talk of the 'body of Christ' – since Christians are not incorporated into the hypostatic union. The Spirit must mediate between Christ and the Church – and that is his *métier* since mediation is his eternal glory – as between Father and Son, Son and Father in the Holy Trinity. There is a danger here that the Christ as Lord of the Church could be seen as awaiting empowerment, merely, from the Spirit *vis-à-vis* his own Church-body, and to that extent be reduced to a *roi fainéant*.

Can Balthasar do better? The basic thesis is already in place: the Spirit is given the Church from the Father through the Son who assures her of his (the Son's) continuous presence by the bestowal of a Spirit who so much points back to the Son (and thereby to the Father) that his characteristic utterance in us is the Son's own fundamental cry, 'Abba, Father' (Romans 8.15). It will readily be seen that, in contradistinction to Mühlen's scheme, Son and Spirit are equally active in the Church, yet in mutually defining ways. 'Neither division, nor identity' is Balthasar's watchword here.

In 1 Corinthians (12.13) the apostle tells his converts that they were 'baptised by the Spirit . . . into one body' and have all 'been given to drink with one sole Spirit' – and Balthasar takes these words as a reflection of

11 *TL* III, p. 262.
12 H. Mühlen, *Una mystica Persona: Die Kirche als Mysterium der Identität des Heiligen Geistes in Christus und den Christen. Eine Person in vielen Personen* (Paderborn 1967²).

the Johannine image of the water of the Spirit which, in the Fourth Gospel,
believers are to lap up from Jesus' *koilia*, his 'heart' (but more literally
'belly', John 7.38) which Balthasar understands as his *corporeality*. Of course
our union with Christ, even Eucharistically, does not mean our taking up
into his physical bodiliness. And yet to judge by a variety of New
Testament texts there *is* a wonderful exchange between our kind of
bodiliness and his:

> That which the Crucified took from us in the body on the Cross, that
> he restores to us inasmuch as he offers to us his transfigured body.[13]

As Pope Pius XII's encyclical on Christ and the Church, *Mystici Corporis*,
insisted, on the Cross Christ offered with himself his mystical members –
and this explains why the 'contents for living' (*Lebensgehalte* – Balthasar
has in mind what Paul terms, in a word with a future, 'charisms') the
exalted Lord will transmit to his Church are all forms of his being given
away (his *Weggeschenktsein*). That the sacrifice of Jesus' life is the fountain
from which the life of the mystical body flows constitutes the deepest
reason why all authentic charisms – ways of life, tasks for living – in the
Church are ordered to the service of others, for the building up of that
body. And yet *charisms* (as distinct from the sacraments and institutions
dominically founded in the days of Jesus' flesh) have always been understood as bestowed by the Spirit. It follows that there is here no distance
between what the Son gives and what the Spirit gives.

The same conclusion imposes itself when we reflect on how the Son
dying on the Cross was the one who breathed out the Spirit, at once to the
Father (Luke 23.46) and to the world (John 19.30). On both counts the
Spirit is Spirit *of the Son*, as the Son returns the Spirit to the Father, his
mission accomplished, and gives him to the world to be henceforth in-
distinguishably Spirit of Father and Son and so the unifying bond for
the Church. Raised by the power of the Spirit (that shows the reality of
the Son's human death, for no man can take up again his life), the risen
Lord shows forth the Spirit as the fullest epiphany in the world of the
eternal Fatherly love and the means of exalting him as man to pneumatic
existence. From now on that 'inversion' of the order of Son and Spirit of
which Balthasar has made so much in his accounts of the Incarnation,
Baptism, public ministry, Passion, death and Resurrection of the Lord,
has no further sense.

Both arguments allow Balthasar to conclude that

> the mystery consists in the fact that in the gift of the Holy Spirit the
> risen Son gives himself as well, as the Son that he is – since one
> could equally say that, vice versa, in the Spirit as Gift the Giver is
> perfectly present.[14]

That for Balthasar demonstrated not only the inseparable co-working of
Son and Spirit in the time of the Church but the grounds for the Spirit's
disdain of anything that smacks of a going back on the bodiliness of the

13 *TL* III, p. 269.
14 *TL* III, p. 272.

Resurrection. And that in turn suggests to Balthasar that the Catholic Church – of all the confessions claiming the Christian name the most 'bodily', thanks to its reliance on such 'hard facts' as not only Scripture and Tradition but also the apostolic and especially the Petrine ministry – must be the true centre of Christendom's unity. The Church is the Church of the Spirit, granted. And yet the Spirit only expounds himself insofar as he explains himself as the reciprocal love of Father and Son in the Son's sending from the Father on the way of the Cross – with all that entails.

The Spirit is *both* the Spirit of Christ *and* his own hypostasis in God. The Spirit's freedom is not to be unsuitably diminished nor inappropriately inflated in relation to the Son's, nor is it to be placed on some parallel line to his.

That is not to deny the reality of a kind of hiatus between the Son's 'going away' from the disciples and the Spirit's coming to them. The Farewell Discourse at the Last Supper speaks clearly of this, and its point, for Balthasar, lies in the need for the universality latent (but only latent) in the particularity of Jesus' earthly existence to become (for the first time) really apparent. But it was hard. Balthasar speaks of this 'true and inexorable withdrawal' as, for the disciples, a spiritual death – an unutterably intense variant, as it were, on the French maxim, *Partir, c'est mourir un peu.* (Still, love of the Saviour should also – such is the complexity of human action and reaction – have allowed them to rejoice.) The Magdalene will not hold onto Jesus; he will pass from the sight of the disciples on the road to Emmaus; he will tell Thomas that they are blessed who believe though they have not seen. And all this is to encourage that radical renunciation, both of the too 'carnal' desires of the self and of Jesus as graspable, controllable, that is the precondition for the greatest gift of all – the Holy Spirit. It is only congruent that the fulfilment the Spirit gives should come after – and from – a mortal wound, since this was how it would be – and was – on the Cross. Deeper still, Balthasar's investigations into the foundation of theological logic in the Trinitarian life have shown that the disinterested love of Father and Son in the inner-Trinitarian *kenōsis* is the 'premise' (*die Voraussetzung*) for the coming forth of the 'absolute, non-kenotic Love-Spirit of God'.[15]

Balthasar will not accept that diremption by which Christ as Head of the Church is accorded the honour of founding her structure, but only the Spirit as Soul of the Church animates her life. That in the Alexandrian school Origen could call *Christ* the Church's soul and St Cyril treat Christ *and* the Spirit as executing this task conjointly ought to alert us. The 'structure' of the Church cannot be understood unless we see it 'in the unity of what the pre-Paschal Jesus has founded . . . and what as the Risen One he gives his Church in the Spirit'.[16] If that unity is to be grasped from a central point, that central point can only be the Sacrifice of the Lord's

15 *TL* III, p. 276. Balthasar appears to agree with the statement that the doctrine of kenosis is what we should count most essential to Christian identity, as made in T. Kolbush, 'Freiheit und Tod: Die Tradition der *mors mystica* und ihre Vollendung in Hegels Philosophie', *Theologische Quartalschrift* (1984), pp. 185–203.
16 *TL* III, p. 280.

death – where the pre-Easter and the Easter Lord intersect. Balthasar has already shown that the charisms flow from the Cross. It is common Catholic teaching that all the sacraments draw on the Cross. But the priestly ministry of the apostleship is perhaps the best example of what Balthasar means: instituted by the pre-Paschal Jesus, it is rendered an abiding charismatic service by the risen Lord. The Twelve, consecrated by Christ's High Priestly Prayer at the Supper Board, are set aside for sacerdotal duties on the foundation of his self-consecration on the Cross.[17] ('For their sake I consecrate myself, that they also may be consecrated in truth', John 17.19.) With such a source, the ministerial priesthood of the Church cannot just be an objective reality of grace; it must be subjectively appropriated in grace as well.

Here Balthasar reaches at last the celebrated 'objective'/'subjective' distinction in matters of the economy of the Spirit which will dominate the ecclesiological chapters of his logic.

---

17 Balthasar depends on André Feuillet's wonderful study of the foundations of the Catholic view of ministerial priesthood in the Johannine corpus: *Le Sacerdoce du Christ et de ses ministres* (Paris 1972).

24

❧❀❧

The Spirit and the Church:
Subjective and Objective

On distinguishing – but not separating

The indisputably Hegelian sound of Balthasar's distinction between the subjective and the objective presence of the Holy Spirit leads him to underline the strictly theological – and so, in itself, quite unphilosophical – provenance of the difference the distinction is meant to articulate. The root of the subjective–objective distinction for *this* Spirit is the twofold rôle of the Holy Ghost in the eternal Godhead: as the subjective 'love-movement' of Father and Son, and as that movement's objective product or fruit. Within the immanent Trinity, the Spirit unifies Father and Son as Love, but points to their distinction as Witness, carrying out both rôles self-identically.

In the economy, however, in its context of kenosis, when a human obedience will be integrated within the inner-divine *disponibilité* of Son for Father, though the Spirit is still sent from the Father, he comes from the Son only in the 'inverted' form of the Son's 'not doing his own will' – constant Johannine refrain. The pictures – the absolute, and the economic Trinity – look remarkably different, yet in fact the reality is just the same. A single love takes two forms only because divine and human natures can never be the same thing. Insofar as Jesus Christ is God he obeys the Father in the sheer Spirit–Love the Father sets before him; but as man this selfsame love takes the form of mandated obedience. Mission from the Father is the economic form of the Father's love for the Son; creaturely obedience is man's invitation to enter this love. These reflections – which draw on the Christological sections of the aesthetics, dramatics and logic – are meant to indicate that, notwithstanding the everlasting root of the distinction between objective and subjective Spirit in the immanent Trinity, that distinction will never amount, even in the economy, to an outright separation. (Balthasar avoids the hard outlines of the German synonym for 'separation', *Trennung*, by using the softer Greek word, *diastasis*.) Indeed, the tension between subjective and objective is often felt most acutely just at the point where it is closest to dissolution – as when the Church feels incumbent her the duty of giving testimony in martyrdom (objective) precisely in those whose love for Christ is most pure (subjective).

It is possible that Catholic Christians – at least since the Donatist crisis of patristic age North Africa – may overplay the objective side of things, insisting on the validity of the 'work performed' in the sacramental Church even by unworthy ministers of grace. Balthasar warns that such notions remain only 'limit concepts'.

> In the New Covenant there is no longer any official cult which is not at the same time personally coloured, and which does not lead into the personal *communio sanctorum* . . .[1]

The *opus operatum* ought always to be a heartfelt *opus operantis*: rite and right feeling belong together. He is far more concerned, though – and no doubt the tendency of post-Conciliar Catholicism on the ground to relativise everything redolent of 'official structures' (doctrinally, liturgically, pastorally) is his target here – that the 'objective' aspect of the Spirit's work can be quite unsuitably underplayed.

> In what is most objective in the Church the divine Subjectivity comes to expression, and not as something rather at the side, but as a norm of love that can never be overtaken by the subject – by the man of earth, man the striver, over whose head it is constantly suspended.[2]

And Balthasar explains that even when the Christian life is at its most subjectively intense, when the person on the road to God feels closest to him, the 'objectivity of absolute love' – embodied in Scripture, the sacraments, Tradition, the ministry – always transcends him or her. That has a very practical corollary: one should never be complacent about the experience of grace. However generously one has responded to the God who gives himself in the sacramental economy of the Church, there is always more to receive, and more to give.

The bi-unity of the Church

'The flesh is salvation's hinge', wrote Tertullian in a famous dictum. Interpreted pneumatologically that means: the true Holy Spirit always refers back to the Word who came *in the flesh* to save us. Once again, this allows Balthasar to privilege the objective holiness the Spirit brings. That holiness – expressed in the first instance[3] in the 'circumincession' of the Spirit-inspired Scripture, Spirit-formed Tradition, Spirit-assisted magisterium – lies always ahead of its subjective correlate. For its part, subjective holiness is only authentic when it aims at the goal which objective holiness holds out. The 'fellowship [better, communion, *koinōnia*] of the Holy Spirit', which Paul wishes his converts in 2 Corinthians 3.13, is primarily objective participation in that Spirit. Only secondarily does it refer to the inter-subjective community sense found among them (though this too is the Spirit's fruit). The primacy of the Spirit in the constructing

---

1 *TL* III, p. 284.
2 Ibid.
3 Balthasar adds parenthetically at this point the holy sacraments and the canons. Thus *TL* III, p. 286.

of the Church is that much clearer if objective holiness and subjective holiness are set in that order.

The difference between the two modes of the Spirit's presence and work, and yet the fine-tuned co-ordination between them, become apparent in those two archetypal representatives of the Church, our Lady and St Peter. Each presents the totality – but in her or his way. Balthasar draws on the ample researches of the Abbé René Laurentin – perhaps the most learned Mariologist of the twentieth century – in bolstering his proposal that, while the whole Church is both Marian and (in Peter) priestly, these two symbolic valencies hardly do more than greet each other and touch.[4] And the reason why the priestly Church (universally priestly in the faithful, ministerially so in the ordained) does not as such, in the literature, evoke the Marian Church has nothing to do with a fear that women would 'get above' themselves and seek the sacrament of Order! Rather, it has everything to do with the specific fittingness of these two symbolic wholes to express on the one hand the objective, on the other the subjective, holiness of the Church. So the two holinesses are certainly distinct. But they are also interrelated. The objective order of the sacramental life and ministry was only encharged to Peter's care after he had made the threefold avowal that he loved Jesus, and received the promise he would imitate Christ's Cross. The ministerial office – quintessence of objective holiness – moves toward its subjective correlate. Likewise, the supreme subjective holiness of the Mother of the Lord also bears a relation to objective holiness – and of a kind that is more foundational still. The perfect subjective holiness of the *Theotokos* is a condition for the very existence of Christ – and *a fortiori* of the Church, in the latter's entire subjective *and* objective order, and so of the objective holiness of sacraments and ministry. So much is this the case that Balthasar presents our Lady as filling in the lacunae of sacramental and ministerial acts, thus showing forth the identity of the Holy Spirit in his twofold aspect – subjective, objective – in the Church.

Less controversially innovatory is his proposal that the interplay of (objective) ministry and (subjective) charisms also represents the 'biunity' of the Church and, thereby, of the Spirit. Actually, Balthasar prefers to speak (and here the fluidity of language in the emergent ecclesiology of the New Testament Church serves his turn well) of charisms *simpliciter*, sorting these into ministerial (*ämtlich*) and non-hierarchical (*nichthierarchisch*) as he goes along. Though the ministries into which the original apostolate unfolds are *sui generis*, their holders are none the less portrayed with charismatic capacities – wisdom in teaching, the discernment of spirits, and the like. Balthasar underscores the varied abundance of the charismata mentioned in the New Testament listing – from something as easily identified as hospitality to something as elusive as 'believing' (evidently understood as a distinctive intensity of the basic Christian life). Taking *prophecy* – the declaration of what God desires now from his Church – as a foundational charism, Balthasar goes beyond the Pauline letters to make it include both authentic theology and mysticism (for, unusually, he sees the latter as always given for the general utility of the Church). Between what Friedrich von Hügel called the

4 R. Laurentin, *Marie, L'Eglise et le sacerdoce* (2 vols, Paris 1953).

'institutional' and 'mystical' elements in religion there can certainly run tensions: yet because both stem from the Holy Spirit – objectively, subjectively – 'they are bearable within the peace of the Church in the same Holy Ghost'.[5]

Objective Spirit

Under the heading of 'objective Spirit', Balthasar outlines the clear contours of the Catholic life: the interlocking threesome of Tradition, Scripture and apostolic office in which Catholic Christians locate spiritual authority; preaching and the Liturgy; the sacraments of the Church; the canons – rules for life together in the ecclesial body; and, last but not least, 'theology' – the Church's patrimony of thought. Though these are but witnesses and instruments of Christ and his Spirit in the Church they are needful if the individual is to enter into the fullness of the subjecthood of the divine Persons sent from the Father. Some words on each are clearly prescribed.

Tradition–Scripture–ministry

This threesome should lend itself to pneumatological analysis, for the Spirit is Lord of Tradition and Scripture, while the ministry is a pre-eminent form of the charismata – his distinctive gifts. Holy Tradition, in Balthasar's view, is essentially *die Selbstübergabe Gottes* – divine self-consigning.[6] As such it neither fades into eventual insignificance (witness the way the mighty acts of God in Israel's favour recovered their actuality by grace on Israel's feasts) nor can it be relegated to a secondary place after Scripture, which is, rather, its testimonial seal. The self-traditioning of God reaches its climax in Christ – the fullness of the divine act and word to the world, as of the world's grace-enabled response to that act and word. If Jesus criticises the 'traditions of men', human falsifications and biassings of the divine testimonies to Israel, it is because he knows authentic Tradition finds its goal in him. The primary form of the spiritual reading of Scripture – the typological, which Balthasar does not nicely distinguish from the allegorical – takes as its aim the 'explanation of the whole "Old Testament" in relation to the fullness of Christ'.[7] And as to the New Testament, Balthasar cites the influential sixteenth-century Louvain theologian John Driedo in calling her Scriptures 'nothing other than the witness of the Church herself', and yet Scripture is the Church's *in the mode of gift,* so that she 'might acquire in [the Bible] a sure criterion for her authoritative tradition'.[8] Indeed, Balthasar is happy – with the Fathers and mediaevals – to speak of Scripture's sufficiency as a Cicerone to revelation, so long as we understand the *place* of Scripture: within the Spirit-endowed Church, where its pages are guarded by a ministry that preaches and explains

---

5 *TL* III, p. 292.
6 *TL* III, p. 294.
7 *TL* III, p. 295. Here Balthasar can refer to his old mentor Henri de Lubac, and notably to *idem, Histoire et Esprit: L'intelligence de l'Ecriture chez Origène* (Paris 1956), and *Exégèse mediévale* II.2 (Paris 1964), pp. 60–84.
8 *TL* III, p. 298. The earlier part of the citation is from Driedo's *De ecclesiasticis Scripturis et dogmatibus.*

their content. It is the *circumincession* of Tradition, Scripture and apostolic office we must get inside. All breach of this charmed circle – for example, in the Reformers' war cry, *Sola Scriptura!* – cuts off our reception of 'objective Spirit'. Just so, without the teaching office of the apostolic ministry, Tradition – as the content of the divine self-gift – becomes unthinkable, for the self-identity of divine revelation escapes through our fingers, running away borne by a thousand divergent interpretations into history's sands. Of course there is such a thing as the Spirit of Christ as our 'interior master' (Augustine's phrase), and so – as night follows day – an 'internal magisterium' in the hearts of the faithful. But that can never be a warrant for atomised individualism: the interior teaching goes on for the sake of the common mission of the Church where the successors of the apostles preside.

It is a mark of the continuing influence on Balthasar of the anti-antiquarian predilections of the *nouvelle théologie* that his account of 'Tradition–Scripture–ministry' is so present- and future-directed. It is against the background of the Spirit's task of expounding the meaning of Christ's existence *for the future* that we have to understand his inspiring of the Scriptures, and his leading into all truth the successive generations of the Church. The Spirit is creative – in the ministerially guarded ongoing interpretation of Tradition and Scripture – because he draws on the Fountain, creating from the 'vitality' of Christ. Exegetical practice, ministerial actions, these must be consciously performed 'in the Spirit' if they are to render the original divine *Selbstübergabe* – and this they can always be thanks to the presence of the Spirit energising the Church at her foundations as the *Immaculata* and the sacrament of Christ.

Preaching and Liturgy

Preaching and Liturgy can be dealt with more briefly for the foundations are already laid in the above of which they are the further expression. The apostles at Pentecost are witnesses and intermediaries of objective Spirit because they do not report, to the international crowd, on religious experiences, however unique and grandiose (Balthasar speaks here in clipped, Barthian accents). Instead, they are heralds through whom God exhorts, speaking as they do in the place of Christ. Writing to Corinth, Paul was exceptionally conscious that the power of his message owed almost everything to the Spirit, and little to his own (as he portrays things) feeble delivery. The one, it seemed, worked through the other – on the model of the weakness of the Cross that makes strong. As Balthasar points out, proclamation (*Verkündigung*) is more than sermonising (*Predigt*) because it implies that the Spirit makes of human language an event in which the mysteries of the Word incarnate and atoning, humiliated and victorious, become actual in the present.

That same event character also attaches to the Liturgy, and to mission to unbelievers. The Word is objectively present by the Spirit in the missionary's speech: but he (or she) must struggle to make that presence thoroughly subjective to the hearers by thinking through what its reception, spiritually, culturally, demands. (There is also the little matter – crucial to the efficacy of mission – of letting the Word be in subjective accord with the Gospel-bearer's life.)

What Balthasar emphasises – and this should call to mind the liturgical dimension of objective Spirit, still to be treated – is that in proclamation and mission it is the 'meta-historical Living One' who is acting: all veridical examples of such action gravitate towards the Omega-point of destiny in Christ.

> Thus every Churchly, every Christian proclamation transcends itself, above all inasmuch as the historical past of the Son's theophany is, in its rendering present by the Spirit, always greater and more mysterious than the words of a sermon could allow someone to grasp; and also because the pneumatic and eschatological Lord is to be grasped only in hope, not in sight.[9]

Of these three aspects of objective Spirit – preaching, mission, worship, the Liturgy is the most obviously turned towards the End. But while insisting on its essentially doxological character, Balthasar also maintains its exotericism. The renewal of the prayer of the One who gave his flesh and blood for the world, its blessing presses beyond the confines of the Church, as phrases from the Mass of the Roman rite themselves attest. Following his favourite exegete – at least in the context of the logic – Heinrich Schlier, Balthasar defines the Liturgy as *leibhaftige Hingabe*, 'bodily self-donation' – and sees there the connexion between Christ on the Cross, the Eucharist in the community and the sacrifice of self in personal living.[10] And returning in his end to his beginning (in this section), Balthasar finds it unsurprising, accordingly, that Paul should have sought in the Liturgy his supreme image for the apostolic preaching in Romans 15: it is the priestly service (*leitourgia*), the sacred office (*hierourgeia*) of the Gospel of God.

The Sacraments

The sacraments are the most obvious example of 'objective Spirit', given their matter-and-form make-up. And yet in order to desire a sacrament and prepare oneself to receive objective holiness by its means there must be, on the part of the individual, some trace of the subjective Spirit (for example, in the contrition of a penitent at Confession, or the faith of parents and Godparents at the Baptism of a child). That for Balthasar is an index of how comprehensively the Holy Ghost is the 'Realiser' of that 'Trinitarian-ecclesial event' which a sacrament is.[11]

But is not insistence on these seven sacred signs as gateways to salvation (exceptional situations aside) a collapse into arbitrariness, with the divine will taken as assigning groundlessly this particular 'space of visible Churchliness' for its action? Say rather it is a matter of the

> positive finitude of the Incarnation-structure of Christ, in which the Church shares as his 'body', and so finds herself endowed with his Spirit and commissioned with corresponding tasks.[12]

9 *TL* III, p. 306.
10 H. Schlier, 'Martyria, Leitourgia, Diakonia', in *Festschrift Volk* (Freiburg 1968), pp. 242–9.
11 *TL* III, p. 310.
12 *Idem.*

By the sacraments the Spirit strives to let men share the objective divine holiness in all the decisive life-situations they encounter or inhabit, introducing them to a holiness which, as he pours it on the Church, will always exceed their subjective grasp.

That – in the context of a pneumatological logic – is Balthasar's fundamental sacramentology, his theology *de sacramentis in genere*. It is time for a word on how, in the perspective of the Spirit, he sees the particular sacraments.

In *Baptism-and-Confirmation*, the Spirit acts as our Introducer (*Einführer*) into salvation's objective mystery. Christologically, we die with Christ, but pneumatologically we are raised in the Spirit. Confirmation intensifies the baptismal gift; more precisely (the difference is notoriously difficult to adjudicate), he confers his charismata now, having regenerated the person in Baptism before. The sacrament of *Penance* is the 'second plank of salvation' – not to be offered just once, however, since the Easter Spirit is, for the Fourth Gospel, essentially the 'objective Spirit of the possibility and licitness of ecclesial pardon'.[13] He also comes to give himself subjectively, restoring the individual to the holy communion of redeemed subjects. The Spirit's absolution is the fontal form of that forgiveness Christians are to show each other in the Church. The *Eucharist* – a sacrament and more than a sacrament – lends itself to pneumatological discussion through the time-honoured issue of the epiclesis – prayer for the Spirit's descent to make the Gifts life-giving. From a survey of early texts indebted to Johannes Betz' *Die Eucharistie in der Zeit der griechischen Väter*,[14] Balthasar concludes that the original epiclesis was addressed to the Logos (as the 'Lord who is Spirit'), asking him to tabernacle in bread and wine as once at Bethlehem; with Athanasius, the Spirit's own distinctive divine Personhood becomes clearer – yet so does his indivisibility from the Son, which then opens the way for the developed Eastern theology of epicletic prayer focused on the Spirit (alone). But as Balthasar points out, the Spirit cannot in fact be made a stranger to the Son, and what might appear grammatically, in 'mature' epicletic formulae, to be the Son's passivity in face of the Spirit's operation is really the Son's 'most fruitful act'.[15] The primacy of objective holiness when compared with subjective becomes manifest once more as Balthasar describes how, by a 'Marian' accord with the Spirit of Christ, the Church allows herself to be included in his (the Son's) self-offering. Just this allowing oneself to be included, however, is what renders Eucharistic participation (subjectively) transformative in daily living. The sacrament of *marriage* places beneath the 'norm' of Christ's espousal of his bridal Church every Christian union of man and wife. It is the Spirit's job to 'change natural eros into the agape that comes from God'.[16] Possibly Balthasar was thinking of Adrienne von Speyr when he speaks in this connexion of a real Christian possibility for spouses to renounce the (in itself evangelically legitimate) use of natural

13 *TL* III, p. 313.
14 J. Betz, *Die Eucharistie in der Zeit der griechischen Väter* = *Katholische Dogmengeschichte* I.1 (Freiburg 1955).
15 *TL* III, p. 315
16 *TL* III, p. 317.

marriage for the sake of some greater supernatural fruitfulness that can issue from this 'greatest friendship' (the phrase is Thomas') between the sexes. The apostle, after all, could be called father and mother of his community, a testimony to an engendering that is 'Christological-ecclesiological' in character. Which brings us to *Holy Order*. The solemn words of the Risen Lord 'Receive the Holy Spirit' (John 20.22) echo and re-echo down the ordination ceremonies of the centuries. For understandable reasons, however, the man in holy orders has been linked more fully to the Son whose *shaliach*, or accredited representative, he is. Balthasar, with assistance from the German dogmatician Gisbert Greshake, attempts to right the balance. In his study *Priestersein* the latter had seen how the ministerial priest stands at the point of intersection between the *auctoritas* of Christ and the *communio* of the Holy Spirit[17] – but the further touch is needed of Balthasar's objective/subjective distinction to grasp how the ministry the ordained receive is not only Christological but pneumatological: 'objective Spirit' (hence the sacramental character of Ordination in its distinctness from personal holiness), while the communion the ordained must realise by their dealings is not only a work of the Spirit but of the pneumatically self-giving Christ. Once again, subjective holiness must not be sundered from objective by the excuse of the *opus operatum* teaching. The objective 'expropriation' of the minister in favour of the Lord and the flock must find subjective expression in a life of love – not simply as a moral duty (this would be a commonplace of exhortation to the ordained) but as an *issue in logic*: the 'inexorable logic of the indivisible unity in God between the objective and subjective aspects of the Holy Spirit'.[18] The dreadful alternative is a functional and ultimately a bureaucratic priesthood. The *sacrament of the sick* for Balthasar – over against the vast majority of modern Catholic writers – is above all a sacrament given in the face of the threat of dying. To his mind, the mediaeval Latin name of the Anointing (*Extrema unctio*) showed a profounder theological insight than the theory or practice of either ancients or moderns. The Church is not in the business of distributing supernatural medicine but of preparing disciples to follow Jesus in a death like his so as (secretly) to rise with him in a resurrection like his. The Last Anointing is the renewal in the face of death of our Baptism into Christ. The Spirit enters this sacrament for precisely that reason: his communication in Baptism (and Confirmation) now becomes literally a life-and-death affair.

Canon Law

Canon Law may seem a bit of a comedown after scaling these heights. But it was the Lutheran exegete Ernst Käsemann, of all people, who called it 'one of the gravest and most fatal mistakes of liberalism to have separated out Spirit and law'.[19] Love – in whose name this divorce is usually declared – is not law's contrary but its radicalisation. The demands of law ennoble – which is why the Old Testament's Holiness Code expects gracious

---

17 G. Greshake, *Priestersein* (Freiburg 1982).
18 *TL* III, p. 322.
19 E. Käsemann, 'Sätze heiligen Rechts im Neuen Testament', in *idem*, *Exegetische Versuche und Besinnungen* 2 (Göttingen 1965⁴), p. 75.

election by God to take flesh in Israel in a righteous order, for Israel must be holy as the Lord their God is holy.[20]

In setting out the foundations of canon law in the New Testament, Balthasar is not afraid to throw into the balance the entire case of the theological logic. He writes:

> The fundamental structure found in the Old Testament comes to its fulfilment in a Trinitarian way in the New as the 'Truth' of the love of God in Jesus Christ goes to the unsurpassable end and the 'Spirit of Truth' interprets for Church and world the law that lies within this love-deed of God. Every appearance of the arbitrary (in the election of one people rather than another) falls away, since God in the love that goes freely to the Cross of Jesus freely reveals his own Essence (as Trinitarian love) for all to see. What he does, that he *is*: wherefore he now receives the essential right – which is at the same time a right based on love – to the creature's loving response in full.[21]

So too, in his obedience to the Father for the brethren from love unto death, Jesus has acquired the 'right' to his exaltation and with it the 'right' likewise to see exalted the brothers and sisters he brings with him. The *communio* between love of God and love of neighbour would be subverted were objective Spirit *not* to fashion, at human hands, a canon law, guardian as that is of the mediations of the Word of salvation in Tradition, Scripture, ministry, of the sacramental mysteries, and of the unity of that charity which in Jesus served men for the Father's sake. Balthasar can cite to good effect the Code of Canons of the Latin Church when he maintains that all the states of life in the Church which the law protects are Spirit-fostered – a sound basis for accepting the dictum of a French theologian of this subject that

> law of the Church is itself holy and has as its end only the preservation of the sovereign presence of the Spirit.[22]

Theology

This is the last of Balthasar's presentations of 'objective Spirit'. It has been a feature of the theological logic – which is, we have noted, a theological ontology where truth is convertible with being – that certain premises of its 'system' must be divinely put in place. Proclamation and justification, for example, are necessary for receiving the truth of the Word and the Spirit. We shall not be surprised to hear, then, that for Balthasar in order to explain the faith it is necessary first to have it. Nor is that primarily a matter of the illuminating power of the Holy Spirit in our hearts, enlightening the mind and warming the will and affections. As the

20 Cf. Leviticus 20.7.
21 *TL* III, p. 326. Something is lost in translation inasmuch as German, unlike English, uses the same word for 'right' as for 'law'.
22 B.-D. Dupuy, 'Esprit-Saint et anthropologie chrétienne', in *Eglise et Esprit: Actes du Symposium organisé par l'Académie internationale de sciences religieuses* (Paris 1969), pp. 307–26, and here at p. 326.

theological aesthetics made clear, the 'objective' light which falls on the
formed content of revelation and makes it radiant to the beholder is the
more important luminary in the Balthasarian heavens. *Wahrheit Gottes* and
Wahrheit des Geistes have transposed these aesthetic categories into those
of truth, speaking of the mediation of divine logic in human logic, and
the exposition of the truth of the Word, Jesus Christ, by the interpreting
Spirit. It is, Balthasar can now say, characteristic of a theology unresisting
to objective Spirit that it knows itself to be set before a truth greater than
which no mind can conceive – but knows too that taking refuge for this
reason in mere apophaticism is forbidden it. The Spirit is always revealing,
again and anew, the meaning of the whole.

The Spirit makes theology possible by changing the context in which
through human language – typically of human understanding at large –
one person responds to another against a backcloth of meaning where the
various components of existence (frequently contradictory) jostle. The Holy
Spirit, in his work as Interpreter, expounds for theology the unity in Christ
of the word who addresses us and the ultimate – because divine – horizon
before which hearers stand. For Christ is not only a human interlocutor,
he is also God from God, substantial Expression of the Father. Here at last
the fear that the language of personal exchange may tell us nothing about
the cosmic background is exorcised. The linguistic act that joins my 'I' to
this 'Thou' strikes supra-linguistic reality. And what a reality! Through
the absolute love revealed in Christ the scrawl of crooked lines which fill
our common horizon reads for the first time plain. How mercy conspired
to exploit sin the volumes of the theological dramatics showed.

In a favoured pun of Balthasar's, only simplicity of eye (*Einfalt*) can let
the complex unity unfold (*einfalten*). Each word of the divine dialogue
must be heard in its total context, from Abraham till now, yet all is summed
up in the *pro nobis* of the Cross. And so the theologians who best embody
objective Spirit stand out: Augustine and Bede; Anselm, William of St
Thierry, Bonaventure; with Pascal, Kierkegaard, Newman among the
'religious thinkers'. Theology in its defensive (with the Fathers) or rational
(with the Schoolmen) mode is not an alternative to sapiential reflexion. It
is only its ante-room, an 'indispensable preamble to praying and confessing
theology'.[23] The Christian search for God proceeds as from those divinely
found. And if Balthasar has a criticism of 'monastic' theology it is that
sometimes it forgot how the starting point is not creaturely desire for God
but the fire the divine Word has set ablaze in us by the Spirit.[24] A better
word for Balthasar's theological *beau idéal* (after all he was never a monk,
though schooled by Benedictines) would be 'mystagogical'. As he says,
the adoring hymns of the Liturgy are in a way the highest expression of
Christian thought, just as for Plato's thought the deepest truths in his
Dialogues were found in their mythopoetic seams. Is not the profoundest
'theology' of Jesus in the gospels located in his High-Priestly Prayer? We
must look to musicality and art for clues as to how (not least in language)
the Spirit keeps the best theological expression eschatological, 'immersed

23 *TL* III, p. 337.
24 In this sense, Balthasar regrets the title of Dom Jean Leclerq's great study, *L'Amour
    des lettres et le désir de Dieu* (Paris 1957).

in the mystery of God in the Jesus Christ of all the ages'.[25] Tantalising final comment!

Subjective Spirit

Balthasar must now launch onto the waters of 'subjective Spirit' which will take him past the floating islands of (in order of treatment) prayer, forgiveness, the 'experience of the Spirit', discernment of spirits and 'testimony of life'. He begins with a word of warning. To avoid Pietism or subjectivistic 'charismaticism', these aspects must never be separated from their presuppositions in objective Spirit. Nor is this simply a matter of observing the demands of Catholic orthodoxy or Church discipline. To emancipate the experience of subjective Spirit from that of its objective counterpart will create only enthusiasts and never saints.

First, *prayer* is 'in' the Spirit. Balthasar takes the moment in the Gospel according to Luke where Jesus 'exults' in the Holy Spirit, pouring out a paean of praise to the Father for the revelation to 'little ones', as the guide to his – and Christian – prayer in its pneumatic reality. The Spirit directs the prayer of Jesus to the Father as also its answering resonance – *Abba*! (Romans 8.16) in the hearts of his adopted brethren.

> The Spirit bestowed on us by way of gift is our possibility not only of speaking in God as creatures but of entering together into that personal dialogue of God which the Spirit is.[26]

This would hardly be possible, though, unless in the Spirit we first listened with the Word who proceeds from the Father. Such listening is the root of a prayer true to Scripture, and it is responded to (and this is also prayer) as the Spirit puts on our lips not human language, simply, but the language of the Word himself. This listening and responding will go on through all eternity, for what we need to know and be thankful for is inexhaustible, as the Spirit testifies with our spirit that we are co-heirs with Christ and so sons of God, and what the Son knows in the Spirit is the unsoundable depths of the love of the Father to whom he returns thanks by an equally limitless 'Eucharist'. The dialogue of prayer 'has dimensions that stretch out beyond our sight, before opening out once more to the limitless space of the Interpreter Spirit'.[27]

Much of Balthasar's theology of prayer is a meditation on Romans 8.17–30. How does the Spirit help us in our weakness – and in any case *what* weakness? If Christians really made their own the prayer of the Son – that the Father's Name be sanctified, his Reign come, his Will be done on earth as in heaven, their prayer would be infallibly heard, as Christ's was in his Easter triumph and all its unfolding implications. At the risk of being thought 'dolorist' (contributing to a cult of suffering), Balthasar thinks our prayer is often inadequate because we do not share sufficiently in Christ's sufferings, do not groan enough with the creation that is in travail until the revelation of the sons of God. It is the Spirit's task to transform

25 *TL* III, p. 339.
26 *TL* III, pp. 341–2.
27 *TL* III, p. 343.

our half-hearted hope into a 'Christologically adequate invocation',
whereupon the Father, 'perceiving in us the intention (*phronema*) of the
Spirit, recognises the adequate content of this prayer of sighing and can
answer it'.[28]

Ecstasies and Corinthian charisms (such things as glossolalia) must,
says Balthasar, echoing Paul, be useful – for the corporate body or for
the individual – and this they can only be if they bear fruit in either the
Christian understanding or the practicalities of the apostolic life. Not that
Balthasar believes that any mystical graces are given purely for the good
of individuals. It is an unusual feature of his theology of mysticism that
he treats all mystic graces as *gratiae gratis datae* – more profoundly
opportunities for others than for the saint herself, even if this can only be
claimed in some historically unverifiable way, as with a figure cut off
from contact with others, like Thérèse of Lisieux.

Those aspects of subjective Spirit that are expressed as, on the one hand,
forgiveness, and, on the other, the *direct experience of the Holy Spirit*, get
shorter shrift. Pardon is a beautiful aspect of evangelical subjectivity. In
the ancient world, the Greeks knew the concept of *excuse* when some
shameful action was unavoidable. For the Roman moralists the remission
of a *warranted* punishment was deemed essentially irrational. Without
denying that the cosmic and social order merits respect, the gospel
relativises its demands in the light of the heavenly initiative in forgiving.
That initiative was directed to us 'while we were still sinners' (Romans
5.10); hence the precept that we should anticipate (possible) response by
forgiving our enemies, turning the other cheek. The disarming strategies
for dealing with enmity recommended in the Sermon on the Mount are
seen by Balthasar as ways of imitating the love exerted on the Cross for
the conversion of men. It is not a question of psychological warfare, but of
'having a share, in the Holy Ghost, in the Cross-attitude (*Kreuzesgesinnung*)
of the Son, nay, of the Father . . .'.[29] That is, presumably, an example of
indirect or tacit experience of the Holy Spirit. What when such experience
becomes direct or explicit? The question, Can we *know* (as individuals)
that the Holy Spirit dwells in us? interested the Fathers, the mediaevals
and Trent (for rather different reasons in each case). It has taken on fresh
actuality, Balthasar thinks, in a secularised world where some moment,
at least, of personalised faith experience strikes many as a *sine qua non* of
believing. Balthasar takes St Thomas' eminently sane comments on the
matter as his starting point. As Uncreated Love, the Holy Spirit can move
supernaturally our created power of love but, given the similarity between
a natural love and a grace-borne love, to be sure that one's delight in
loving comes from divine charity is not easy: one can only 'conjecture on
the basis of probable signs'.[30] The Gifts of the Spirit – a major theme in
Thomas' dogmatics – are in the same boat: reflexion by their recipient on
their origin is by no means plain sailing. All we can be guided by in
assessing such matters is the overall drift or complexion of a life lived
self-spendingly in faith.

28 *TL* III, p. 345.
29 *TL* III, p. 349.
30 Thomas Aquinas, *De Veritate*, q. 10, a. 10c.

The likelihood that certain experiences are supernatural touches to the soul's quick, or pith, or powers, turns, then, on the whole complex of a Christian's life. Balthasar thoroughly approves of the epoch-making study *L'Expérience chrétienne* by the French diocesan priest Jean Mouroux, a book that, virtually single-handedly, restored to Catholicism a balanced doctrine of experience after the inflation of the subject in Modernism and its deflation in Integrism.[31] 'Christian experience', rightly understood, is a constellation in the life of a person as a whole, a pattern produced in someone's existence by the Spirit. Spiritual 'tastings' of the divine are, in their primitive immediacy, ambivalent. They can be judged aright only from the vantage point of the totality of a life. If you are looking for manifest examples of Spirit-possession, Balthasar concludes, you must go not to the enthusiasts but to the martyrs.[32]

So claims to manifest experience of the Spirit here and now worry Balthasar if they are taken out of a total context – but also if they are removed from the attitude of openness to the eschatological finishing of the Spirit's work in subjects that we call hope. Still, this does not prevent him, as an experienced spiritual director in the Jesuit tradition, from essaying a brief theology of the *discernment of spirits* which must necessarily be undertaken at some discrete time and place.

The discernment of spirits is *the* great theme of the Ignatian *Exercises*, and it is entirely predictable that Balthasar as both a patrologist and a former Jesuit should emphasise their ancient lineage in this respect. Throughout the Old Testament and inter-testamental literature the need to distinguish between good and evil spirits, true prophecy and false, is ever at hand. Concern with the distinctive signs of spirits of light and of darkness – the former move us toward what is good and heavenly, the latter produce spiritual bewilderment and impotence, is a feature of desert monasticism, diffused through the classic spiritualities of the Church by Athanasius and Diadochus, John Cassian and Gregory the Great. Discerning that distinction of spirits is a key charism in the Letters of Paul. Balthasar sums up the Pauline doctrine of discernment as a study of an empowerment entrusted to the 'inner vigilance, subtlety of response but also ecclesiality, *Kirchlichkeit*, of each Christian alive'.[33] It is never a stab in the dark: for the authentic Spirit bears fruits, and brings with him such recognisable signs as brotherly love, respect for the Lord and the apostolic ministry established in his name, and confidence in proclaiming the gospel – which, 1 John adds, is always a gospel about the Son of God come in the flesh. This is vital background for the Ignatian attempt to find, in the evaluation of experiences of spiritual strengthening and/or disturbance, signs for the way the individual Christian should walk in his or her elected path to God. Consonant with his stress on the need for totality-thinking in spiritual judgment, Balthasar

31 J. Mouroux, *L'Expérience chrétienne: Introduction à une théologie* (Paris 1952). For an account inspired by Mouroux's work, see A. Nichols, *The Shape of Catholic Theology: An Introduction to its Sources, Principles and History* (Edinburgh and Collegeville, Minn. 1991), pp. 235–47.
32 Here Balthasar picks up a theme in the spiritual theology of the French Dominican Marie-Jean Le Guillou. See the latter's *Les témoins sont parmi nous: L'Expérience de Dieu dans l'Esprit-Saint* (Paris 1976).
33 *TL* III, p. 359.

underlines Ignatius' care not to equate prematurely all 'consolations' with
positive divine leading. In growth towards holiness, the proof of the
pudding is in the eating. Unlike some modern popularisers of the Ignatian
method, Balthasar is not afraid to give due prominence to Ignatius' concern
for 'thinking with the Church'. The way of life we choose must be among
those revered by our Mother the Church – the 'hierarchical' Church, the
saint of Manresa would add. Here too subjective and objective Spirit go
hand in hand.

That is not the only form the discernment of spirits takes. There is also
the question raised by the Charismatic Movement with its appeal to
dramatic 'Pentecostal' experiences. Balthasar finds a nugget of authentic
'subjective Spirit' in the Charismatic Renewal though his overall judgment
is rather negative. The emphasis on glossolalia is perverse, given Paul's
insistence that charisms are to be ranked according to utility. The basic
phenomenon – producing speech-like sound under the force of religious
feeling – is known outside Christianity, and its fascination is questionable.[34]
Xenoglossia – the speaking of languages unknown to the speaker but known
to the hearer – is what actually went on at the first Pentecost, and something
far more valuable (if one can get it!). Nor is Balthasar more impressed by
miracles of healing. In the gospels these are essentially enacted parables
of the healing of the soul; in the time of the Church, the generous
acceptance of physical suffering and death is usually more fruitful for the
Kingdom than is the recovery of health. If Balthasar's discussion of these
charismata is surprisingly unnuanced (glossolalia is surely an effective
symbol of the loosing of the tongue in praise, and the healing of bodies
can point to the resurrection of the flesh in the Age to Come), his own
previously expressed opinions on the gift of prophecy mean that here at
least he must be less withering!

The Charismatic Renewal, if it is to enjoy a place in the sun within the
Catholica, must, for Balthasar, shed its unbalanced emphasis on gifts
known, certainly, yet not in fact highly prized, in the primitive Church.
The enjoyment of Pentecostal gifts (even when this imbalance is corrected)
can be more widely misleading, however, ecclesiologically. The Church,
first, does not begin absolutely with Pentecost, but with the Annunciation
and the Cross. Next, it is characteristic of the Spirit of Pentecost to drive
her out onto the streets of the human city, not to make her spiritually
warm inside. Lastly, subjective Spirit must never be separated from
objective. These are criteria of authentic Churchmanship which Catholic
charismatics ignore at their peril.

What would a manifestly Pentecost-based renewal be like in
Catholicism, then? It would understand that the Spirit of Christ always
sends us back to the Cross, where alone the Resurrection is accessible. It
would recognise that spiritual gifts only make sense as intensifications
of faith, hope and (above all) love. It would avoid like the plague all
Konventikeltum, 'conventicle-ism', aware that the Spirit is given for mission
to the wide world. It would strenuously oppose the contrasting of

34 Balthasar makes much use of the critique of Neo-Pentecostalism by K. G. Rey,
Gotteserlebnisse im Schnellverfahren: Suggestion als Gefahr und Charisma (Munich 1985).
For the incidence of 'speaking in tongues' outside the Church, see J. G. Dunn, *Jesus
and the Spirit* (London 1975), p. 304.

charismatic (hurrah!) with juridical (boo!), knowing the Church to be an organic totality. It would abandon the attempt to found ecumenism simply on a spiritual experience – for the Church is visible sacrament, and not just invisible communing in the Spirit.

The last sphere of discernment of spirits Balthasar evidently felt he must touch on concerns the Spirit of Christ and the power of the State. Since both Christian and Church are in the world (here Balthasar looks ahead to the theme of the next chapter of the theological logic), they cannot avoid the question of their relation with worldly power. The Saviour had power, as the gospels take various opportunities to confirm, but he held it and exercised it as a responsibility before the Father – to be carried out as the needs of the Kingdom required. On the Cross his power to reconcile the world with God was hidden – a major theme, this, of the theological aesthetics – under its seeming opposite, the impotence of the Crucified. The *plena potestas* the Word made man has received from the Father in the Spirit is shared by the risen One with his Church. But this doctrine must never be disassociated from the words of Jesus about how the greatest must seem the smallest, the servant of all. Power – and thus freedom – is given the Church not that she may become minatory, but that she may build up even the 'brother who is weak' (cf. Romans 14.13–15; 1 Corinthians 8.7–13). The Church has to give witness before the world and its qualitatively different power – and this she does, most triumphantly, most fruitfully, when she is rejected by the world and even violently suppressed. (We see here how far Balthasar is from being an apostle of Christendom – curious in one whose whole work turns on a spiritual synthesis of Christianity and culture.) How does the discernment of spirits enter here? Chiefly, it would seem, in the need to establish – in a situation of tension between the holy power of the Church and the worldly power of a State whose rationale is meant to be the common good – where that divine Power which regulates all such conflicts would have us go.

One last variety of 'subjective Spirit' remains to be treated, and this is what Balthasar calls *Lebenszeugnis*: the witness of a Christian life well lived. The credibility of witnessing with the Spirit to the love of God which found its perfect Witness in Jesus Christ depends, for Balthasar, on the credibility of our charity, or what he terms – so as to bring out its distinctively Catholic Christian character, *die kirchliche Liebe*, 'ecclesial love'. To co-testify with the Spirit who is the reciprocal love of Father and Son can only be done by a love that is a life's devotion. Take the 'disciple whom Jesus loved' as an example. What is he save a 'Grünewald finger' (the reference is to the late mediaeval German artist's Isenheim altar, where the elongated finger of the Baptist points to a pockmarked Crucified for the weal of the inmates of a lazar-house), who sends back his readers to the self-testifying of the Spirit, water, blood, flowing from the Saviour's riven side as the love of Father and Son extends 'to the end' (cf. John 13.1). No matter whether John the Beloved was a martyr or not, it is the dying for love that counts, whether all at once, at a crash, or lingering-out, in daily mortification.[35]

---

35 E. Peterson, 'Zeuge der Wahrheit', in *idem, Theologische Traktate* (Munich 1951), pp. 167–224.

25

❦

The Spirit and the World

Balthasar's pages on the topic are few and far between – which some might regard as a tell-tale sign of too ecclesiocentric an author. But here we have to remember how for Balthasar the Church is essentially mission to the world – so the criticism needs to be retrenched. That the boundary between Church and world can be permeable is indicated when Balthasar closes his ecclesiological section with the remark that henceforth – since the Incarnation and Pentecost – the norm which is Christian love will affect all successive ethics, even atheistic ones.[1] It is unavoidable because it is unforgettable.

Yet the Spirit is not confined to an overflow from the Church. His range is as vast as the world – in creation and salvation alike. Balthasar wants to stay faithful to this affirmation. But he also wishes to uphold the distinctiveness of the New Testament revelation of the Spirit of the Father and the Son, and not permit this to be sucked back into a less differentiated Old Testament account of the 'Spirit of God'. These two concerns, simultaneous and in a certain tension, determine what he makes of the cosmic pneumatologies of such Protestant writers as Wolfhart Pannenberg, Charles Raven and John Taylor. In the movement of *ressourcement* to which Balthasar himself belongs, it was Henri de Lubac who, with the aid, above all, of the Greek Fathers, had recovered an ampler eschatology where the Spirit presses a world that is fundamentally redeemed by Christ to its wondrous consummation.[2] Human nature, including, through the human body, cosmic nature, already joined to the Father in the Church 'intensively', thanks to the redemptive work of the Son, must become so united *extensively* – and this begins to happen as the creation, with its human heart, 'groans' in expectation of its liberation, doing so by indebtedness to the moving of the Spirit. Now, as Balthasar comments, this thought, if 'absolutised', brings us to liberation theology with its view of the Spirit as the 'motor of change in history and of society's life'.[3] The danger that this may eviscerate the specifically New Testament account of the action of the Spirit of Christ is palpable, and has its cosmic (rather

---

1 *TL* III, p. 380.
2 H. de Lubac, *Catholicisme: Les aspects sociaux du dogme* (Paris 1938).
3 Cited from C. Schütz, *Einführung in die Pneumatologie* (Darmstadt 1985), p. 100, at
   TL III, p. 385.

than world-historical or social-political) counterpart in theologies, or
religious philosophies, which seek to relate the Spirit to the process of
evolution in physical nature.

The notion that the Spirit may be hailed as the true *anima mundi* sought
in vain by the Pythagoreans, Plato, the Stoics, Plotinus and the Arabs
from Alkindi to Averroes exercised distinct appeal for the twelfth-century
School of Chartres. For a while the great Abelard himself entertained
it, though the Council of Sens gave it a good knock on the head. (This
was only the Council of an ecclesiastical province, but the reception of its
anathema in the collection of authoritative magisterial texts known collo-
quially, from its first editor, as 'Denzinger', testifies to widespread approval
of its douche of cold water in the hierarchical Church and among her
approved divines.)[4] Pannenberg, as a Lutheran systematicism concerned
to open a dialogue with natural science and contemporary (physical)
cosmology, draws on the Anglo-American attempts to fuse evolutionary
theory with Christian doctrine,[5] but more fundamentally – in Balthasar's
view – seeks to complement Teilhard de Chardin's Christologically
conceived 'evolution to the Omega Point' with an account of the divine
action in the evolutionary process that does greater justice to the rôle of
the Spirit.[6] The self-transcendence of a creature in a 'life-field' *vis-à-vis*
the evolutionary future and ultimately, in the human animal, that movement's absolute climax is Pannenberg's *punctum insertionis* for the
Spirit. Though reassured by the attempt to find a specifically cosmic rôle
for the Spirit, but this time on inner-biblical grounds, in Karl Barth (an
author who can scarcely be accused of affinity with pantheism), Balthasar
remained anxious that Pannenberg's efforts, while well meant, would
end in rendering down the New Testament Spirit in his essential Christ-
relatedness, to the level of the Old Testament *Spiritus Creator*. The same
reservations apply to the Anglican authors already mentioned.[7]

Balthasar has another niggle – and it is not a minor one. Such speculations seem to go well beyond the limitations of Christian revelation
which, after all, does not offer enlightenment on all subjects – even all
theological subjects! – without exception. But this caution, as found here
in the theological logic, was hardly observed by Balthasar himself, when
writing the more speculative closing sections of the theological dramatics.
In fact, Balthasar only takes his own advice semi-seriously. The chief
objection to Pannenberg's cosmological Pneumatology is not that it fails
to observe a proper apophaticism, but that its cataphatic content is not
that of the heart of the New Testament, itself the heart of Scripture.

4 H. Denzinger, *Enchiridion symbolorum, definitionum et declarationum de rebus fidei et morum*, ed. P. Hünermann (Freiburg 1991[37]), pp. 324–6.
5 As laid out in, for example, A. M. Ramsey, *From Gore to Temple* (London 1960), and E. C. Rust, *Evolutionary Philosophies and Contemporary Theology* (Philadelphia 1969).
6 W. Pannenberg, 'Kontingenz und Naturgesetz', in A. M. Müller and W. Pannenberg (eds), *Erwägungen zu einer Theologie der Natur* (Gütersloh 1970); *idem*, 'Ekstatische Selbstüberschritte als Teilnahme am göttlichen Geist', in C. Heitmann and H. Mühlen (eds), *Erfahrung und Theologie des Heiligen Geistes* (Hamburg 1974), pp. 176–92; *idem*, 'Der Geist des Lebens', in *Glaube und Wirklichkeit* (Munich 1975), pp. 31–56; *idem*, 'Gott und die Natur', *Theologie und Philosophie* 58 (1983), pp. 481–500.
7 C. G. Raven, *The Creator Spirit* (London 1962); J. V. Taylor, *The Go-Between God* (London 1972).

If the Spirit of the New Covenant as Christ's Spirit is portrayed as a Spirit of humility, service, descent to the lowest place and so to the place where life is given away in atonement for all, then it will be possible only with difficulty, in the context of the created universe's evolution, to style that Spirit the Spirit of ascent, of the self-transcendence of (logos-bearing) forms and so for good or ill the Spirit of power, the Spirit of victory to the strongest.[8]

The cosmic, evolutionary march, with its 'hetacombs of victims', seems to have little to do with the Spirit of Jesus. If a principle be sought for that forward- and upward-moving *élan* of the evolutionary process, then Balthasar would prefer to locate it on the side of creation rather than of the Trinitarianly divine. The cosmic imperative beloved of German Romanticism, *Stirb und werde*! ('Die and become!') *can* be applied to the central event of salvation, the Paschal Mystery. Indeed, *avant la lettre* it *was* so applied by St Paul – and the Saviour himself. But that is not to say that the Cross and Resurrection of the Lord are simply the supreme application of a fundamental truth in a nature religion, or the sovereign instance of a law of human history. The projection of the intra-historical events of salvation onto the evolutionary background is no wise way to attempt a clarification of the unity of the divine plan.

Neither Good Friday, nor Easter, nor Pentecost can be turned into speculative principles. For here it is not a matter of a supreme kind of transcendence, but of the overcoming – possible only from the side of God – of the contradiction between divine love and human sin. Only from this vantage point does it become definitively clear what the Holy Spirit is.[9]

By all means let the Creator Spirit be accorded his universal range. But that Spirit ever bears the 'stigma' of the Cross and Resurrection. That alone is his give-away sign.

8 *TL* III, p. 392.
9 *TL* III, p. 305.

26

✧❋✧

Return to the Father

Balthasar's last word in *Theologik* III is given, appropriately enough, to the overall *goal* of both subjective and objective Spirit. That goal he finds alluded to in Ignatius of Antioch's Letter to the Romans, when that arche-type of primitive Christianity, a charismatic bishop on his way to martyr-dom, writes of 'a living water that murmurs within me, Come to the Father'.[1] Our goal, like that of the Son made man, and with him of all creation, is *Heimkehr*, going home, return to the Father's house. It is a piece of intellectual audacity to put together, as Balthasar does, this text from the second-century Antiochene Christian with a fragment of Novalis' poetry:

> Die Lust der Fremde ging uns aus,
> Zum Vater wollen wir nach Haus.
>
> Desire for a strange land has left us;
> we want to go home to the Father.

But then the Greek Fathers and the German Romantics are perhaps the most constant wells of Balthasar's inspiration, sacred and profane. To avert criticism, he insists that *Sehnsucht*, nostalgia for the Fatherly house, is not flight from the world. For the home for which we long is all creation's final resting place, that eternal Sabbath which is far from mere inactivity, since the Trinitarian love never rests, either in God or in his saints.

To preserve his discourse from the taint of pietism, Balthasar scrutinises the various ways in which an ultimate Source – as it were, a 'Father' – for all things has been conceived. He treats it as more or less a law of religious development that the more reflective a religious tradition is the less likely is it to rest content with merely affirming the multiplicity of things. Instead, it will seek out that unity which bears them all. This can be very differently done: reducing the multiple to mere appearance (as with Parmenides or Gautama); synthesising the many in the shape of Ideas themselves unified by a Good lying beyond being (as in Plato); conceiving an absolutely One transcending all other unity of being and spirit as its source (Plotinus). In one sense, Balthasar is inclined to think, all these apparently so diverse

---

1 Ignatius, *To the Romans*, 7, 2. I take this as the leading theme of my short commentary on the Apostles' Creed, *Come to the Father. An Invitation to share the faith of the Catholic Church* (London 2000).

positions – philosophically, religiously – are variants of the same. All manifest the 'ultimate drive of the world's being as thinking being' oriented to its own wellspring.[2] From the standpoint of divine revelation, that is a distinctly limited quest – yet not one without value, even where the depiction of the divine Maker is concerned: how could it be for a Christian anything other than deeply touching when Plotinus portrays that Source as expending its entire riches, even to the very boundary of nothingness (which is where, for Plotinus, matter, as the One's most distant emanation, has its 'place'). It is a phenomenon of human religiosity (including in its philosophical form) that a 'goad of memory', *ein Erinnerunggsstachel*, whereby the finite being that has gone forth from the Source is recalled to its origin, plays a key part in what the Neoplatonists called *epistrophē*, turning back to the One.[3] And this is where Balthasar can make the transition to the salvation-historical faith of Israel and the Church. Among the Hebrews, that prick of memory took the form of an inability to forget Israel's beginnings, the hour of her birth at the Sea of Reeds, in the marvel of the Exodus escape. So deeply rooted was that remembering that it could survive all her later infidelities, as the voice of Torah called Israel home. God was Israel's originating Father through no mythic cosmogony but a historic act of adoption of the people. And he was her goal as the final Rest (cf. Psalm 95) to which she was to travel on pilgrimage – along with, so certain prophecies had it, the other nations of the world.

The New Testament proclaimed for all the world to hear what some few prophetic oracles had stammeringly uttered. But it proclaimed it in a paradoxical way. All who believe in Jesus can become sons in the Son. Here Israel's confession of God as her Father is both personalised and intensifed to an extraordinary degree (in Jesus's claim to be *the* Son, absolutely) and yet universalised (since the sonship is now open, through the grace of Christ, to all who would desire it – and this not only as individuals but as bearers of responsibility for all). 'Not individuals only but the story of the world, must be borne to their home in the mansions of the Father.'[4]

In no way does this render nugatory the speculations of other religions and philosophies about the ultimate Source (and Goal). On the contrary, it shows those aspirations to be supremely worthy, while the rejection of such thinking – in Positivism and atheism – is alone contemptible. The latter views of the world in renouncing 'every transcendent Omega for history, are incapable of dialogue in regard to the final meaning of the individual as of universal existence'.[5] Nevertheless, analysis of the portrayal of this Source and Goal in traditions as diverse as Zen Buddhism and Platonism show them – so Balthasar suggests, giving examples of how such analysis might proceed – to be schematisms. They lack life since they do not acknowledge

> the one thing that cannot be hypothesized or constructed from the side of the world: the Trinitarian love become visible in Jesus Christ

2 *TL* III, p. 400.
3 *TL* III, p. 401.
4 *TL* III, p. 403.
5 Ibid.

as the essence of all being – the Father as self-loving and outpouring Source, first of all in the Absolute itself, and then, by way of demonstration of the fact that this outpouring is disinterested love, in the free surrender of the Son for an estranged world and hence for its fetching home.[6]

That is why St Thomas could legitimately structure his masterwork, the *Summa Theologiae*, on the *exitus-reditus* pattern, by an Egress and a Return. Let no one object, adds Balthasar, that here Alpha and Omega, Source and Goal, are only brought together in a fashion accessible for us through a doctrinal construct – the Trinity. Let the 'fanatics of absolute unity' (he means, uncomplimentarily at this point, Jews and Muslims) recognise that God cannot be substantial Love unless he has a Beloved generated in self-giving (that was studied in *Theologik* II) and unless, too, the perfect disinterest of their union can be shown in a 'Third' (as *Theologik* III has attempted), the Fruit and Witness of the unity of their 'generative and thankful love'.

The mystery of the divine love founds everything but has itself no further foundation. Here Balthasar comes back to his original starting point. In *Theologik* I, he had argued that (in my précis):

> worldly truth's lack of final foundation derives from its reception of its ground from something that is not itself – namely God – whereas, while the divine truth is equally without foundation, this is only in the sense that God's truth rests on nothing other than itself, nothing other than its own infinity.[7]

Now, however, in the light of the further propositions put in place by the theological logic when considering the truth of the Son and of the Spirit, we can go further and refine the terminology of truth and infinity by that of love itself. It is love that is the fount of all intelligibility – and therefore, adds Balthasar, in a phrase to scandalise areligious rationalists, of all rationality.[8] *Theologik* – and so the trilogy as a whole – will not end in sheer apophasis, baffled cessation of thought before the Mystery of truth which is also (compare *Theodramatik*) the Mystery of goodness and the Mystery (compare *Herrlichkeit*) of beauty as well. No, because as various exclamations and imperatives in the Pauline Letters suggest, this love *offers itself to knowledge* (cf. Romans 11.33; Ephesians 3.18–19), at any rate if the 'knowledge' we are speaking of

> stays open to the marvel of a love ... which issues eternally from itself, without ground or reason.[9]

If the Spirit 'searches the depths of God' (1 Corinthians 2.10), that Spirit is given us as the Spirit of Christ to enable us, after our fashion, to 'search'

---

6 *TL* III, pp. 403–4.
7 See above, p. 58.
8 *TL* III, p. 406.
9 *TL* III, pp. 406–7. Balthasar finds the perfect expression of such a noetic in Gregory of Nyssa's commentary on the Song of Songs, anthologised by Balthasar himself as *Der versiegelte Quell* (Einsiedeln 1984[3]).

likewise. Nor will such searching be merely tentative, much less in vain: as a co-searching with the Holy Spirit it will be real exploration of *der väterliche Liebesabgrund*, the 'abyss of the Father's love'.[10]

It is with that Fatherly love – though seen as it must be, Trinitarianly (no Person of the triune Godhead is ever alone)[11] – that Balthasar will end. In the trilogy's closing paragraph he sums up his own theological vision 'paterologically', for it is to the Father that the truth of Word and Spirit leads:

> Through the glory of the Son we shall see appear the abyss of the glory of the love of the invisible Father, and this in the twofold figure of the Holy Spirit of love, while we, as born of the Son, shall exist in the fire of that love where Father and Son meet, and in that way, together with the Spirit, we shall be at the same time that same love's witnesses and its doxologists.[12]

10 *TL* III, p. 408.
11 For the inappropriateness of the suggestion of a feast of God the Father in the liturgical calendar, see M. Caillat, 'La dévotion à Dieu le Père: Une discussion au XVIIe siècle', *Revue d'Ascétique et de Mystique* 20 (1939), pp. 35–49, 136–57.
12 *TL* III, p. 410.

27

Epilogue to the Trilogy

Balthasar's 'Epilogue' to the Trilogy is a free-standing if short book in its own right. In it he abjures the 'American' ambition to offer a 'digest' of the whole. (I have to hope that his shade accepts less quizzically the homage offered by my own threefold commentary!) His aim, rather, is to justify the departure from the tradition of theological pedagogy whereby he has laid out what is in effect his 'Church dogmatics' not in the form of a series of tractates on discrete doctrinal areas (the Trinity, Christology, grace and so forth) but from the vantage point of the transcendentals.[1] His initial justification for his approach is thrown off in a few words. It is the easiest way to ensure the transition from a 'true philosophy' to the biblical revelation.

That 'transition' he calls, in the context of his Epilogue, *Schwelle*, 'threshold', and it provides him with the architectural metaphor underlying the structure of this small study. He will begin in an atrium or entrance hall (*Vorhalle*) where a variety of voices can be heard discussing the central human questions. From there he will in due course cross the threshold (in the sense of the transition from philosophy to revelation just explained), and finish in – a cathedral (*Dom*). From *Vorhalle*, across *Schwelle*, to *Dom* – that is the path the book will travel taking over again as it were the mental trajectory Balthasar followed in conceiving and writing the trilogy.

Atrium

In the atrium where Balthasar would place us, being a Christian is simply one option among the many world-views to which speakers from diverse hustings or market stalls would persuade us. As a self-consciously post-Christendom thinker, Balthasar would have us make the decision for Christianity – if at all – by the weight of *rein geistige Argumente*, 'pure spiritual-intellectual arguments', alone.[2] (He recognises, however, that reliance on the force of argument can be counter-productive, since the desire to find apodeictic proof of the truth of the gospel would leave no

1 H. U. von Balthasar, *Epilog* (Einsiedeln–Trier 1987), p. 7.
2 *Epilog*, p. 11.

room for the free act of faith and – he adds, typically, of *Hingabe*, 'surrender'.) But how are we to assess the competing claims that assail our ears in the entrance hall? The approach Balthasar advocates is what he calls the 'method of integration'. If one presentation of truth is able to integrate another within itself, but the reverse is not the case, then go with the more comprehensive view.

> The person who can integrate the maximum truth within his view can lay claim to the highest reachable truth.[3]

But can this method prevent Christianity itself from being absorbed, as one component, within some 'higher' synthesis, in the style of Hegel's epistemological ideal of 'absolute knowing'? Hegel's mistake lay not in his commendation of ever-intenser and more comprehensive integration but in his failure to accompany this with the recognition of a comparable freedom for facts to have their say. And where positive facticity is concerned, the revelation found in the moment of creation and its continuation in the uniqueness of the history of Israel – the people who carried the creation-idea – and of Israel's Christ is clearly no *bagatelle*. By combining the method of integration with suitable attention to facts in their uniqueness we should be able to avoid both irrationality and rationalism – though the task is arduous; and in different ways thinkers so various as Schelling and Barth, Rahner and the contemporary German psychologist of religion Eugen Drewermann, failed to do it justice.

Balthasar considers how things may be better done. And here he draws attention to the tradition of Augustine and Thomas. For them, the original form of created spirit is instinct with a 'dynamism' energetically ordered to the vision of God, such that, supported by grace, man turns in the direction of something that nature can never furnish yet God can put at his disposal – and does so when by the free divine initiative God shows to man a revelation that at once corrects and fulfils the use of human powers, raising these onto a new and hitherto unheard of plane. Managing the relations of the ideas of nature and of grace in that tradition involves a notoriously bumpy ride – as Balthasar's colleagues in the crisis over *la nouvelle théologie* had found to their cost in the 1940s and 1950s.[4] Balthasar believes the difficulties can be overcome if one bears in mind that already set within purely natural freedom is the grace of that divine self-opening whose radiance permeates all history from its 'Christological centre' – for that concept resolves the antinomy otherwise found in the notion of a God-directed nature whose immanent goal natural powers cannot attain. (It is typical of Balthasar that this attempted mediation between the *nouvelle théologie* men and the Neo-Scholastics should emphasise the three themes of freedom, history and Christ.)

Theologically, then, we can justify Balthasar's proposed use of our time in the atrium – attending to the ever-wider integration of natural truths, but also to facts in their ('supernatural'?) uniqueness. Strolling through

---

3 Ibid.
4 See A. Nichols, 'Thomism and the *Nouvelle Théologie*', *The Thomist* 64 (2000), pp. 1–19.

the atrium in the late-twentieth-century West, what conversations shall we actually overhear?

The one question that it would be spiritual and intellectual death *not* to hear put is that of the meaning of the human conversation-partner himself. Amazingly – but hardly unaccountably, the fault lies with the sway of Positivism, that is often *die unbestellte Frage*, the question nobody asks. It is typical of Positivism – whether in the natural or the human sciences or in Marxism (for Balthasar regards Marxism as a form of sociological Positivism) – to take the human as a given. The question of what meaning a being can have that *of its essence asks after meanings* (including scientific meanings) is either unnoticed or disclaimed as scientifically unanswerable (of course!) and put to one side. Not that this is only a modern Western sin: Balthasar thinks that, in the Far East, Confucianism and Shintoism have functioned as a 'psychological–sociological ethic' which tended to suppress – or at any rate not to raise – *die Seinsfrage*, the question of being. (Hence the survival power of these ethical traditions which could find a host in various religious and areligious systems.) But if philosophy is to be reduced to anthropology, or dissolved by scepticism, is it worth our joining in the polylogue in the atrium at all? The game is only worth the candle if people are willing to raise the question of the meaning of man in such wise that they do not exclude *a priori* the finding of some single ultimate meaning, one that throws light in the process on the totality of what is.

Balthasar now reviews the principal answers given in human history to this key 'philosophical-religious question'. He aims to convince the reader that the various traditions of human religiosity and speculative thought contain valid elements and yet the schemata in which these elements lie embedded resist integration one with another for the simple reason that their basic postulates rule each other out. For being and meaning cannot simultaneously be construed monistically (as with the Indian philosophies), esoterically (as with Gnosticism and the Sufis) and tragically-pathologically (as with the Greek and Norse mythologies and Mahayana Buddhism). Moreover, features of these overall views are destructive of the *humanum*, whether by abolishing individuality (the first), waging war on finitude (the second), or generating despair of life (the third). The thought then occurs whether what no human system can integrate might be brought together by a free self-opening of the divine.

For Balthasar, it is no part of the rationale of the Judaeo-Christian revelation to 'stop the holes in reason'.[5] And yet simply through its own character as a disclosure of being and meaning than which no greater can be conceived the Word of God might be able to provide the integrative framework which neither culture nor natural philosophy can supply. Its tones are those of 'fully living, unconditional, unquestionable authority';[6] it enters history, then, with a call for absolute obedience, and its content is a far distant promise. It specifies a transformation of behaviour even as it binds a people in a relation of reciprocal giving with their covenant Lord. This faith – Abrahamic, Mosaic – resembles nothing in the religions of the

5 *Epilog*, p. 22.
6 *Epilog*, p. 23.

nations. At once sustained and further challenged by renewals of the divine utterance, it comes to its unsurpassable climax in the Word's Flesh-taking, unthinkable but supremely fact. From this vantage point is it conceivable that the valid elements in the other religions and their attendant philosophies might at last find the integration previously sought in vain?

Balthasar thinks so. Thus, Christianity affirms with Judaism and Islam the infinite qualitative difference between God and the creature; it accepts with those monotheistic faiths that God has revealed himself over and above his showing of his hand in creation, and done so freely, in loving kindness to man. It rejects – with the orthodox versions of Judaism and Islam – any aspiration to the substantial divinisation of the creature, or that creature's emptying of its creaturehood (*Entwerden*). It locates the origin of the Eastern religions' desire for such unmaking in the inconceivability (to them) of any finite being's possessing abiding worth when placed beside the 'all-being' God. And here it can see further than either Judaism or Islam. Thanks to its central confession that God is love ultimately because he is in his own life *Hingabe und Fruchtbarkeit*, 'surrender and fruitfulness' – the divine Trinity, it knows that God can give the Other room, and so can find for the finite other too a space of freedom even within his own unity. In this way Christianity does not only draw the sting of what is poisonous in the Oriental religions, it also justifies for the first time the Jewish and Islamic conviction about the mercy of God.

Such 'acceptance of the positivity of the other'[7] is crucial to Balthasar's analysis. It enables the Christian faith to fill in the *lacunae* in the great religions. It can acknowledge the personhood of the created spirit, and not seek the human interlocutor of God simply in collectivities – the people of Israel, the Islamic *umma*, though certainly the human person in their relation to God is always to be understood in their communal setting. It can find in suffering and death, those foundational aspects of finite existence, not mere negativities but bearers of a positive meaning – since the ultimate revelation of divine love is inseparable from a Cross. To suffer and die – and this is a lesson which the Oriental religions need to learn quite as much as the remaining Abrahamic faiths – can be the 'meaningful, fruitful, deed of love'.[8] The transience of things ceases to be a motive for indifference, carefully cultivated, as in the Taoist, Stoic and Sufi ethics, but a message of readiness to do the sweet will of God in whatever daily circumstance presents. (Balthasar cannot but think here of the *Exercises* of his master, St Ignatius.) The ethical ways of Shintoism and Confucianism also find their proper place, their imperatives now warmed by the courage to offer in all the situations of social living something beautiful for God, in imitation of Christ.

Implicitly at least, Christology has been crucial to the claims (for Christianity's greater power of integration) Balthasar has here presented. The *homoousion*, as understood at Nicaea and Chalcedon, is a necessary condition for grasping the positive charge of creaturely otherness before God, and the turning of suffering and death into atoning (at-one-ing)

7 *Epilog*, p. 29.
8 *Idem*.

agencies for a world estranged from him. In the Resurrection is shown what was on the Cross achieved, and man in his body–soul unity invited to share that transfiguration.

> Salvation is not from finitude; rather is it the taking up of the finite (and so of the other) into the infinite, which, in order to be a life of love, must have the Other as such (the Word, the Son) in itself, as likewise it must have the union of the Other with the One (which it does in the Spirit).[9]

When we compare such an evocation of the divine Mystery with the earthly forms of love we can see at least that it is not a contradiction in terms. At the same time, however, Balthasar is keen not to make of this unique Singularity something the world could construe from its own side. The process of integrating the meaning-fragments of existence with the gospel's aid can never be made into a stringent proof of the truth of Christian faith – precisely because to perceive the Christian revelation as true can only come about through a free decision borne by grace. That element of trust is nevertheless no last-minute concession to the irrational. All personal communication of truth, on whatever level, requires *some* kind of trusting.

Threshold

In the atrium of Balthasar's edifice we have developed, through hearing and responding to the representatives of other religions and philosophies, a new style of Catholic apologetic. Its byword, found in two variants, is *Wer mehr (Wahrheit) sieht, hat (tiefer) recht*: 'Whoever sees more (truth), is (more deeply) right.'[10] Balthasar is not so blithe as to suppose, however, that Buddhists and Jews, Muslims and Nietzscheans will simply accept that the 'method of integration' leads to recognition of the superior power of the Christian fact to make sense of the rest, and capitulate accordingly. All kinds of objections could be posed at every point – and, if we bear in mind how uncomfortable a thing it is to switch *Weltanschauung* or change religious ships midstream – quite certainly will be.

For example, one could imagine a Buddhist judging silence to be a better response to a bewildering world than some unverifiable theory about its ultimate ground, or a Muslim deciding that respect for God's transcendence should dissuade us from attempting to bridge the gap between unconditioned and conditioned in a Christology and Triadology, or any thinking person taking the line that the human condition does not permit overall views of Providence, so that Balthasar's spiritual-intellectual maximalism must be deemed to overreach itself. Perhaps after all, despite the 'method of integration', less can actually mean more.

And Balthasar adds for good measure a ragbag of other awkward questions. Is it self-evident that man is the final stage of evolution? Does the 'Western' concern with personality really deserve the weight the Balthasarian apologetic has given it? Does not the factual condition of the

9 *Epilog*, p. 31.
10 For the two versions of Balthasar's maxim, see *Epilog*, pp. 11, 35.

world contradict the affirmation (by Bible and Balthasar) that it was made 'very good'? And more besides.

Faced with this host of difficulties, Balthasar changes tack. Instead of getting people to concentrate on the ultimate goal of human existence (with a view to persuading them that the Christian version thereof is the most comprehensively integrated account of the same), he now asks them to think about what is the most primary and seemingly obvious of all topics – the *being* which is the first thing mind knows. From this – the most universally common of all starting points – can he manage to take his interlocutors with him across the threshold? Can he bring them from and through philosophy to the revelation of the Holy Trinity in Jesus Christ our Lord?

The attempt to do so will also be a *post hoc* justification of the trilogy: aesthetics, dramatics, logic. 'Attempt' because, as readers of the opening section of *Say It Is Pentecost* (and even more of *Theologik* I!) will be aware, writing a fundamental ontology is no easy matter. It requires at one and the same time breadth of experience of the real, fertility in concept formation, lucidity in the making of distinctions. Not the categories in which we classify things and their relationships but the being such categorialisation presupposes is the El Dorado of metaphysics. Balthasar links being's elusiveness to its simultaneous wealth and poverty (it is what is most all-embracing and therefore richest, nought save nothing falls outside its fullness; it is also what is poorest, since it seems to lack all further determination). That is why the history of metaphysics can submit so weird and wonderful a series of reports on it, everything from the Absolute to the illusory play of *maya*. Balthasar's hope is that divine revelation will help him by throwing theological light on being in such a way that *philosophical* illumination occurs – just as he also hopes that philosophical exploration of being will act as a *praeparatio evangelica* bringing the unbeliever via meditation on the beautiful, the good, the true across that 'threshold' into faith. And naturally, by this stage in his overall enterprise he has not only the first volume of the theological logic but the entire trilogy to give him confidence that this is indeed a viable endeavour.

What Balthasar does in *Epilog* is to press into service three distinctions of which much has been made in *Theologik* I – that between being and beings, between appearance and hiddenness in being, and between being and its polarities – in order to help us grasp three foundational powers of being, which are, in turn, its capacity for 'self-showing' (*Sich-zeigen*, compare the 'beautiful'), for 'self-giving' (*Sich-geben*, compare the 'good') and for 'self-saying' (*Sich-sagen*, compare the 'true'). If he can show that the transcendental properties of being at large, available in principle to all human beings for their perusal, point graphically to their own supreme fulfilment in the Christian revelation, he will surely have fulfilled his promise to lead the enquirer along a route that passes from the entrance hall of religious–philosophical discussion, across the threshold, to the inner sanctuary of Catholic Christian believing, what he calls, in the structuring metaphor of *Epilog*, the 'cathedral'.

Despite his evident distaste that *Epilog* might be treated as a digest of the trilogy at large, Balthasar's pages on the ontological distinctions he favours sum up in short compass materials set out more capaciously else-where.[11] As a good Thomist (in this respect, as others) he emphasises the real (and not merely formal) distinction between 'being as reality' (*Sein als Wirklichkeit*) and 'individual essences' (*die einzelnen Wesen*) which may or may not be fully realised by the sustaining gift of being (an aborted baby, for example). The fuller the power given the greater the energy of self-realisation, as is shown by that increasing interiority (plant in its eco-system, beast in its environment, human being in its life-world) we encounter as we move up the 'scale of being' – until, in man, we find being become self-aware (not only *an sich* but *für sich* too). If there is here a partial warrant for acknowledging man as in the divine image and likeness, Balthasar warns against any easy inference that (common) being, conjecturally realised in the subsistent archetype of the human spirit, *is* God. That way would lie idolatry. We know the two elements of *Weltsein*, what it is to be the world, only in their distinct deficiencies – that of *Sein*, what is bestowed, as well as that of *Wesen*, what receives. Combining the two will not make that ontological deficit disappear! We must not absolutise the finite so as the more readily to 'construct' God.

> It is enough that we know that no finite thing, even when realised, has posited itself [in being]: it has as horizon . . . a Ground to which it is indebted.[12]

The being an essence receives is not only an *An-sich* (and in the case of spirited creatures like the human being a *Für-sich* as well). It is also a *Mit-sein*, a being-with others (and in the case of man, a *Für-ein-ander(es) Sein*, a being for the other, whether personal or impersonal – Englishmen or Birman cats, the poor or antiques). That sets up a contrast of inner and outer which is the semantic presupposition of 'communication'. One can go out of oneself towards another, and in that act 'realise' one's 'within'. From this the distinction between appearance and hiddenness both arises and takes its power. For in order to give oneself, one must also protect the giver – where 'protect' does 'not imply hold something back but make possible the gift'.[13] In communication, the other lies open to me as a 'mystery lying beyond all concepts', its very objectivity a trusting appeal to my 'ontic love', to service it by letting it flower in my space, even as, reciprocally, it does service to me by bringing home to me my difference, in this way giving me to myself, enabling me to see self and others 'in the encompassing light of being, being as the real'.[14]

Thus there returns with force the problem of the unity of being, which the real distinction between being and beings left unresolved. If we introduce into the contrast of common being, on the one hand, and the individually realised, on the other, the concept of *polarity*, we see that the two poles define each other's need (being's to be received, the individual's to be realised), and in this fashion point to an ultimate identity which is their ground. That polarity is not, however, the sign of sheer creaturely

11 *Epilog*, pp. 38–45.
12 *Epilog*, p. 41.
13 *Epilog*, p. 42.
14 *Epilog*, pp. 42–3.

defect – how problematic it is not to be God! For the radical difference
which the real distinction brings about in the world's being is also what
allows for the 'solidarity, traffic and exchange of beings amongst
themselves, for their mutual inhabitation'.[15] And that in turn is the first
step towards what in free beings we know as love.

The question which this particular progression of ideas raises is, What
in that case must the Ground of being and beings, the absolute Identity,
be like? It would be hubristic of philosophy to claim to answer that query.
But this at least can be said: where the polarity of being is taken seriously
– where justice would be done both to being and beings – the fruitfulness
of love has to be considered a shadowing forth of something, however
inexpressible, in the *Urbild*, the divine Archetype itself.

On these bases – a selective summation of the philosophical doctrine of
Truth of the World – Balthasar moves forward to portray being as transcendentally self-showing, self-giving, self-saying, with all the implications
those neologisms carry for his three projects – the theological aesthetics,
theological dramatics, theological logic.

First, *self-showing*. All worldly being is epiphanic (here upholders of
the real distinction must concur with the poets: Claudel, Goethe and
the anonymous author of Psalm 19 in the Hebrew Bible). Some thing's
Erscheinungsgestalt, its 'form of appearing', expresses not only its essence
and not only the *Gesamtwirkliche*, or ecosystem, of the world to which it
belongs, but also beyond this that Ground to which Balthasar's
phenomenological description and ontological analysis have directed us:
the subsistingly real. That is why truly to take in something – from amoeba
to astral body, via azalea, anteater, Andrew and Andrea – produces *das
Staunen*, 'amazement'. In a form we call 'beautiful' the 'Unknown-Real'
makes itself known, intimates a reference to itself, and does so by that
combination of radiance and a pointing beyond itself which splendid form
always conveys. There can be superficial beauty – *Schein*. But in order to
be epiphany there must be *Erscheinung*, which is more, the showing
through of depths in being, suggesting the inner linking of the
transcendental 'beauty' to its fellow-transcendentals 'goodness' and 'truth'.
Balthasar warns that the ability to perceive this demands spiritual culture
(*Bildung*) – sensitivity to the meaning of images (*Bilder*), the capacity to
read forms as wholes. But the prize is great. The 'transcendental epiphany
of the world's being' anticipates the 'structure of the revelation of absolute
reality, whose midpoint is occupied by the form of Christ'.[16] Only
when through the 'unity of imagination' (the phrase is taken from the
classical German philosophers) the many images of the New Testament
are allowed to open up the *Ding an sich* of Jesus Christ in his full reality do
we gain access to the manifold dimensions conveyed by his form. In
him, as man, the 'worldly structures' of form and light serve the epiphany
of the 'structure' of the Absolute itself – for his humanity is the embodiment of his identity as the Trinitarian Son. In his Ascension the 'appearing'
(*die Erscheinung*) disappears, to make us understand that this was the
disclosure of the Absolute; and yet the Spirit has to interpret this form

15 *Epilog*, p. 45.
16 *Epilog*, p. 49.

and this alone as the definitive epiphany of that same Absolute, since the Son abides, though bodily invisible, in Church and world. Where the Absolute 'lights up and takes form' in the finite we are dealing with more than beauty.[17] We are dealing (here the title of the theological aesthetics seems unavoidable) with *glory*, and the response must be no longer 'plain' wonder and rapture, but worship.

Next, *self-giving*. The connexion between the beautiful and the good is easily traced: what shows itself by that token communicates itself, and in that sense gives itself. And while by no means rejecting the Aristotelean–Thomist definition of the good as that which all things seek, Balthasar holds that it is characteristic of beings endowed with knowledge and freedom to seek the good not only because they need it, or because it will satisfy, but also so to win it as to be its bestowers in self-giving. The good is the transcendental norm of all bestowing and being bestowed.

Reflection on this theme leads Balthasar to the conclusion that love is as much man's due as are water and sunlight to a plant – yet can one have a claim in justice (a 'right') to that which is only present if freely offered? From here arises those conflicting demands and accusations which are the root of drama – whether on a miniature family scale or in the vast panorama of world history. The theatre – as the theological dramatics proposed – is where that range of drama is represented. The good bestows itself – that is its nature – but *how* does it enter into freedom? One can speak of an example making an impression, but there is something deeper to which such diverse *loci* as Greek tragedy, the Buddhist notion of the *boddhisatva* and the Judaeo-Christian practice of an intercessory prayer accompanied by self-offering attest. In all these cases, direct influence is renounced, for recourse is had to a Ground in which everything is founded – even the freedom of another man. This finds its apogee in the vicarious substitutionary action of the Cross of Christ where kenosis, self-emptying, is power, the power of One dying that others may live. St Irenaeus will call its effect *suasio*, 'suasion', and St Augustine masterfully expounds it in the *De Spiritu et littera*, explaining it neither as compulsion nor as enticement from without, but as the 'laying open of the innermost freedom of the heart, which consists precisely in the love of God and one's neighbour'.[18] Through the Love-Ground of God – the Holy Spirit – the capacity of the human heart for its own most proper (*eigenst*) freedom finds gracious release. The *Sich-zeigen* of being is fulfilled in its *Sich-geben*, just as, in Origen of Alexandria's *Commentary on the Gospel of John*, it is because the light of Christ is love that it can 'take our darkness into itself, in order to expel it from our souls'.[19]

But for a spiritual being to 'make known its inwardness' language is required, and not simply 'externalising itself in appearing or deed'.[20] And so finally we come to *self-saying*. If self-showing and self-giving are truly transcendental determinations of being then they will be found across its entire gamut – and like, say, Schelling, Balthasar delights in fact to trace

17 *Epilog*, pp. 51–2.
18 *Epilog*, p. 56.
19 Origen, *Commentary on the Gospel of St John*, at 1, 5.
20 *Epilog*, p. 59.

in the plant and animal kingdoms *Vorstufen* – preliminary steps – of their happening in man (as well of course as their supreme exemplification in the divine). With 'self-saying' that might seem a little tricky. But this is to forget the analogues of speech in the pre-human world – in, for example, mimicry and gesture. Indeed, Balthasar insists that this capacity, essentially linked as it is to transcendental 'truth', is not only the locus of an end, an evolutionary top-notch in the family tree of life. It is also the place of a beginning, since for those aware that all things come to be through the divine knowing (the divine Word), every being is an utterance in the language of God. As to man, the gates of the human senses – eye *and ear* – stand ever open for a word to address us: to suit us, it must be both sensuous and intelligent, the word of mind or heart. In our response, the medium of our thinking and judging is language on which, remarks Balthasar, citing a hero of *Herrlichkeit*, J. G. Hamann, 'the entire capacity for thought reposes'.[21] In human dialogue, one can give or communicate in the sense of share (*mit-teilen*: one of the numerous instances of German punning in this text) even in poor words. 'Through the narrows of image-bound words souls can meet each other and exchange.'[22] Stillness and silence play their part here as well: one can belong to another without hearing oneself talk (another pun: *ge-hören, sich hören*). For linguistic subjects are free to scatter signs in the field of speech as they will. Such freedom necessarily raises the topic of the truth or falsehood of what is spoken: consonant with the ontologically oriented epistemology he has developed in the opening volume of the logic, Balthasar renews his insistence that it is only as things are measured by absolute Spirit – by God – that they are 'true'. The light in which we weight things in speech must participate in that primordial uncreated Light if we are not to betray their truth.

Looking back from the 'threshold' at his treatment of the transcendentals, Balthasar is inclined to award a certain primacy, within their interdependent unity, to *pulchrum*, the beautiful, since it best represents the epiphanic character of the world's being (though in another sense the beautiful is, with the good and the true, simply an aspect of this radiant appearing). In shining form something shows itself as meaningful (compare *verum*, true), and a gift to the world (compare *bonum*, good). Not fully satisfied with this account, he appeals to another to correct it. *Each* of the three transcendentals can claim a priority: the beautiful in the work of art; the good in an act of total devotion; the true in authentic speech as it illuminates being. Correspondingly, we must develop three primary attitudes: wonder at the beautiful; thankfulness for the good; faith in the true.

As he looks toward the final section of *Epilog*, 'Cathedral', Balthasar does not forget the apologetic, missionary purpose declared at the outset of this work. The polarity of being and beings, never absent from an account of any of these transcendentals, leads us to seek a final unity, grounding both poles. (It has sometimes been asked why Balthasar did

---

21 *Epilog*, p. 61. For a more contemporary mentor, Balthasar turns to T. Kobusch, *Sein und Sprache: Grundlegung einer Ontologie der Sprache* (Leiden 1986).
22 *Epilog*, p. 62.

not make his trilogy a tetralogy by adding a treatise on divine revelation in the perspective of *unum*.) Unity is the first of the transcendentals: it undergirds all the rest. In the divine Source to which the dialectic of being and beings directs our gaze, 'God's glory is his self-giving, and this again is his truth'.[23] That identity of the three has for presupposition, however, the divine freedom (God is the archetype of spirit), and this is a freedom to show himself, give himself, speak himself, not ineluctably but *as he wills*. Here we cross the boundary into the sanctuary, where we shall hear more of the Father's Son who is his Word (his self-utterance), his Expression (his self-manifestation) and his Child (his self-giving), and of the Spirit in whose fruitful love, the difference between the Persons of Father and Son remaining, the unity of God is regained in enhanced guise. Meditating on the processions and missions of Son and Spirit will lead Balthasar to re-think yet again that issue of the relative priority of the transcendentals, and settle finally on the primacy of *bonum* which in God is the divine love.

Cathedral

Consonant with his conviction that fundamental and dogmatic theology should never be sundered, Balthasar has anticipated, on the edge of the 'threshold', some of what he calls, in a deliberate paradox, the 'sacred public *arcana* of Christian revelation'.[24] These *arcana*, 'secrets', are as un-expected as any esoteric teachings of some mystery religion. But unlike the latter, they are entirely exposed to public view – and are so in a special manner on the Cross of Christ which Balthasar echoes Paul in calling the folly of God, wiser than the wisdom of men. Despite the *preambula fidei* of the 'method of integration' and a metaphysics of being as beautiful, good, true, through which Balthasar has taken us, when we cross the threshold into the heart of the Church's sanctuary that divine folly should make us stumble. We should enter in a state of shock.

Proclaimed at the altar of this 'cathedral' are three inter-connected doctrinal themes: 'Christology and Trinity', 'The Word becomes flesh' and 'Fruitfulness'. These pages allow us a last look at those few dogmatic points – from among the vast array presented in the trilogy at large – that were closest to Balthasar's heart, most fed his Christian imagination.[25]

Jesus Christ could not say, I am the Truth (the Johannine 'I Am' central to the theological logic), unless everything in the world bore a necessary reference to him, and this can only be the case if he is the *analogia entis* – the analogical sharing of finite being in Infinite being – in his own person. As Son of the Father, he is 'the total epiphany, self-giving and self-utterance of God', and so can be, within the world's being, in the midst of the finite, the 'adequate sign, giving, statement, of God'.[26] For the endorsement of

23 *Epilog*, p. 66.
24 *Epilog*, p. 69.
25 In this way, *Epilog*, pp. 69–98, resembles his short commentary on the Apostles' Creed, *Credo: Meditationen zum Apostolischen Glaubensbekenntnis* (Freiburg–Basel–Vienna 1989²).
26 Ibid.

his claim he draws attention not only to his miracles but also to his human destiny as a whole – the way he works by mirroring the ever-working Father (cf. John 5.19) and does so up to the climax of his Cross and Resurrection.

> So the entirety of Jesus's being human becomes a self-utterance and self-giving of God, so unique – both in speaking . . . and in deliberate silence, in action as in passion – that from his highness (the appearing glory) and perfect servanthood . . . the truth of his whole being can be read off, with a certainty that does not exclude faith but includes it.[27]

Thanks to the interpretative work of the Holy Spirit, we can see through this Icon to the Father, and Balthasar insists on the *erscheinende Leiblichkeit*, the bodily appearance, of the Logos as the instrument of the revelation of God, not least in the Resurrection where he must show himself Victor over death in his victimhood in dying, and thus disclose the mighty divine power.

The transcendentals irradiate the human Jesus, just as they reign in the self-disclosure of God. That the two poles, finite and Infinite, come together in Christ does not mean, though, that the ontologist from now on has God in his eye. The real 'identity' of God lies in his tripersonality whose vitality, yes, the transcendentals unfold but who remains beyond everything we might infer from *Seiendsein*, the being of beings – which is how Balthasar understands and accepts the assertion of Gregory of Nyssa and Dionysius the Aeropagite, that God is 'beyond being'. Only so can he in sovereign freedom turn to being, attend to it, *serve* it (so Balthasar dares to write) in his perfect love – a love constituted by the inner-Trinitarian relations and by nothing less than that (or rather *Them*). That is why what Jesus reveals is the triune Love, and there especially where un-love withstands it – though he wills to draw its sting and bury it for ever in death and hell. For in the Word incarnate forms of love that the world treats as contrary one to another are reconciled and atoned in a New Testament fulfilment of the many facets of Old Testament man-before-God, a fulfilment that could not have been dreamed of till it happened (a leading preoccupation, this, of the first and last volumes of the aesthetics). It is the poor in spirit alone (certainly not the majority of historical-critical scholars!) who see this complexity with truly divine simplicity.

The circumincession in Christ of all the transcendentals points, since he is the Father's Word, to the riches of the love of God – his nature as triune Communion. Hence the shockingness of the claim that this Word is in the Incarnation *flesh*, flesh on which my salvation turns, mortal flesh, flesh laid low in death as mine will be. But the Passion of Christ was only possible in the body: first, because (so Balthasar thinks) the soul's pain is made possible by its embodiment; second, because the world-redeeming rationale of the Passion of Christ could only be realised through a unity, given in matter, between the Logos Incarnate and those human beings he entered solidarity with us in order to save. The Incarnation has, through

27 *Epilog*, p. 70.

the body, cosmic corollaries. Christ's Headship, as the New Adam, over his 'body', the Church, on the one hand, and, on the other, his cosmic Lordship, are 'only comprehensible in a reciprocal movement of both magnitudes'.[28] All the blood and tears of sacrifice on a cosmic scale, the witless sacrifices of animals, the conscious if not always willing sacrifices of human beings, are embraced in the *absolute Hingabe*, the unconditional self-giving, of the Logos on the Cross, ushering the anthropic cosmos into the realm opened by Christ's substitutionary yet all-embracing act.

But then, as if to dissuade us from getting carried away on a wave of *Teilhardisme*, Balthasar rubs our noses in the hard particularity of Jesus' body. That is the thing about bodies: they force us to recognise that the other is not myself. It is a new Kierkegaard, rather than a second Teilhard, we listen to when we hear Balthasar on the scandal that 'out of this bodily present man the personal Word of God himself speaks', confounding our assumption that 'God is in heaven and we on earth, since God is spirit and we body, or if he be body then certainly not this individual, mortal body, comparable with all others'. But so it is, all in the cause that a 'definitive self-showing, self-saying, self-bestowing' might occur.[29] And so it continues, in the abiding outpouring of the body and the blood in the Holy Eucharist.

No religion, Balthasar thinks, other than the Christian one, can cope with death, since no other can know death as love.

That forms, in the case of the Atonement, no bad transition to the last motif in Balthasar's 'Cathedral' and thus the closing theme of *Epilog*: 'fruitfulness'. A favoured image of the German Romantic poets, Balthasar has found it indispensable for expounding the good that comes from the Christian mysteries – and indeed the absolute Good that is the most Ancient of them all, the Holy Trinity.

The transcendentals can be understood as ways in which being lies open, and the sign *par excellence* of this *Sich-eröffnen* of being is fruitfulness. The cosmic fruitfulness of nature is linked with dying (literally, for some species for which death occurs in the intercourse that brings life). Now the ontology presented in the theological logic has not hesitated to see in such cosmic fruitfulness an echo of the primordial mystery of being, its Trinitarian composition. But when Jesus Christ comes to express the triune God and pour forth this primal mystery in finite acts, he breaks that natural circle of bearing and dying, dying and bearing, by an action that is no less bodily yet has another meaning. On the Cross, dying was fruitful, bringing forth not more life that will die again but a new life belonging to the 'everlasting, triunely fruitful life of God'.[30] The divine Fruitfulness which at sundry times in the past – culminating in the motherhood of the Virgin – rendered humanly fruitful in a supernatural mode those who were barren, now begins to shower forth its blessings in new and unheard of ways, in Mary's spiritual motherhood of the Church and John the Beloved Disciple's contemplativity, in the sacramental Church, which continues

28 *Epilog*, p. 80.
29 *Epilog*, p. 82.
30 *Epilog*, p. 87.

Christ's bodily presence in the world and for the world, and in the seven sacraments, none of which makes sense save as a mediation of the work of the salvation-bringer in his Paschal Mystery.

Yet we cannot end in a Samuel Palmer landscape, all nature bathed in the translucence of grace, as a people, solemn but happy, files from church into a countryside paradisially bejewelled. The theological dramatics have shown how, where divine love is most manifest, human hatred is worst released, and that message of the Johannine corpus (and notably the Apocalypse), backed up as it is, alas, by observation, gives Balthasar pause. Divine fruitfulness, it seems, has not carried away in its beneficent stream the daily abuses of human freedom – not even (or especially?) in Christendom. Must we assume, then, that the world will continue tragic to the end and be, in the meta-historical End, frozen, like figures in Dante's *Inferno*, in that state? Congruent with Catholic teaching and the sources of revelation which control and limit what that teaching may say, Balthasar can only suggest grounds for hope (not pillars of certainty). If St Cyril and the Council of Chalcedon are right, then the Incarnation has altered all humanity's position (though with this nothing is as yet said about the *individual*'s freedom). Again, in the Atonement the Son has shown love to be stronger than Hell, enduring for the salvation of all deeper alienation from the Father than any mortal could. But third, the Pentecostal Spirit, the Spirit of the atoning Christ, can enter human freedom from within since he is not only its norm but its source. And fourth, we do not know the power of finite freedom to resist the soliciting love of God to the bitter end. Among the witnesses Balthasar summons to his side on a point much contested by faithful Catholics who would rather be his friends,[31] none is briefer or more affecting than the French playwright Gabriel Marcel's: 'J'espère en Toi pour nous': 'I hope in Thee, for us.'[32]

31 Among the literature, see J. Ambaum, 'An Empty Hell: The Restoration of All Things. Balthasar's Concept of Hope for Salvation', *Communio* 18 (1991), pp. 35–52; J. R. Sachs, 'Current Eschatology: Universal Salvation and the Problem of Hell', *Theological Studies* 52 (1991), pp. 227–54; G. Fessard, 'Eternal Damnation or Universal Salvation', *Communio* 23 (1996), pp. 579–603; as well as Balthasar's own *Was dürfen wir hoffen* (Einsiedeln 1989²), and *Kleine Diskurs über die Hölle* (Ostfildern 1987).
32 Cited at *Epilog*, p. 98.

28

Postword

Balthasar's trilogy is a great forest where I have attempted – for my own edification, and education, as well as for that of others – to make the contours of the wood visible despite the profusion of the trees. It is impossible not to be impressed by the architectonic way in which the materials of Scripture and Tradition are pressed into service with a view to seeing the total content of divine revelation in the perspective suggested by the three transcendentals: the beautiful, the good, the true. Not that the full range of the monuments of Tradition is exploited: Balthasar privileges his first love, the Fathers of the Church, and after them the mediaeval doctors, and the approved mystics of the Church of all ages. The Liturgy, Eastern and Western, and the iconography of the Church are, despite their evident congeniality to him, less invoked than one might like. The philosophical underpinnings of the aesthetics and dramatics, already laid in *Wahrheit der Welt* and – so it transpired when the latter work re-appeared as the first volume of the theological logic – never repudiated, may be compared with those found in Balthasar's younger contemporary, Pope John Paul II. Both men aimed so to use phenomenology as to ground phenomena in real ontology, but while Pope Wojtyla's philosophy is Thomas catalysed by Scheler and thus strongest in the ethical domain, Balthasar's is Thomas fructified by Goethe and Schelling, and therefore especially concerned with cosmology in its relation to subjecthood and interiority. The whole of *Theologik* I could be described as a meditation on a somewhat throw-away remark of Thomas' in the Commentary on the Sentences: *res corporales sunt in anima nobiliori modo quam in seipsis*, 'bodily things are in the soul in a more noble fashion than they are in themselves'.[1]

What the reader who comes to the trilogy from a background in humane letters will marvel at is the range of reference which can integrate into the dramatics a myriad dramatic constructions suggested by actual plays, and into the aesthetics rich raids on the mythopoetic, the common fund of images understood (or at any rate understandable) by members of the race. But Balthasar is no Chateaubriand, seeking to impress the secular critic with the genius of Christianity via his own. The entire trilogy is

---

1 Thomas Aquinas, *In libros Sententiarum*, I, dist. 3, q. 4, art 4, corpus. I am indebted for this reference to my Cambridge Dominican confrère, Fr Edward Booth.

controlled by a deep feeling of docility towards divine revelation where all issues from the love of God that posits form – and thus founds all analogical discourse in dogmatics – from its own side.[2] It is consciousness of that practised *betende Theologie*, 'theology on one's knees', as well as confidence in the mystical insights suggested by Adrienne von Speyr, which excuses, if it does not wholly justify, the innovatory passages on the interrelation of Trinitarian theology and eschatology that make the final volume of the theological dramatics both compelling and disturbing to read.

It falls to the theological community of the *Catholica*, under the guardianship of the magisterium, to evaluate those particular novelties in Balthasar's work. His conviction that theology should not cry off the effort of *cataphatic* exploration of the ultimate divine mystery by a premature appeal to the *apophatic* need for restraint before its greatness was always matched by a willingness to *sentire cum Ecclesia*, 'think feelingly with the Church'.

Meanwhile, as we enter a new millennium, there is much here – incredibly much – to inspire a Catholic Christianity that seems often lacking in the power to move its adherents or attract what should be its converts – move and attract imaginatively, dramatically, intellectually. I hope that, through the effort of *haute-vulgarisation* my three commentaries have involved, many clergy and laity will find resources in Balthasar to do just that.

---

2 The theme of this is Manfred Lochbrunner's marvellous study, *Analogia caritatis: Darstellung und Deutung der Theologie Hans Urs von Balthasars* (Freiburg–Basel–Vienna 1981).

᳟᳟᳟

Select Bibliography

General studies of Balthasar

R. Gawronski, *Word and Silence: Hans Urs von Balthasar and the Spiritual Encounter between East and West* (Edinburgh 1995).

J. Godenir, *Jésus, l'Unique: Introduction à la théologie de Hans Urs von Balthasar* (Paris–Namur 1984).

E. Guerriero, *Hans Urs von Balthasar* (Milan 1992²).

M. Kehl and W. Löser (eds), *The von Balthasar Reader* (Et New York 1982).

B. McGregor and T. Norris (eds), *The Beauty of Christ: An Introduction to the Theology of Hans Urs von Balthasar* (Edinburgh 1994).

A. Moda, *Hans Urs von Balthasar: Un' espozione critica del suo pensiero* (Bari 1976).

E. T. Oakes, *The Pattern of Redemption: The Theology of Hans Urs von Balthasar* (New York 1994).

J. O'Donnell, *Hans Urs von Balthasar* (London 1992).

J. Saward, *The Mysteries of March: Hans Urs von Balthasar on the Incarnation and Easter* (London 1990).

D. L. Schindler (ed.), *Hans Urs von Balthasar: His Life and Work* (San Francisco 1991).

A. Scola, *Hans Urs von Balthasar: Uno stile teologico* (Milan 1991); Et *Hans Urs von Balthasar: A Theological Style* (Edinburgh 1995).

Studies of Balthasar's logic and related themes

E. F. Bauer, 'Hans Urs von Balthasar (1905–1988): Sein philosophisches Werk', in E. Coreth, W. M. Neidl, G. Pfligersdorffer (eds), *Christliche Philosophie im katholischen Denken des 19. und 20. Jahrhunderts*, III *Moderne Strömungen im 20. Jahrhundert* (Graz 1990), pp. 285–304.

L. S. Chapp, *The God who Speaks: Hans Urs von Balthasar's Theology of Revelation* (San Francisco, 1997).

213

R. CHIA, *Revelation and Theology: The Knowledge of God in Balthasar and Barth* (Berne 1999).

J.-P. DISSE, *Metaphysik der Singularität: Eine Hinführung am Leitfaden der Philosophie Hans Urs von Balthasars* (Vienna 1996).

A. F. FRANKS, 'Trinitarian *analogia entis* in Hans Urs von Balthasar', *The Thomist* 62 (1998), pp. 533–59.

P. IDE, *Être et mystère: La philosophie de Hans Urs von Balthasar* (Brussels 1995).

W. KLAGHOFER-TREITLER, *Gotteswort im Menschenwort: Inhalt und Form von Theologie nach Hans Urs von Balthasar* (Innsbruck–Vienna 1992).

——, *Karfreitag: Auseinandersetzung mit Hans Urs von Balthasars 'Theologik'* (Innsbruck–Vienna 1997).

M. LOCHBRUNNER, *Analogia caritatis: Darstellung und Deutung der Theologie Hans Urs von Balthasars* (Freiburg–Basel–Vienna 1981).

W. LÖSER, 'Being Interpreted as Love: Reflections on the Theology of Hans Urs von Balthasar', *Communio* XVI (1989), pp. 475–90.

R. MENGUS, 'L'"Epilogue" de Hans Urs von Balthasar (1905–1988)', *Revue des Sciences Religieuses* 62 (1988), pp. 252–64.

J. PALAKEEL, *The Use of Analogy in Theological Discourse: An Investigation in Ecumenical Perspective* (Rome 1995).

E. PÉREZ HARO, *El misterio del ser: Una mediación entre filosofía y teología en Hans Urs von Balthasar* (Barcelona 1994).

U. J. PLAGA-KAYSER, *'Ich bin die Wahrheit': Die theologische Dimension der Christologie Hans Urs von Balthasars* (Münster 1998).

M. SAINT-PIERRE, *Beauté, bonté, vérité chez Hans Urs von Balthasar* (Quebec 1998).

G. DE SCHRIJVER, *Le merveilleux accord de l'homme et de Dieu: Etude de l'analogie de l'être chez Hans Urs von Balthasar* (Leuven 1983).

Index of Subjects

ana-logic 69, 117
  and understanding about the
    Incarnation 95
analogy, and the hypostatic union of
  the Logos 114–18
analysis, as part of human knowledge
  of worldly truth 58–9
angelology 26, 120
animal life, interiority of being 24–5
'Apocalypse of the German Soul'
  (Balthasar), God as the object of
  human existence 16
apophaticism, as description of the
  Incarnation 78–80
apostles
  parental relationship with
    individual churches 178
  preaching 175, 176
arts, fulfilment in Jesus Christ 95, 97–8
assumptio 112
atheism, rejection of God 192
Atonement 210

baptised, temptation 121
Baptism 177
beauty
  relationship to being 53, 206
  relationship to truth 38
  and the relationship of truth and
    being 11
becoming, in the hypostatic union of
  the Logos 111–14
being
  concrete individuals and their
    relationship with universals 40–1
  expression in personal existence
    46–8
  knowability 55

being (cont.)
  meditation about as precursor to
    Christian faith 202
  mystery 51–4, 57
  personality 46
  reactions to divine being 206
  revelation in subject–object
    relationships 15–22
  and truth 9–13
  see also divine being; man
believers
  experience of the Holy Spirit 182–3
  incorporation into Christ 167–8
Bible
  New Testament, as revelation of
    God's love 179
  Old Testament, theme of
    personality 167
  Pneumatology 135–7, 139–40, 148–9
body language 106
Buddhism
  negative theology 78
  selflessness 163

Canon Law 178–9
Cappadocian Fathers 140, 148
cata-logic 117
  Jesus Christ
    as the key to the Trinitarian
      structure of history 95, 98–9
    and reconciliation between
      creation and God 95, 96–7, 99
Chalcedon, Council (AD 451) 210
Chalcedonian definition 81
Charismatic Renewal 184–5
charisms 168, 170, 173
Christian Fathers, negative theology
  78–9

215

Christian life
  grace 172
  testimony to the presence of the
    Holy Spirit 185
Christianity
  arguments for as the ground of
    faith 197–8
  historical nature and universal
    validity 152–4
  recognition of separation between
    God and creation overcome in the
    love of the Trinity 200–1
Christology
  explanation by Pneumatology
    135–8
  involvement in Pneumatology
    131–3
Church
  Balthasar's wish to work with the
    Church through theologic 212
  Catholic Church 169
  catholicity 166
  as Christ's body 116–17, 118, 135
  as expression of love within the
    Trinity 160
  and the Holy Spirit 167–72
    gifts 161
    objective holiness 172–81
    subjective holiness 172–4, 181–5
    universal communion through the
      Holy Spirit 154
    work under the guidance of the
      Holy Spirit 129
  as link betweeen the God the Father
    and the world 187
  mission and the believer's
    participation through
    justification 165
  roles of God the Son and the Holy
    Spirit 167–70
  and the State 185
  and the world 162–4, 166–7
Church Fathers, Pneumatology 138,
  140–1
communication, as means for giving a
  sense of being to individual
  essences 203
Confirmation 177
Confucianism 199, 200
Constantinople, fall (1453) 99
Constantinopolitan Creed 156
constellations 45
contemplation, as response to Jesus
  Christ's teaching 76
cosmos *see* creation

created beings, truth measured by
  God 206
creation 15
  Christ's lordship 116–17, 118
  goal as return to God the Father
    191–4
  as image of the Trinity 77, 91–4
  participation in the divine nature 86
  relationship with Trinity through
    the Incarnation 2–6
  as revelation of God 26, 57–9
  unlikeness to God 77–8
the Cross
  as the climax of the Incarnation
    115
  and the contradiction of sin 120–1

damnation 48
death, as love 209
Dei Filius (Vatican I) 3, 4n
Dei Verbum (Vatican II) 4n
Descent into Hell 120–1, 122
Devil, personality 120
dialogue
  as basis for understanding the
    Trinity 71–2
  inadequacies as reflection of the
    Incarnation 73
difference, in the Trinity and in
  creation 94, 95
Diognetus, Letter to 166
discipleship, as response to Jesus
  Christ's teaching 76
divine being
  distinctiveness from individual
    essences 203–4
  nature shown by the transcendentals
    of self-disclosure 204–7, 208,
    209–10, 211
  revelation through images 37–41
    distortions 35–7
    in language 41–3
  unicity reflected in personal
    individuality 40
  see also being
divinisation 150
dying, sacrament 178

Epilog (Balthasar), justification of
  Balthasar's approach to
  dogmatics 197
essence, and existence 27, 45–6, 47–8,
  77
essences
  distinctiveness from being 203–4

essences (*cont.*)
  sense of being through
    communication with each
    other 203
essentialism, within the Trinity 81–6,
  87
eternal life 48
Eucharist (Mass) 153, 177
evolution, and the role of the Holy
  Spirit 188–9
existence, and essence 27, 45–6, 47–8,
  77
experience, Holy Spirit's activity in
  human experience 152
Extrema unctio 178

faith
  as freedom 165
  in the hypostatic union of the
    Logos 111
  as recognition of Jesus Christ's
    revelation of God the Father 109
  and the revelation of being through
    images 43
faithfulness, as an attribution of
  God 85
Filioquism 86–7, 145, 155–7
flesh
  importance in the Incarnation 208–9
  language, as expression of the
    Incarnation 105–6
  redemption as the whole counsel of
    God 101–3
  and salvation 172
forgiveness 182
freedom
  interrelationship with justification
    and sanctification 164–5
  as the truth of being 10
  as the truth of revelation of objects
    23–7, 28, 29, 30, 31
  as the truth of the self-revelation of
    subjects 28–31
  within the Trinity and humanity as
    nature of the Holy Spirit 158–9
fruitfulness, and divine being 209–10

Gift, as nature of the Holy Spirit
  157–8
glory, as an attribution of God 85
glossolalia 184
God
  concept 16–17
  counsel, in the redemption of the
    flesh 101–3

God (*cont.*)
  as His own foundation 193
  holiness 165
  knowledge about humanity as the
    basis of existence 18–19
  knowledge of creation 30–1
  and the Logos 81–9
  Luther's concept 122
  as measure of truth in created beings
    206
  mystery, as revealed in the
    Incarnation 63–5, 67–8, 69
  revelation in creation 26, 57–9
  revelation in finite truth 56
  unity as love 99
  unlikeness to creation 77–8
  see also God the Father; God the Son;
    Holy Spirit; Incarnation; Jesus
    Christ; Logos; Trinity
God the Father
  activity in the Incarnation 112,
    147–9
    implications 150–5
  hypostasis within the Trinity 81,
    83–4
  icon seen in Jesus Christ 107–9
  monarchy 156–7
  return to the Father as the goal of the
    Holy Spirit for creation 191–4
  revelation 73–4
    and Gift of the Son through the
      Holy Spirit 157–8
    through Jesus Christ 76, 111, 113
    Christ's teaching 75, 76–7
  will to salvation fulfilled in Jesus
    Christ 107
  see also God; God the Son; Holy
    Spirit; Incarnation; Jesus Christ;
    Logos; Trinity
God the Son
  activity
    in relation to that of the Holy
      Spirit 140, 147–9
    implications 150–5
  as gift 143
  role in the Church 167–70
  see also God; God the Father; Holy
    Spirit; Incarnation; Jesus Christ;
    Logos; Trinity
Godhead, attributes 84–5
good, relation to the mystery of
  being 53
goodness
  in creation and its relation to the
    Trinity 91–4

goodness (*cont.*)
  and the relationship of truth and
    being 11
grace
  caritas 70
  and human freedom 159
  within the Christian life 172
  work 5

Hebrews, Letter 113, 115
Hegelianism, and negativity 120
Hell 10–11, 120–1, 122
heresy, partial apprehension of
    truth 32
Hermas, Pneumatology 138
Hinduism 163
history
  as expression of truth's totality
    48–9
  Trinitarian structure 95, 98–9
Holiness Code 178–9
holiness in the life of the Church
  objective holiness 174–81
  objective and subjective
    holiness 172–4
  subjective holiness 181–5
holism 13
Holy Saturday 122
Holy Spirit
  being 144–5
    Church Fathers 140–1
    mediaeval Fathers 141–3
    modern period 143–4
    New Testament 139–40
  epiclesis 177
  as Gift 157–8
  gifts in personal life and in the
    Church 161
  as Interpreter of God the Father 74
  and Jesus Christ
    activity 135–8, 139, 147–9
      implications 150–5
    continuation of the work of the
      Logos 127–9
    as interpreter of Jesus Christ as
      revelation of the Trinity 208
    as interpreter of the parables 76
    role in the Incarnation 63–5, 67,
      112
    task to conjoin the world with the
      Logos 99
  relationship to the world 187–9
  role 210
    within the Church 167–70, 171–2
      objective holiness 174–81

Holy Spirit (*cont.*)
    in objective and subjective
      holiness 172–4
    subjective holiness 181–5
    within creation 193–4
  salvation of the world and the
    Church 162
  and the Trinitarian structure of
    history 98
  and the Trinity
    as freedom of the Trinity and
      freedom within humanity 158–9
    hypostasis within the Trinity 81,
      83–4, 86–7
    and love within the Trinity
      159–60, 171
    as revealer of Father–Son
      relationship in the Trinity
      129–30
  see also God; God the Father; God the
    Son; Incarnation; Jesus Christ;
    Logos; Trinity
homoousion 200–1
human beings
  freedom
    abuses not abolished by Divine
      fruitfulness 210
    given through the Holy Spirit 159
  interiority of being 25–6
  knowledge of God 16–22
  nature 199–201
  spiritual development through
    physical growth 41–2
  union with the Logos 116
  see also man
human knowledge, perception of finite
    and infinite truth 58–9
human nature
  as directed by God and oriented
    towards God 198
  exaltation in the Incarnation 112
Humani Generis (Pius XII) 4n

I–Thou relationships
  and personality 70, 71
  as reflection of the Trinity 71
iconoclast controversy 107–8
icons *see* images
identity, in the Trinity 93–4
images
  as expression of the hypostatic
    union of the Logos 109
  as expressions of the divine 105, 106
  Jesus Christ as the image of God the
    Father 107–9

images (*cont.*)
  prohibition in the Old Testament as
      the precursor to Jesus Christ as the
      image of God 76
  as revelation of the truth of
      mystery 37–41
      distortions 35–7
      through language 41–3
  and the subject–object relationship
      in the revelation of God 19–22
immutability, in the Godhead 112
Incarnation 101, 102, 210
  ana-logic as understanding about
      the Incarnation 95
  contradiction 103–5
  and the contradiction of sin and
      obedience 119–23
  as described by negative
      theology 78–80
  expression in the language of the
      flesh 105–6
  as expression of the relationship
      between Trinity and creation 2–6
  as fact 111–12
  as the fulfilment of myth 106–7
  and the Holy Spirit 148–9, 150
  as the icon of God the Father
      108–9
  as image of divine being 39
  importance of the flesh 208–9
  inadequately reflected in dialogue
      between the human and the divine
      73
  as the overcoming of difference in
      creation and between creation and
      God 95–7
  as revelation of God's mystery 63–5,
      67–8, 69
  symbolic nature of revelation of God
      the Father 109
  and the Trinity 65, 68, 69–72, 149,
      151–2, 160
  see also God; God the Son; Jesus
      Christ; Logos; Trinity
incorporation 150
inculturation 162
integration, method 198
intellectual activity, in the Logos
      112–13
Islam, recognition of separation
      between God and creation 200
Israel, salvation history 192

Jesus Christ
  advent 28

Jesus Christ (*cont.*)
  communion with believers through
      the sacraments 176–7
  disclosure of the divine
      attributes 84–5, 87
  form revealed by the Spirit 154–5
  as founder of new relationship
      between the world and God 95, 99
  as fulfiller of arts and sciences 95,
      97–8
  as fulfilment of God the Father's will
      to salvation 107
  as fulfilment of Tradition 174
  historical nature and universal
      authority 152–4
  as the image of God 21, 107–9
  as infinite truth 63–5, 68, 69
  as the key to the Trinitarian
      structure of history 95, 98–9
  as the means of leading all creation
      to sonship to God 192
  parables, as revelation of God the
      Father 110
  Passion, as overcoming of the
      contradiction between divine love
      and human sin 189
  power 185
  as revelation of the Trinity 73–4,
      202, 204–5, 207–9
  and the role of theology 180–1
  sacrifice and its results in
      justification 165
  as self-expression of the Logos 74–9
  summary of the Torah 67
  symbolic nature of his revelation of
      God the Father 109
  words, as revelation of God the
      Father 111
  see also God; God the Father; God the
      Son; Holy Spirit; Incarnation;
      Logos; Resurrection; Trinity
John, St
  Gospel
      dialectic 104
      and the Incarnation 63–5, 67
      Pneumatology 127, 135–8, 149
      theme of sight 108
      use of 'flesh' 101, 103
  letters 121
Judaism
  approaches to understanding about
      God 71–2
  recognition of separation between
      God and creation 200
justice, as an attribution of God 85

justification 179
  interrelationship with sanctification
    and freedom 164–5

Kantianism, subject–object relation
    20
kenosis 169, 171, 205
  in the Incarnation 112, 113
  within the Trinity 92
  and in creation 92, 93
knowledge
  comparison between divine and
    human knowledge 30–1
in the subject–object relationship as the
    revelation of God 16–22

language
  analogy 77
  as expression of the Incarnation
    105–6, 109–11
  as revelation of being 41–3
Last Supper, Farewell Discourse 169
Law
  misery 121
  radicalisation by love 178–9
liberation theology 164, 187
lies, as attack on truth's unity 49
light, as property of truth 18
Liturgy 176
logic
  Balthasar's understanding 95
  as reflection of God 69, 71
  relationships between divine and
    human logic 73
Logos
  as the focal point for creation 93
  hypostatic union 101–3
    as becoming 111–14
    contradiction in the Incarnation
      103–5
    expression in the language of the
      flesh 105–6
    as the fulfilment of myth 106–7
    as the icon of God the Father
      107–9
    nature and expression in
      language 109–11
    use of analogy 114–18
  as key to nature of human beings
    199–201
  as revelation and Gift of the Father
    157–8
  self-expression through Jesus Christ
    74–9
  within the Godhead 81–9

Logos (*cont.*)
  work continued by Holy Spirit
    127–9
  see also God; God the Father; God the
    Son; Holy Spirit; Incarnation; Jesus
    Christ; Trinity
love
  as an attribution of God 84, 85, 86–7,
    88
  divine love, contradiction with
    human sin overcome by Christ's
    Passion 189
  experience 16
  in the Incarnation 67, 68, 102, 103,
    119–20
  radicalisation of law 178–9
  as reflection of God 71
  relationship to the mystery of being
    52, 53
  relationship to truth 29–30, 31–3
  and the revelation of being through
    images 43
  shown in Christ's death 209
  as testimony to the presence of the
    Holy Spirit in Christian life 185
  as the unity of God 99
  within the Trinity 82–5, 144–5, 150,
    157–8, 159–60
    as the essence of creation 192–3
    as overcoming of separation
      between God and creation
      200–1
    as procession of the Son and the
      Spirit in creation 92
    and the role of the Holy Spirit 171
    self-giving 205
Luke, St, Pneumatology 137, 149
Lutheran-Catholic dialogue 164, 165

man
  co-inherence with all creation as
    difference from God 102–3
  as microcosm of the world's
    macrocosm 102
  relationship with the Logos 88
  see also being; human beings
marriage 177
Marxism 199
Mass (Eucharist) 153, 177
measure, as property of truth 18
mercy, as an attribution of God 85
metaphors, as expression of the
    hypostatic union of the Logos 110
mind 15
ministries, in the Church 173

ministry–Tradition–Scripture, within
    the Church 174–5
miracles 184
Monopatrism 145, 155
Monothelite controversy 113
mystery
    relationship to truth, and its
        revelation through images 35–43
    as shown in the truth of being 10,
        51–4, 57–8
mysticism 173, 182
myths, as evidence of immediacy of
    the divine 106–7

nature
    philosophy 24–6
    as the truth of being 10, 11–12
    see also phenomenology
negativity, and Hegelianism 120
Neoplatonism
    mysticism 78, 79
    union with the one as the goal of
        creation 192
New Testament *see* Bible
New Theology 48–9, 198
Nicaea, Council (Seventh Ecumenical
    Council, 787) 108
non-Christian religions
    Christianisation 162–3
    denial of worth of being in creation
        200
    rejections of Christianity
        understandable 201–2
    views of creation's union with the
        Good seen as schematisms 192–3
non-contradiction, principle, as
    applied to the Christian character
    121–2
nouvelle théologie 48–9, 198

obedience, contradiction in the
    Incarnation 119–23
object–subject relationships
    freedom of the object in self-
        revelation 23–7, 28, 29, 30, 31
    freedom of the subject in self-
        revelation 28–31
    and the revelation of being 15–22
Old Testament *see* Bible
omnipotence, as an attribution of God
    85
Ontologism 17
Ordination 178
orthodoxy 150–2
orthopraxy 150–2

Palamism 74, 141–2
    lack of truth 85
parables
    as revelation of God the Father in
        Jesus Christ 110
    as revelation of the Kingdom of God
        in Jesus Christ 76–7
participation
    in the God–world relationship 58
    as the truth of being 10
Passion, work of the Holy Spirit
    148–9
Paul, St (apostle) 78, 79, 80, 82, 85,
    121, 135, 167, 168, 173, 189
    Church's mission, in Philippians
        162–3
    discernment of spirits 183, 184
    Ephesians 115, 162
    Pneumatology 137, 140, 149
    preaching 175, 176
Penance 177
personal existence, as expression of
    being 46–8
personal life, and the Spirit's gifts 161
Personalism 143
    within the Trinity 81–6, 87
personality
    and the I–Thou relationship 70, 71
    achieved through mission of the Son
        and gift of the Spirit 154
    in the Old Testament 167
Persons 140–3, 144
    individuality, as reflection of divine
        unicity 40
    relationship within the Trinity 132,
        133n, 140–3, 144, 155–6
    see also Trinity
phenomenalism 36
phenomenology
    as revelation of the truth of being
        10, 11–12
    and theologic 211
    see also nature
philosophy
    aims, and links with theology 4
    approaches to the Incarnation 67
    systems, and creation's knowledge
        of God 5–6
Platonism 192
Pneumatochian controversy 128
Pneumatology
    explanation of Christology 135–8
    inclusion of Christology 131–3
polarity
    in being 27

polarity (*cont.*)
  between characteristics of essences,
    as indicator of the unity of being
    203–4
polytheism, and divine unity 4–5
Positivism 6
  neglect of consideration of human
    nature 199
  rejection of union with God 192
practice, and theory 77
prayer 181–2
  as response to Jesus Christ's
    teaching 76
pre-Christians, temptation 121
preaching 175–6, 179
priesthood 173
  ministerial priesthood 170, 172, 178
prophecy 173
prudence, importance for attitudes to
  truth 31–3
Pythagoreans, analogical teaching 117

rationalism, relationship to truth
  12–13
reconciliation, as the overcoming of
  difference in creation and between
  creation and God 95–7
religion, as hindrance to human
  acceptance of God's revelation 17
Resurrection
  as evidence of God's might 115
  as fulfilment of the Incarnation 105
  Holy Spirit's revelation 150
  as transfiguration of creation 96–7
  see also Jesus Christ
revelation
  and creation's knowledge of God 4
  in the God–world relationship 58

sacraments 176–8, 210
saints, communion, as the kingdom of
  truth 49
salvation 201
salvation *see* reconciliation
salvation
  and flesh 172
  God the Father's will fulfilled in
    Jesus Christ 107
sanctification, interrelationship with
  justification and freedom 164–5
Scholasticism 9–10
  links with theological logic 1–2
science, conjectural nature 99
sciences, fulfilment in Jesus Christ 95,
  97–8

Scripture–Tradition–ministry, within
  the Church 174–5
sectarianism, partial apprehension of
  truth 32
self-giving, characteristic of being
  205–6
self-saying, characteristic of being
  205–6
self-showing, characteristic of being
  204–5, 205–6
selflessness, Christian elements in
  Buddhism 163
Sens, Council 188
service, in self-revelation of being 23
Shintoism 199, 200
sick, sacrament 178
silence, importance for the revelation
  of God in the Incarnation 79–80
sin
  contradiction, in the Incarnation
    119–23
  contradiction with divine love
    overcome by Christ's Passion 189
  effects on creation's knowledge of
    God 4n
Son of Man *see* Jesus Christ
speech 41
spirits, discernment 183–5
State, and the Church 185
subject–object relationships
  freedom of the object in self-
    revelation 23–7, 28, 29, 30, 31
  freedom of the subject in self-
    revelation 28–31
  and the revelation of being 15–22
symbols, as expression of the
  hypostatic union of the Logos
  109
synthesis, as part of human knowledge
  of worldly truth 58–9

temptation, in the Incarnation 114
theologic, nature of Balthasar's
  theologic 211–12
theological aesthetics 179–80
  basis in theological logic 1–2
  concepts 9
  interrelationship with the dramatics
    and logic 164
  objective 65
theological dramatics
  basis in theological logic 1
  concepts 9
  objective 65
Theological Idealism 5

theological logic
  importance for Balthasar's aesthetics
    and dramatics 1
  objective 65, 67–8
  as reflection of the Trinity 69
  Trinitarian basis 1–2
theology
  approaches to the Incarnation 67
  importance for the aims of
    philosophy 4
  negative theology as descriptive of
    the Incarnation 78–80
  role of the Spirit 179–81
theory, and practice 77
thought, relationship with being as
  governed by truth 10–11
time, effects on relationship between
  essence and existence 47–8
Torah, Jesus Christ's summary 67
Tradition–Scripture–ministry, within
  the Church 174–5
transcendentalism, importance for
  recovery of sense of truth 11
transcendentals
  in creation and their relation to the
    Trinity 91–4
  relation to the mystery of being
    52–4
  see also unity, truth, goodness
Trinity
  as basis of theological logic 1–2
  differences within 70
  and the exploration of truth 10, 11
  freedom of the Father–Son
    relationship as shown by the Holy
    Spirit 128, 129–30, 158–9
  image in creation 91–4
  and the Incarnation 65, 68, 69–72
  love
    as the essence of creation 192–3
    as the overcoming of separation
      between God and creation
      200–1
    role of the Holy Spirit as love
      171
    self-giving based on love 205
    within the Trinity 82–5, 144–5,
      150, 157–8, 159–60
  otherness reflected in creation
    77
  personalism and essentialism within
    the Trinity 81–6, 87
  reflection in theological logic 69
  relationship with creation through
    the Incarnation 2–6

Trinity (*cont.*)
  revelation in Jesus Christ 73–4,
    114–16, 118, 202, 204–5, 207–9
  role in prayer 181–2
  and the structure of history 95,
    98–9
  as understood by dialogue 71–2
  see also God; God the Father; God
    the Son; Holy Spirit; Incarnation;
    Jesus Christ; Logos; Persons
trust
  in Christian faith 201
  and loving relationships 52
truth
  administration 31–2
  and being
    as non-hiddenness of being
      51–2
    relation to the mystery of being
      53
    revelation through images 43
    in subject–object relationships
      15–16, 18
    as unveiling of being 47–8
  in creation and its relation to the
    Trinity 91–4
  as freedom
    in the self-revelation of objects
      23–7, 28, 29, 30, 31
    in the self-revelation of subjects
      28–31
  God as the measure of truth in
    created beings 206
  Jesus Christ as infinite truth 63–5,
    68, 69
  as mystery, and its revelation
    through images 35–43
  personal nature 46–7
  relationship between finite and
    infinite truth 55–9
  totality, expression in history 48–9
  validity in the universal and
    personal 45–6
  worldly truth, human knowledge
    about 58–9
'Truth of the World', as introduction to
  aesthetics and dramatics 9

unbelief 120
unity
  characteristic of being 207
  in creation and its relation to the
    Trinity 91–4
  in the hypostatic union of the Logos
    115–16

universals, relationship with concrete
    individuals 40–1

value, in creaturely existence 26–7
Vatican I, *Dei Filius* 3, 4n
Vatican II, *Dei Verbum* 4n
vegetative life, interiority of being 24,
    25
veracity, in self-revelation of human
    beings 25–6
volition, in the Logos 112, 113–14

wisdom, as an attribution of God 85,
    87–8

world
    and the Church 166–7
    derivability from the Trinity 88–9
    macrocosm represented in man's
        microcosm 102
    relationship to the Holy Spirit
        187–9
    salvation
        and the Church 162–4
        as objective of the Incarnation 114

xenoglossia 184

Zen Buddhism 192

Index of Names

Abelard, Peter 188
Albert the Great, St 150
Althus, Paul 121
Ambaum, J. 210n
Andresen, C. 142n
Anselm of Canterbury, St 81, 180
Anselm of Havelberg 98
Aquinas, Thomas, St 1, 4n, 5, 17, 19, 26, 68, 69n, 76, 82, 88, 96, 113, 114, 116, 140, 142, 150, 165, 182, 193, 198, 211
Aristotle 1, 141
Athanasius, St 140, 147, 156, 177, 183
Augustine of Hippo, St 56n, 69, 72, 73, 76, 82, 84, 88, 91, 98, 104, 128, 150, 159, 166, 180, 198, 205

Barth, Karl 4, 84, 91, 110, 118, 131, 188
Basil of Caesarea, 'the Great', St 129, 141
Bede, St 180
Betz, Johannes 98n, 177
Blondel, Maurice 68
Bonaventure, St 82, 87, 88, 91, 95, 97–8, 99, 103, 149, 180
Bouyer, Louis 133, 142n
Breton, S. 141n
Bruaire, Claude 83, 132
Buber, Martin 70, 71, 72
Bulgakov, Sergei 92, 147–8

Caillat, M. 194n
Calvin, John 143
Cassian, John 183
Cattaui, G. 69n

Cavaliero, G. 103n
Chesterton, G. K. 12, 28, 47, 107
Claudel, Paul 69, 103
Clement of Alexandria 138
Coleridge, Samuel Taylor 38
Cyril of Alexandria, St 101, 108, 128, 148, 150, 169
Cyril of Jerusalem, St 138, 140

de Chardin, Teilhard 188
de la Potterie, Ignace 136n
de Lubac, Henri 3, 98, 99, 163n, 174n, 187
de Tilliette, Xavier 107
Denys the Areopagite 108, 208
Denzinger, H. 188
Diadochus 183
Dionysius the Areopagite 108, 208
Dumeige, G. 70n
Dunn, J. G. 184n
Dupuy, B.-D. 179n
Durrwell, François-Xavier 133n, 139, 145

Ebeling, Gerhardt 111
Ebner, Ferdinand 71, 72, 73
Eckhart, Meister 86
Eliot, T. S. 10
Eriugena, John Scotus 56n, 96, 97
Ernst, Cornelius 105
Eusebius of Caesarea 108

Fessard, G. 210n
Feuillet, André 170n
Fichte, Johann 55–6n
Florovsky, Georges 108
Fries, H. 98n

Gandillac, M. de 69n
Goethe, Johann Wolfgang von 24, 37
Gregory the Great, St 183
Gregory Nazianzen, St 98, 148
Gregory of Nyssa, St 13, 193n, 208
Gregory Palamas, St 74, 141
Greshake, Gisbert 178
Grünwald, Matthias 185
Guardini, Romano 37, 106n
Guimet, F. 70n

Hamann, J. G. 206
Haubst, Rudolph 99
Hegel, G. W. F. 1, 67, 70–1, 73, 96,
    99, 128, 131–2, 141, 143–4, 161,
    198
Heidegger, Martin 83
Heitmann, C. 150n, 188n
Hippolytus, St 138
Hitler, Adolf 163
Homer 4
Hugh of St Victor 98
Husserl, Edmund 27

Ignatius of Antioch 79, 191
Ignatius Loyola, St 152, 183–4, 200
Irenaeus of Lyons, St 74, 102, 113, 138,
    147, 205

Jesus Christ *see* Subject Index
Joachim of Fiore 91, 98–9
John of the Cross 80
John Paul II (Pope) 2n, 163, 211
John, St *see* Subject Index
Jüngel, Eberhard 110, 132

Kant, Immanuel 6, 36, 110
Käsemann, Ernst 178
Kasper, Walter 107, 132–3
Kierkegaard, Søren 46, 180
Koch, J. F. Schmucker von 106n
Kolbush, T. 169n

La Croix, J. 143n
Laurentin, René 173
Le Guillou, Marie-Jean 183n
Leclerq, Jean 180n
Leonard, André 132
Léthel, François-Marie 75
Lewis, C. S. 107
Luneau, A. 98n
Luther, Martin 119, 121–2, 123, 165

McDermott, John 163n
Madaule, J. 69n

Manaranche, A. 141n
Marcel, Gabriel 71, 210
Marion, Jean-Luc 83
Maritain, Jacques 22
Mark, St 137
Marx, Karl 99
Matthew, St 137
Maximus the Confessor, St 75, 95, 96,
    97, 108
Millet-Gérard, D. 69n
Moltmann, Jürgen 129
Mouroux, Jean 183
Mühlen, Heribert 140, 142, 150n, 167,
    188n
Müller, A. M. 188n
Mussner, Franz 108

Nédoncelle, Maurice 143
Newman, John Henry 11, 180
Nicholas of Cusa 56n, 95, 99
Nichols, A. 1n, 147n, 155n, 183n,
    191n
Nietzsche, Friedrich 6
Novalis 191
Novatian 138

Ockham, William of 85
Origen 108, 169, 205
Ortega y Gasset, José 106

Pannenberg, Wolfhart 131, 132, 187,
    188
Pascal, Blaise 180
Patfoort, A. 155n
Paul, St (apostle) *see* Subject Index
Péguy, Charles 49
Peter, St (apostle) 173
Picard, Max 79
Pius XII (Pope) 4n, 48, 168
Plato 117, 141, 180, 191
Plotinus 4, 56n, 191, 192
Porrée, Gilbert de la 85–6
Porsch, Felix 136n
Preiss, T. 143n
Przywara, Erich 3

Rahner, Karl 5, 79, 104, 112, 163
Ramsey, A. M. 188n
Ratzinger, Joseph 99, 150n
Raven, Charles G. 187
Rey, K. G. 184n
Richard of St Victor 70, 73, 95, 142
Ricoeur, Paul 109–10
Rondeau, M.-J. 142n
Rosenzweig, Hans 71–2

Rupert of Deutz 91, 95, 98, 104
Rust, E. C. 188n

Sachs, J. R. 210n
Scheeben, Matthias Joseph 72n, 73
Scheffczyk, L. 98n
Schelling, Friedrich 19, 75, 107, 133
Schleiermacher, Friedrich 55–6n
Schlette, H. R. 154n
Schlier, Heinrich 116, 136n, 176
Schneider, Reinhold 164
Schütz, C. 187n
Siewerth, Gustav 92, 106
Smalley, B. 98n
Söhngen, Gottlieb 110
Stenzel, Julius 141n
Swedenborg, Emmanuel 99
Swete, H. B. 145

Tauler, John 80
Taylor, John 187

Tertullian 101, 138, 166
Theodore of Studion, St 108
Thomas Aquinas, St 1, 4n, 5, 17, 19, 26,
    68, 69n, 76, 82, 88, 96, 113, 114, 116,
    140, 142, 150, 165, 182, 193, 198,
    211
Thunberg, Lars 96
Tromp, Sebastian 148

Victorinus, Marius 133n
Virgin Mary 123, 165, 166, 173
von Hügel, Friedrich 173–4
von Schönborn, Christoph 108
von Speyr, Adrienne 112, 113, 119,
    120, 122, 123, 130, 133n, 135, 148,
    177–8, 212

Welte, Bernhard 104
Wendebourg, Dorothea 142n
William of St Thierry 180
Williams, Charles 103